# Hume's Abject Failure

# Hume's Abject Failure

## The Argument Against Miracles

JOHN EARMAN

**OXFORD**
UNIVERSITY PRESS

2000

# OXFORD

UNIVERSITY PRESS

Oxford   New York
Athens   Auckland   Bangkok   Bogotá   Buenos Aires   Calcutta
Cape Town   Chennai   Dar es Salaam   Delhi   Florence   Hong Kong   Istanbul
Karachi   Kuala Lumpur   Madrid   Melbourne   Mexico City   Mumbai
Nairobi   Paris   São Paulo   Shanghai   Singapore   Taipei   Tokyo   Toronto   Warsaw

and associated companies in
Berlin   Ibadan

Copyright © 2000 by John Earman

Published by Oxford University Press, Inc.
198 Madison Avenue, New York, New York 10016

Oxford is a registered trademark of Oxford University Press.

Library of Congress Cataloging-in-Publication Data
Earman, John.
  Hume's abject failure : the argument against miracles / John Earman.
     p.   cm.
  Includes bibliographical references and index.
  ISBN 0-19-512737-4; ISBN 0-19-512738-2 (pbk.)
  1. Hume, David, 1711–1776—Views on miracles.
  2. Miracles.   I. Title.
  B1499.M5 E37   2000
  212—dc21      99-049345

9 8 7 6 5 4 3 2 1
Printed in the United States of America
on acid-free paper

For the S.D.F.H., B.B., and F.M.C.

# *Preface*

An impressive amount of ink has been spilt over Hume's "Of Miracles." It is almost universally assumed, by Hume's admirers and critics alike, that "Of Miracles" offers a powerful and original argument against miracles. On the contrary, I contend that Hume's argument is largely derivative, almost wholly without merit where it is original, and worst of all, reveals the impoverishment of his treatment of inductive reasoning. Hume scholars will no doubt be enraged by this charge. Good! There has been much too much genuflecting at Hume's altar.

If the only purpose of the present work were to bash "Of Miracles," it would not be worth the candle. But in fact, Hume's essay does have the virtue of bringing into focus a number of central issues in induction, epistemology, and philosophy of religion. It is my contention, however, that a proper treatment of these issues requires the use of the probability calculus that was being developed by Hume's contemporaries but of which Hume was largely unaware. In Part I of this monograph, I provide a detailed critique of "Of Miracles" from the perspective of the version of this apparatus developed by Thomas Bayes and Richard Price ("Bayesianism"). Part II reproduces some not easily obtained early writings on the Bayesian analysis of eyewitness testimony. Also included are documents that set the historical context in which Hume was working; without this context, a fair evaluation of Hume's contribution is impossible. Readers will also want to consult Tweyman (1996) which reprints selections from tracts, from 1752–1882, reacting to Hume's essay.

The selections from primary texts in Part II are arranged as follows. The first selection, from Locke's *Essay Concerning Human Understanding*, sets the general problem of which miracles is a special case; namely, how is belief to be apportioned when uniform experience conflicts with eyewitness testimony? The next three selections from Spinoza, Locke, and Samuel Clarke illustrate the conflicting conceptions of miracles and their role in Christian apologetics that were extant in Hume's day. Next come selections from Thomas Sherlock and Peter Annet, which give some of the flavor and substance of the eighteenth-century miracles debate in Britain. This is followed by the text of Hume's "Of Miracles"; the changes that Hume made in various editions are recorded. Then come excerpts from two of the contemporary reactions to Hume's essay. The first, by

George Campbell, is better known and rhetorically more forceful; the second, by Richard Price, though less well known and not as rhetorically successful, is more philosophically interesting and gave Hume greater pause. Finally, there are three selections, from Anonymous (George Hooper?), Laplace, and George Babbage, that illustrate attempts to use the probability calculus to quantify the effects of eyewitness testimony and, in particular, the effects of multiple witnessing in boosting credibility and the effects of error, self-deception, and deceit in diminishing credibility. Except where noted otherwise, the italics in the text is from the original author.

I hope that the present work will be found useful by students in the history of philosophy, in epistemology, and in philosophy of religion. Toward this end, the bibliography contains a representative sample of references to recent literature on Hume's miracle argument. I have not attempted to respond to all of this literature—that would require a book in itself. Rather, I have attempted to present an analysis that, whatever its other merits and demerits, is self-contained and thematically unified.

In criticizing Hume's argument against miracles, I have occasionally been subjected to a kind of reverse inquisition: since I attack Hume, must I not have some hidden agenda of Christian apologetics? I find such inquisitions profoundly distasteful since they deflect attention from the real issues. I am not averse, however, to laying my cards on the table. I find much that is valuable in the Judeo-Christian heritage, but I find nothing attractive, either intellectually or emotionally, in the theological doctrines of Christianity. If I had need of Gods, they would be the Gods of the Greeks and the Romans. The attack on Hume is motivated purely by a desire to set the record straight and frame the issues in a way that makes discussion of them more fruitful—but I must admit, after a bit of soul searching, that the sharpness of the attack is in part a reaction to what I see as pretentious sneering.

I gratefully acknowledge the helpful comments on earlier drafts of my essay received from a number of people. If I tried to name them all I would be sure to insult some by forgetting them. But I would be remiss if I did not give special thanks to Richard Gale, Rodney Holder, Colin Howson, Philip and Patrica Kitcher, Noretta Koertge, Laura Ruetsche, David Schrader, and Teddy Seidenfeld.

*Pittsburgh, Pennsylvania*                                                                     J. E.
*March 2000*

# Contents

Abbreviations    xi

PART I    HUME ON MIRACLES

1. Introduction    3
2. Hume's Religious Orientation    4
3. The Origins of Hume's Essay    6
4. The Puzzles of Hume's Definitions of "Miracle"    8
5. Conceptions of Miracles    9
6. What a Miracle Is for Hume    12
7. The Eighteenth-Century Debate on Miracles    14
8. The Structure of Hume's Essay    20
9. Hume's Straight Rule of Induction and His "Proof" against Miracles    22
10. Hume, Bayes, and Price    24
11. Bayes and Bayesianism    26
12. The Bayes-Price Rejection of Hume's Straight Rule    29
13. Hume's Stultification of Scientific Inquiry    30
14. The Indian Prince    33
15. Hume's Maxim    38
16. What Is Hume's Thesis?    43
17. Hume's Diminution Principle    49
18. Multiple Witnessing    53
19. More Multiple Witnessing    56
20. What Is Right about Hume's Position    59
21. Fall Back Positions for Hume    61
22. Probabilifying Religious Doctrines    65
23. Hume's Contrary Miracles Argument    67
24. Conclusion    70

Appendix on Probability    75
Notes    77
Works Cited    87
Additional Bibliography    93

PART II   THE DOCUMENTS

John Locke, *An Essay Concerning Human
Understanding*, Book IV
    Chapter 15, "Of Probability"   97
    Chapter 16, "Of the Degrees of Assent"   99

Benedict De Spinoza, *A Theologico-Political Treatise*
    Chapter 6, "Of Miracles"   107

John Locke, "A Discourse of Miracles"   114

Samuel Clarke, "A Discourse Concerning the Unalterable
Obligations of Natural Religion, and the Truth and Certainty of
the Christian Revelations"   120

Thomas Sherlock, *The Tryal of the Witnesses of
the Resurrection of Jesus*   125

Peter Annet, *The Resurrection of Jesus Considered:
In Answer to the Tryal of the Witnesses*   132

David Hume, *Enquiry Concerning Human Understanding*
    Section 10, "Of Miracles"   140

Richard Price, *Four Dissertations*
    Dissertation IV, "On the Importance of Christianity and
    the Nature of Historical Evidence, and Miracles"   157

George Campbell, *A Dissertation on Miracles*   176

Anonymous (George Hooper?), "A Calculation of the Credibility of
Human Testimony"   193

Pierre Simon Laplace, *A Philosophical Essay on Probability*
    Chapter 11, "Concerning the Probabilities of Testimonies"   194

Charles Babbage, *Ninth Bridgewater Treatise*
    Chapter 10, "On Hume's Argument against Miracles"   203

# *Abbreviations*

|       |                                                                                                         |
|-------|---------------------------------------------------------------------------------------------------------|
| *A*     | Anonymous, "A Calculation of the Credibility of Human Testimony"                                         |
| *CDM*   | Campbell, *A Dissertation on Miracles*                                                                   |
| *DM*    | Locke, "Discourse of Miracles"                                                                           |
| *E*     | Hume, *Enquiry Concerning Human Nature*                                                                  |
| *ECHU*  | Locke, *Essay Concerning Human Understanding*                                                            |
| *FD*    | Price, *Four Dissertations*                                                                              |
| *L*     | Grieg (ed.), *Letters of David Hume*                                                                     |
| *NBT*   | Babbage, *Ninth Bridgewater Treatise*                                                                    |
| *NL*    | Klibansky and Mosser (eds.), *New Letters of David Hume*                                                 |
| *ONR*   | Clarke, "A Discourse Concerning the Unalterable Obligations of Natural Religion, and the Truth and Certainty of the Christian Revelations" |
| *PEP*   | Laplace, *Philosophical Essay on Probabilities*                                                          |
| *RJC*   | Annet, *The Resurrection of Jesus Considered: In Answer to the Tryal of the Witnesses*                   |
| *T*     | Hume, *Treatise of Human Nature*                                                                         |
| *TPT*   | Spinoza, *Theologico-Political Treatise*                                                                 |
| *TW*    | Sherlock, *Tryal of the Witnesses of the Resurrection of Jesus*                                          |

The second page number in the text refers to the reprints in Part II of this work.

PART I

*Hume on Miracles*

1

*Introduction*

---

Section X ("Of Miracles") of Hume's *Enquiry Concerning Human Under-standing*[1] is a failure. In philosophy, where almost all ambitious projects are failures, this may seem a mild criticism. So to be blunt, I contend that "Of Miracles" is an abject failure. It is not simply that Hume's essay does not achieve its goals, but that his goals are ambiguous and confused. Most of Hume's considerations are unoriginal, warmed over versions of arguments that are found in the writings of predecessors and contem-poraries. And the parts of "Of Miracles" that set Hume apart do not stand up to scrutiny. Worse still, the essay reveals the weakness and the poverty of Hume's own account of induction and probabilistic reasoning. And to cap it all off, the essay represents the kind of overreaching that gives philosophy a bad name. These charges will be detailed and supported below, but at the outset I want to elaborate on the last one.

An apt analogy for Hume's project is the search for a "demarcation cri-terion." As originally conceived by the logical positivists, such a criterion would separate genuine assertions having cognitive significance from meaningless gibberish. More recently, there has been a quest for a crite-rion to cleave genuine science from pseudo-science. The history of these twin quests has been a history of failure.[2] One of the morals to be drawn from a failure to find a litmus test of the pseudo-scientific is relevant here: namely, it does not much matter what label one sticks on a particular as-sertion or an enterprise;[3] the interesting questions are whether the asser-tion merits belief and whether the enterprise is conducive to producing well-founded belief.[4] The answers cannot be supplied by a simple litmus test, but can only be reached by detailed, case-by-case investigations.

Admittedly, however, such investigations are often unrewarding and can be downright tedious. Charles Berlitz's *The Bermuda Triangle* (1974) sold several million copies. Larry Kusche's *The Mystery of the Bermuda Triangle—Solved* (1986) was never a bestseller. It is a careful, if plodding, examination of the claims made about the mysterious disappearance of ships and airplanes in the region known as the Bermuda Triangle. In case after case, Kusche shows that there is no mystery at all (e.g., the *Raifuku Maru* was seen by another ship to sink in a raging storm) or else that the only mystery is over which of several commonsense explanations is correct. It is not very exciting reading, and after a few chapters the reader hankers after a silver bullet that will spare us further details by putting a merciful end to all the nonsense.

And so it is with alleged miracles. Joe Nickell's *Looking for a Miracle* (1993) casts a skeptical eye on the Shroud of Turin, weeping icons, bleeding effigies, etc. A few chapters are enough to make the reader yearn for a quick knock out blow to spare us further tedium. Hume himself, at the beginning of his miracles essay, confesses the desire to deliver such a blow. Dr. Tillotson, he informs us, supplied a "decisive argument" against the doctrine of transubstantiation that served to "*silence* the most arrogant bigotry and superstition" (*E* 110; 141). "I flatter myself," Hume wrote, "that I have discovered an argument of a like nature which, if just, will, with the wise and learned, be an everlasting check to all kinds of superstitious delusion, and consequently, will be useful as long as the world endures" (*E* 110; 141).[5]

The temptation to fashion such an argument is understandable. But it should be resisted. Any epistemology that does not allow for the possibility that evidence, whether from eyewitness testimony or from some other source, can establish the credibility of a UFO landing, a walking on water, or a resurrection is inadequate. At the same time, of course, an adequate epistemology should deliver the conclusion that in most (all?) actual cases, when all the evidence is weighed up, little credibility should be given to such events. Hume's account of inductive reasoning is incapable of satisfying these dual demands. The tools needed for a better account were being fashioned at the very time that Hume wrote his *Enquiry*, and in succeeding years, they were honed on Hume's skeptical attack on the problem of induction and on his treatment of the problematics of eyewitness testimony. The aim of the current essay is not simply to bash Hume—a comparatively easy exercise—but also to indicate how, given the proper tools, some advance can be made on these problems. The contribution to philosophy of religion is incidental but, I hope, non-negligible.


2

## *Hume's Religious Orientation*

Hume's views on religion have been extensively documented, and there is no need to rehearse the discussion here.[6] But a few remarks relevant to the motivation behind "Of Miracles" are in order.

There is some evidence that the youthful Hume struggled against religious feeling.[7] If there was such a struggle, there is not much doubt about how the mature Hume resolved it. If we take Philo's pronouncements in *Dialogues Concerning Natural Religion* (1776) as a guide, the mature Hume was a theist, albeit of a vague and weak-kneed sort. He seems to have been convinced by the argument from design of the proposition "*That the cause or causes of order in the universe probably bear some remote analogy to human intelligence*" (227). But he was also convinced that the argument does not permit this undefined intelligence to be given further shape or specificity, and certainly not the specificity that would be needed to support any inference "that affects human life, or can be the source of any action or forbearance."[8]

Hume's inconsequential theism was combined with an abhorrence of organized religion, which Hume saw as composed of superstitions that have had almost uniformly baneful effects for mankind. When Cleanthes averred that "Religion, however corrupted, is still better than no religion at all," Philo responded as follows:

> How happens it then, if vulgar superstition be so salutory to society, that all history abounds so much with accounts of its pernicious conse- quences on public affairs? Factions, civil wars, persecutions, subversions of government, oppression, slavery: these are the dismal consequences which always attend its prevalency over the minds of men. (220)

Given such an animus toward organized religion, it is easy to understand why Hume would want to attack religious miracles, for the argument from design and the cosmological argument were supposed to establish the existence of God while miracles were supposed to serve as indicators of what kind of God exists.[9] But how to attack? Only the most benighted theists failed to recognize the pitfalls of eyewitness testimony to miracles. Thus, in chapter 37 ("Of Miracles, and Their Uses") of the *Leviathan* (1668), Hobbes cautioned that

> For such is the ignorance and aptitude to error generally of all men, but especially of them that have not much knowledge of naturall causes, and the nature and interests of men; as by innumerable and easie tricks to be abused. (203)

Nor was there any need to point to improbabilities in the cases of the miracles of Jesus—as we will see below, that ground was well trodden by Hume's contemporaries. What was left was to launch an in-principle attack on the possibility of establishing the credibility of religious mira- cles. The strong desire to strike a toppling blow against one of the main pillars of what Hume saw as baneful superstition led him to claim more than he could deliver, and it blinded him to the fact that in stating his arguments against miracles he was exposing the weaknesses in his own account of inductive reasoning.

# 3

## The Origins of Hume's Essay

Hume's *Treatise of Human Nature* (1739–1740) was written during a three-year stay (1735–1737) in France, first at Reims and then at La Flèche. It was at the latter that Hume received the inspiration for his essay on miracles, as he confessed to George Campbell, the author of *A Dissertation on Miracles* (1762), one of the better contemporary responses to Hume's essay:

> It may perhaps amuse you to learn the first hint, which suggested to me that argument which you have so strenuously attacked. I was walking in the cloisters of the Jesuits' College of La Flèche, a town in which I passed two years of my youth, and engaged in a conservation with a Jesuit of some parts and learning, who was relating to me, and urging some nonsensical miracle performed in their convent, when I was tempted to dispute against him; as my head was full of the topics of my *Treatise of Human Nature*, which I was at that time composing, this argument immediately occurred to me, and I thought that it very much gravelled my companion; but at last he observed to me, that it was impossible for that argument to have any solidity, because it operated equally against the Gospel as against the Catholic miracles;—which observation I thought proper to admit as sufficient answer. (*L*, Vol. 1, 361)

Since there are many distinct arguments in Hume's miracles essay, it is impossible to tell with certainty which of them he meant when he says that "*this* argument immediately occurred to me." But given that his head was "full of the topics" of his *Treatise*, the most reasonable supposition is that he was referring to the "proof against a miracle" he gives in Part 1 of his essay (to be discussed in section 9), a proof that he touted to be "as entire as any argument from experience can possibly be imagined" (*E* 114; 143).[10]

While in France, or shortly after his return to London in 1737, Hume must have produced a draft of the miracles essay, for on 2 December 1737, he mailed a copy to his cousin, Henry Home. Hume had considered including the essay in the *Treatise*, but as he explained to Henry, he had decided against it, for fear of the reaction of his readers.

> Having a frankt Letter I was resolv'd to make Use of it, & accordingly enclose some Reasonings concerning Miracles, which I once thought of publishing with the rest, but which I was afraid would give too much Offence even as the World is dispos'd at present . . . I beg of you show it to no Body, except to Mr. Hamilton[11] . . . & let me know at your Leizure that you have receiv'd it, read it, & burnt it. I wou'd not even have you

make another nameless Use of it, to which it wou'd not be improper, for fear of Accidents. (*NL* 2)

The essay that appeared eleven years later in the *Enquiry* was probably an extensively revised version of the one sent to Henry, for both the style and the content of the published version indicate that it dates from the 1740s (see Burns 1981 and Stewart 1994). Hume was obviously not satisfied with the earlier version he mailed to his cousin. He wrote: "Tell me your Thoughts of it. Is not the Style too diffuse? Tho as that was a popular Argument I have spread it out much more than the other parts of the Work" (*NL* 2). Whatever modifications it underwent before publication, the printed version is also diffuse and somewhat disjointed. But Hume's strong writing style gives a first impression of a logical unity. This impression vanishes almost entirely upon careful reading. In the various editions of the *Enquiry*, "Of Miracles" underwent several changes; all are minor as measured in words, but some are significant in content, as will be remarked in the appropriate places below.[12]

Commentators have wondered why Hume chose to include "Of Miracles" in the *Enquiry* when he had declined to make it part of the *Treatise*. The question is not well formed since we do not know what the "it" contained and how much it differed from the published version. Still, this has not prevented speculation. Norman Kemp Smith (1948, 45) hypothesizes that the decision to publish flowed from Hume's desire for the *Enquiry* to have a wider appeal and notoriety than the *Treatise*, which had fallen dead-born from the press. The most straightforward explanation is to take Hume at his word when he wrote to Henry Home in 1748 of his "indifference about all the consequences that may follow" from the publication of the *Enquiry* (*L*, Vol. 1, 111). Supporting such an indifference explanation is another letter of 2 October 1747 to James Oswald:

> Our friend, Harry [Henry Home], . . . is against this [publication of the *Enquiry*]. But in the first place, I think I am too deep engaged to think of a retreat. In the second place, I do not see what consequences follow, in the present age, from the character of an infidel; especially if a man's conduct be in other respects irreproachable. (*L*, Vol. 1, 106)

It may well have seemed to Hume that there was not much to fear. The original version of the miracles essay was presumably toned down, for when he sent this version to Henry in 1737, he wrote: "I am at present castrating my Work, that is, cutting off its noble Parts, that is, endeavoring it shall give as little Offence as possible; before which I could not pretend to put it into the Drs [Bishop Butler's] hands" (*NL* 3). There is in fact little in the published version to give offense if the standard of comparison is, say, the unrelenting attacks on the resurrection of Jesus by Woolston (1727–1729) and Annet (1744a, 1744b, 1745, 1747) (see section 7, this volume). Hume's essay is also an attack on this miracle, but the attack is indirect and follows his tongue-in-cheek remark to his Jesuit interlocutor from La Flèche who protested that Hume's argument operated equally against the Gospel miracles as against Catholic miracles: "which observation I thought proper," Hume replied, "to admit as sufficient answer." Nevertheless, Hume seems to have been too sanguine since in 1751 he was denied a professorship at Glasgow.[13]

# 4

## The Puzzles of Hume's Definitions of "Miracles"

Hume provides a definition of his subject not at the beginning of the miracles essay but several pages into Part 1, where he declares that "A miracle is a violation of the laws of nature" (E 114; 143). After offering a "proof" against miracles in this sense, Hume gives a second definition, which he indicates is more accurate than the first: "A miracle may be accurately defined, *a transgression of a law of nature by a particular volition of the Deity, or by the interposition of some invisible agent*" (E fn 115; 154). This second definition is buried in the middle of a long footnote, the main purpose of which is to reject subjectivist conceptions of miracles, such as Locke's (see section 5). As will be seen below (section 9), the element of supernatural causation is irrelevant to Hume's "proof" of Part 1, and this explains, perhaps, why the second definition is relegated to a footnote. It does not explain, however, why the second definition is given at all. The main focus of Hume's essay is on eyewitness testimony. But when witnesses report having been present at a miracle—say, the raising of a man from the dead—they are typically testifying to the occurrence of a naturalistically characterized event and *not* to supernatural intervention as a cause of the event. In response, it might be said that the *belief* of the witness that the alleged event is due to supernatural causes is relevant to an assessment of the credibility of that witness. That is certainly so, but it does not follow that the opinions of the witness should be made part of the definition of 'miracle', especially since (to repeat) the purpose of the footnote that contains the second definition is to take the position that the issue of whether or not a miracle has occurred is a matter that does not turn on the opinions of particular witnesses.

There is an even more obvious and troubling puzzle about Hume's first definition: if a miracle is a violation of a law of nature, then whether or not the violation is due to the intervention of the Deity, a miracle is logically impossible since, whatever else a law of nature is, it is an exceptionless regularity. Where then is the need for a complicated essay on the credibility of miracle stories?

I will return to these puzzles below. But first I need to explore more of the context in which Hume was operating.

# 5

## Conceptions of Miracles

The idea behind Hume's first definition of 'miracle' as a violation of a law of nature goes back at least as far as St. Thomas Aquinas, who took a miracle to be an occurrence that "lies outside the order of nature" (*Summa Theologica*, Q. 110, Art 4; Pegis 1944, 1022). In his *Theologico-Political Treatise*, Spinoza follows this tradition in defining a miracle as "contrary to the order of nature." But he concluded that a belief in miracles was always due to ignorance; and worse, such a belief was a tacit confession of unsound conceptions of nature and of God and ultimately serves atheism rather than theism.

> [A]s nothing is necessarily true save only by Divine decree, it is plain that the universal laws of nature are decrees of God following from the necessity and perfection of Divine nature. Hence, any event happening in nature which contravened nature's universal laws, would necessarily also contravene the divine decree, nature, and understanding; or if anyone asserted that God acts in contravention to the laws of nature, he, *ipso facto*, would be compelled to assert that God acted against his own nature—an evident absurdity.[14] (*TPT* 83; 108)

The conclusion is evident: "[I]t most clearly follows that miracles are only intelligible as in relation to human opinions, and merely mean events of which the natural cause cannot be explained by a reference to any ordinary occurrence, either by us, or at any rate, by the writer or narrator of the miracle" (*TPT* 84; 109). And further: "[W]e cannot gain knowledge of the existence and providence of God by means of miracles, but . . . we can far better infer them from the fixed and immutable order of nature" (*TPT* 86; 111).

For our purposes, there is a crucial implication of Spinoza's view of laws that can be stated in purely secular terms: "nothing happens in nature which does not follow from her laws" (*TPT* 84; 109). Spinoza held to a strong form of determinism that allowed for no contingency in nature. This is contrary to the modern conception of determinism according to which laws allow for contingency in "initial conditions" and necessitate only conditionals of the form "If the initial conditions are such-and-such, then the state at a later time will be so-and-so." But this difference makes no difference for present concerns. If laws of nature are conceived as universal truths, applying without exception to all space and all time, then a miracle as a violation of a law of nature is a contradiction in terms. As Spinoza himself put it, "[W]hatsoever is contrary to nature is also contrary to reason, and whatsoever is contrary to reason is absurd and, *ipso facto*, to be rejected" (*TPT* 92; 114). Since the point is statable in secular terms and does not require Spinoza's notion that laws are decrees of God, it was available to Hume as well. Before turning to the puzzle of why Hume did not avail himself of it, and thus reduce his miracles essay to a single paragraph, some other matters need to be addressed.[15]

When Spinoza wrote that the term 'miracle' "is only intelligible as in relation to human opinions," he meant to dismiss the subject. Locke begins his "Discourse of Miracles" (1706) with an almost identical definition: "A miracle then I take to be a sensible operation which, being above the comprehension of the spectator, and in his opinion contrary to the established course of nature, is taken by him to be divine" (*DM* 256; 114). But Locke's intent was quite the opposite of Spinoza's since for Locke miracles are the "foundation on which believers of any divine revelation must ultimately bottom their faith" (*DM* 264; 119). To the objection that what will be a miracle for one spectator will not be a miracle for another, Locke says:

> [T]his objection is of no force, but in the mouth of one who can produce a definition of miracle not liable to the same exception, which I think is not so easy to do; for it being agreed that a miracle must be that which surpasses the force of nature in the established, steady laws of causes and effects, nothing can be taken to be a miracle but what is judged to exceed those laws. Now everyone being able to judge of those laws by his own acquaintance with nature, and notions of its force (which are different in different men), it is unavoidable that that should be a miracle for one, which is not so to another. (*DM* 256–57; 114)

Some members of the Royal Society, such as Robert Boyle (1686) and John Wilkins (1699), continued to hew to the definition of 'miracle' as a violation of the laws of nature. They held the charming but muddled idea that miracles are a meeting place for science and religion since natural philosophers, as arbiters of what counts as a law of nature, are best placed to judge what counts as a violation of a law. By contrast, Newton's disciples Samuel Clarke (1705) and William Whiston (1696), and arguably Newton himself, maintained a view closer to Locke's on which 'miracle' marks an epistemic rather than an ontic category.[16] Such a view seems to undercut the use of miracles as direct demonstrations of the active presence of God in human affairs. But to be puzzled, as some commentators are (see, for example, McKinnon 1967), as to how miracles, non-ontically conceived, can have religious force is to fail to appreciate the strategy adopted by the liberal Anglicans in the late seventeenth and the eighteenth centuries. Their concern was less with providing proofs and demonstrations and more with providing grounds for reasonable belief (see section 22). Miracles, non-ontically conceived, could further this goal by serving as evidence for the existence of God and for his designs and purposes. For Locke and the Newtonians, these miracles gained their religious force from their combination with prophecy, from their timing and coincidence, and from contextual factors.[17] But the general evidentiary function of such miracles is independent of the details of Christian apologetics.

Suppose, for the sake of illustration, that there is a well developed theology based on the existence of a god called Emuh, who promises an afterlife in return for certain religious observances in this life. Suppose that this theology predicts that on such-and-such a day Emuh will send a sign in the sky. And suppose that on the appointed day, the clouds over America clearly spell out in English the words "Believe in Emuh and you will have everlasting life," while the same message is spelled out in French over France, in Deutsch over Germany, etc.[18] Then even though these cloud formations may not contravene any of the general principles taken at the time in question to be laws of nature and, indeed, may be explicable in terms of those principles, it would not be untoward to take these extraordinary occurrences to be support for Emuh theology.

Those who have read Hume may be tempted to dismiss such examples as lying outside of the ambit of Hume's argument against miracles since the phenomena at issue would be counted by Hume as marvels rather than miracles. But as we will see shortly, Hume has a hard time maintaining a principled marvel vs. miracle distinction. And in any case what matters is not how Hume classified examples but how the major participants in the eighteenth-century miracles debate classified them. Unless Hume's argument applies to examples generally taken at the time to be miracles and unless it shows that the occurrence of such events lack credibility and/or that these events, even if their occurrences are rendered credible, cannot serve as the basis for a reasonable belief in religious tenets, his essay must be judged a failure in context.[19] Hume's essay shows no sensitivity to the nuances of the changing roles of miracles in Christian apologetics. No such sensitivity was required, Hume thought, because if religious miracles can never be rendered credible (as he proposed to show), then none of the contentious theological issues about miracles is ever reached.

Hume's first definition of 'miracle' as a violation of a law of nature seems intended in part as a rejection of Locke's epistemic conception in favor of an ontic conception. If correct, this would have left him free to follow the secularized version of Spinoza's line and dismiss miracles as contradictions in terms. That he does not do this should be a signal that the first reading of Hume can be misleading. Hume unquestionably rejects Locke's subjectivism. Whether or not a miracle occurs is for Hume an issue that does not turn on the event being discoverable by us, much less on our opinions of it: "A miracle may either be discoverable by men or not. This alters not its nature and essence . . . The raising of a feather, when the wind wants ever so little of a force requisite for that purpose, is as real a miracle [as the raising of a house or ship], though not so sensible with regards to us" (E fn 115; 154). But first appearances to the contrary, 'miracle' for Hume marks an epistemic category in the sense that it is relative to evidence, although for Hume it is not relative to the evidence that any particular person possesses.

# 6

## *What a Miracle Is for Hume*

Hume commentators have tied themselves in knots trying to explain Hume's first definition of 'miracle' in a way that makes sense of his essay. We can cut part way through the knot by noting that no amount of logic chopping can avoid the fact that for all of the participants in the eighteenth-century debate on miracles, Hume included, a resurrection is the paradigm example of a miracle. In the very paragraph where Hume first defines 'miracle,' he says that "it is a miracle, that a dead man should come to life" (*E* 115; 143). What is more revealing is the reason he gives: "because that has never been observed in any age or country." To finish cutting through the knot, we need to do a little logic chopping of our own.

By a *law statement* let us understand a statement asserting the obtaining of some lawlike regularity (e.g., Newton's "Second Law," which asserts that the total impressed force acting on a body is equal to the product of the body's mass and its absolute acceleration).[20] And let us say that L expresses a law of nature if L is a law statement and is true.[21] A *miracle statement* M is a statement that expresses an exception to a true law statement L in the sense that M asserts the occurrence of an event or particular state of affairs, which assertion is incompatible with L. The conundrum should then be obvious: If Newton's "Second Law" does in fact express a law, then the statement M that an apple jumped off of the table even though the net impressed force on the apple was zero is a miracle statement; but by definition, M cannot be true.[22] Case closed; no further argument is needed, certainly not a lengthy essay focused on the unreliability of eyewitness testimony. It is no help to say that a law statement is intended to express a causal or physical necessity, so that L should be understood to be prefixed with a natural necessity operator $\boxed{N}$.[23] For even if this is the proper way to understand Hume's concept of law of nature, it seems that for any interesting sense of natural necessity, $\boxed{N}$L entails L. Adding the box in front of L deepens rather than resolves the conundrum.

To dig our way out of this conundrum, let us call L a *presumptive law statement* just in case (i) L is a law statement and (ii) "uniform experience" (to use Hume's phrase) speaks in favor of L in that many instances of L have been examined and all of them found to be positive. Now define a *Hume miracle* to be an event that has a faithful description M such that M contradicts some presumptive law statement. The virtue of this definition is that the paradigm case of a miracle—a resurrection—is a Hume miracle since "No person who has died returns to life" was a presumptive law for Hume.[24] (Even here Hume might seem to be begging the question, as George Campbell complained in his *Dissertation on Miracles* [1762]: "I leave it . . . to the author to explain, with what consistency he [Hume] can assert that the laws of nature are established by a uniform experience (which experience is chiefly the result of testimony), and at the same time allow that almost all human histories are full of the relations of miracles and prodigies, which are violations of those laws" [*CDM* 32; 185]. For a modern version of this complaint, see Armstrong [1992].)

This virtue seems to be matched, however, by two serious drawbacks. The first is that a proof of the nonexistence of Hume miracles would seem to prove too much since it seems to make it impossible to overturn any presumptive law. That is correct; but that is exactly the position to which Hume's account of inductive reasoning leads him, as I will argue in section 9. The second apparent drawback of the proposed definition of a Hume miracle is that it seems to blur Hume's distinction between miracles and marvels, the latter being rare and unusual events. That Hume took this distinction to be important is evident from the fact that it figures not only in the *Enquiry* but also in the *Treatise* (see Bk. II, Pt. I, sec. 2) and the *History of England* (see ch. 10). In one sense this apparent drawback is merely apparent, for on the account of induction I attribute to Hume (see section 9), the probability of a Hume miracle is flatly zero, which leaves room for marvels defined as events with tiny but nonzero probabilities. On the other hand, it is true that events one would intuitively want to count as marvels fall under the definition of a Hume miracle. But this is just another way of bringing out the point that Hume's account of induction commits him to an awkward position.

My proposed reading of Hume also seems to have the defect of leaving no role for Hume's second definition of 'miracle'. There is, I claim, no role for it in Part 1 of Hume's essay or in much of Part 2, for the key issue for Hume is whether it is possible to establish the credibility of the occurrence of certain kind of event, *naturalistically characterized*. What then can be the purpose of Hume's second definition? As already mentioned, that a witness *believes* the event she reports to be divinely caused is relevant to her credibility, and the credibility of witnesses is focus of Hume's concern, especially in Part 2. Further, Hume's second definition prepares the way for his fall-back position to the effect that even if the credibility of a miracle can be established, this cannot serve as the foundation of religious doctrines (see section 21).

Some modern commentators urged that law statements contain silent provisos that allow for exceptions of a supernatural origin, e.g., "All As are Bs (provided that there are no supernaturalistic interventions)" (see Clarke 1997). A miracle as a naturalistic violation of such a law is still a contradiction in terms (since it shows that the law is not a law after all), and a miracle as a supernaturalistic violation is also oxymoronic (because of the proviso it is not a violation at all). But the present proposal does allow one to say that a miracle is a violation of the unsilent part of the law statement and is, perforce, of supernatural origin, thus allowing us to make sense of both of Hume's definitions. Perhaps this is what Hume should have said, but it is not what he did say. Nor does it make sense of his pronouncement that a resurrection is a miracle because it is not observed in any age or country.

Admirers of Hume never tire of trying to saddle miracle enthusiasts with a dilemma stemming from the very definition of 'miracle'. Although there are many versions of the dilemma, I have yet to find one that can rightly be attributed to Hume and, at the same time, has any real force. Here is one example courtesy of Martin Curd (1996), who has urged that a tour through various attempts to define 'miracle' reveals that "one of Hume's characteristic positions is vindicated: miracles cannot rationally persuade anyone to accept theism if that person is initially neutral on the issue" (183). The reason, according to Curd, is that either a miracle is defined as a violation of a law of nature, in which case a miracle is logically impossible and therefore is not rationally believable, or else the definition must involve an element of divine causation, in which case it is not possible to justifiably believe in the occurrence of a miracle without first accepting theism. Although this position does have a vaguely Humean ring to it, it was not in fact Hume's position in "Of Miracles"; if it had been, the essay would have had to have been considerably different. My reading of Hume allows an escape between the horns of Curd's dilemma. A Hume miracle, such as a resurrection, is certainly not a contradiction in terms, and one can justifiably believe in the occurrence of such an event without already being committed to theism. Further, once it is rendered credible, such a miracle can serve as inductive evidence for theism, or so I will argue in section 22.

But this is getting ahead of the story. The important thing about Hume's concept of miracles is how it functions in his arguments against them. Before I examine the details of the arguments I need to set them in the context of the eighteenth century debate.

## 7

## *The Eighteenth-Century Debate on Miracles*

"Of Miracles" is often treated as if it were a genuinely original piece of philosophy. But although it does contain some original insights and is cast in Hume's characteristically forceful prose, it is in fact a largely derivative work. Apart from questions of priority, a fair evaluation of Hume's treatment of the issues must start from the way in which they were conceptualized by his predecessors and contemporaries.[25]

There are many echoes of Locke in Hume's essay. To name two, Locke's definition of miracles is surely one reference point of Hume's own definition, and Locke's king of Siam is transmuted into Hume's Indian prince (see section 14). But more fundamentally, Hume owes to Locke the formulation of the general problem of which miracles is a special and especially thorny instance. There are, according to Locke's *Essay Concerning Human Understanding* (1690), two sources of credibility: "*common observation in like cases,* and *particular testimonies in that particular instance*" (*ECHU* 377; 103). But what if these sources pull in opposite directions? Locke was well aware of the difficulty created when such a conflict arises: "The difficulty is, when testimonies contradict common experience, and the reports of history and witnesses clash with the ordinary course of nature, or with one another; there it is, where diligence, attention, and exactness are required, to form a right judgment, and to proportion assent to the different evidence and probability of the thing" (*ECHU* 377; 103). Having stated the problem, Locke has little to offer beyond the pious admonition to diligence, attention, and exactitude. The evidences are

> liable to so great variety of contrary observations, circumstances, reports, different qualifications, tempers, designs, oversights, &c., of the reporters, that it is impossible to reduce to precise rules the various degrees wherein men give their assent. This only may be said in general, That as the argument and proofs *pro* and *con,* upon due examination, nicely weighing every particular circumstance, shall to anyone appear, upon the whole matter, in a greater or lesser degree to preponderate on either side; so they are fitted to produce in the mind such different entertainments, as we call *belief, conjecture, guess, doubt, wavering, distrust, disbelief,* &c. (*ECHU* 377; 103)

Locke's waffling was unavoidable, for without the help of the probability calculus, which was being developed when Locke wrote his *Essay* but of which he was largely innocent, it is impossible to state any precise rules for "nicely weighing" the evidence. Unfortunately, Locke abandons his caution and modesty precisely where it was needed most. He writes:

> Though the common experience and the ordinary course of things have justly a mighty influence on the minds of men, to make them give or refuse credit to anything proposed to their belief; yet there is one case, wherein the strangeness of the fact lessens not the assent to a fair testimony given to it. . . . This is the proper case of *miracles,* which, well attested, do not only find credit themselves, but give it also to other truths, which need such confirmation. (*ECHU* 382; 106)

While it is impossible to say whether or not Hume was biting on this bait, it is indisputable that Hume had read Locke's *Essay* and had advertised his own *Treatise* as an improvement on Locke's account of probabilistic reasoning (see section 10).[26]

The bait was offered afresh in a dispute that erupted in the years 1727–1729 with the publication of Thomas Woolston's *Six Discourses on the Miracles of Our Savior.*[27] Woolston used the device of having his friend the "Jewish Rabbi" set out the reasons for thinking that the story of the resurrection of Jesus is undermined by "absurdities, improbabilities, and incredibilities." The rhetoric is inflamatory: "Was, or can there be, any imposture more against sense and reason palm'd upon the understanding of mankind?" (12); "[S]uch a manifest and indisputable Mark and Indication of Fraud, as not to be equall'd in all or any of the impostures that ever were attempted to be put upon the World" (15). Leslie Stephen may have been a bit severe in characterizing Woolston's performance as that of a "mere buffoon jingling his cap and bells in a sacred shrine" (1962, Vol. 1, 195),[28] but Woolston was certainly foolish to turn his undisguised sarcasm on church authorities. Here is a sample:

> Bishop Gibson is for the Messiahship of Jesus, who cast the Devils out of the Madmen, permitted them to enter into the Herd of Swine, that ran violently down a Precipice, and were choak'd in the Sea: How great a Miracle it was thus to cure the Madmen, the Bishop may know best, being perhaps better acquainted with the Devil than I am; but was it not for the Pity to the Swineherds, for their Losses, I could even now laugh at the Thoughts of the Hoggs running and tumbling down-hill, as if the Devil drove them: But leaving the Bishop calmly, decently, and seriously to admire the Wisdom and Justice of his Jesus in that Act, I am for the spiritual Jesus, who, according to the typical Form of that Story, exorcis'd the furious and diabolical Tempers out of the Jews and gentiles of old, whom no Chains of Reason could hold from doing violence to Christians till they were converted; and tho' He permitted the like persecuting and diabolical Spirits to enter into Ecclestiastical Swine; yet will they be precipitated into the Sea of the Knowledge of God, wherein they will be absorpt with divine Visions and Contemplations. (56–57)

Woolston was convicted of criminal blasphemy. He died in 1733 in prison, unable to pay his fine of £100. Gasking (1978) has suggested, not implausibly, that Hume had Woolston's fate in mind when he wrote to his cousin Henry Home in 1737 that he had forborne from including an essay on miracles in his *Treatise* (recall section 3).[29]

While there is little of any theoretical interest in the *Six Discourses*, there is much that is of decisive interest to Hume scholars to be found in one of the many attempted rebuttals of Woolston. Thomas Sherlock's *Tryal of the Witnesses of the Resurrection of Jesus* was first published in 1728 and subsequently went through fourteen editions. Sherlock's well chosen conceit was a trial in which the Apostles, alleged witness to the resurrection, stand accused of giving false evidence. Mr. A, councel for Woolston, puts the case against them, while Mr. B serves as their defense attorney. A jury hears the evidence and renders a verdict. The "not guilty" verdict is no surprise. But what is remarkable about Sherlock's pamphlet is that it succeeded in framing the objections to the resurrection miracle, and to miracles in general, in a form that was at once more forceful and much more philosophically interesting than anything Woolston had managed.

The prosecutor, Mr. A, puts a rhetorical question: "[W]hen the Thing testify'd is contrary to the Order of Nature, and, at first sight at least, impossible, what Evidence can be sufficient to overturn the constant Evidence of Nature, which she gives us in the constant and regular Method of her Operation?" (*TW* 58; 127). There is a distinct echo here of Locke: "Though to a man whose experience has always been quite contrary, and who has never heard anything like it, the most untainted credit of a witness will scarce be able to find belief" (*ECHU* 367; 99). The illustration Locke gives in his *Essay Concerning Human Understanding* is a possibly apocryphal tale:

As it happened to a Dutch ambassador, who entertaining the king of Siam with the peculiarities of Holland . . . amongst other things told him that the water in his country would sometimes, in cold weather, be so hard, that men walked upon it, and that it would bear an elephant, if he were there. To which the king relied, *Hitherto I have believed the strange things you have told me, because I look upon you as a sober fair man, but now I am sure you lie.* (*ECHU* 367; 99)

The defense attorney, Mr. B, answers the prosecutor's charge that testimony ought not to be admitted in cases where it is contrary to the order of nature by claiming that this principle leads to absurd results in cases like the one described by Locke.

For instance; a Man who lives in a warm Climate, and never saw Ice, ought upon no Evidence to believe that Rivers freeze and grow hard in cold Countries; for it is improbable, contrary to the usual Course of Nature, and impossible according to the Notion of Things; and yet we all know that this is a plain, manifest Case, discernible by the Senses of Men, of which therefore they are qualify'd to be good Witnesses. . . . And what has the Gentleman [Mr. A] said upon this Occasion against the Resurrection, more than any man who never saw Ice might say against an hundred honest Witnesses, who assert that Water turns to Ice in cold Climates? (*TW* 60; 128)

Mr. B then draws a general moral from the example: "It is very true that Men do not so easily believe, upon testimony of others, things which to them seem improbable or impossible, but the reason is not because the thing itself admits of no Evidence, but because the Hearer's pre-conceiv'd Opinion outweighs the Credit of the Reporter, and makes his Veracity to be call'd into question" (*TW* 60–61; 128). Sherlock illustrates his moral with an example:

[F]or instance, it is natural for a Stone to roll down-hill; but a Stone moving up-hill is as much an Object of Sense as a Stone moving down-hill; and all Men in their Senses are as capable of seeing, and judging, and reporting the Fact in one Case as in the other. Should a Man then tell you that he saw a Stone go up-hill of its own accord, you might question his Veracity, but you could not say that the thing admitted no Evidence because it was contrary to the Law and usual Course of Nature; for the Law of Nature form'd to yourself from your own Experience and

Reasoning, is quite independent of the Matter of fact which the Man testifies; and whenever you see facts yourself which contradict your Notions of the Law of Nature, you admit the facts because you believe yourself; when you do not admit like Facts upon the evidence of others, it is because you do not believe them, and not because the Facts in their own nature exclude all Evidence. (*TW* 61; 128)

The controversy started by Woolston was kept on the boil by Peter Annet's *The Resurrection of Jesus Considered, In Answer to the Tryal of the Witnesses* (1744a), which repeated Woolston's charge that the Gospel accounts are riddled with inconsistencies, "improbabilites and absurdities" (59). (With Woolston's fate in mind, Annet did not attach his name to his pamphlet but signed it "by a Moral Philosopher." He eventually got his comeuppance 1762 when he was sentenced to be pilloried for the sentiments expressed in his *Free Enquirer* [1761].)[30] Annet's response to the *Tryal* was attacked by Chandler (1744) and Jackson (1744), and later by West (1747), and Annet responded in turn to the first two attacks (see Annet 1744b, 1745).

Hume must surely have known about this controversy if only in general terms, and thus it is not surprising that his essay concentrates on the ability of eyewitness testimony to establish the credibility of miracles. Whether or not he read and was influenced by the particular works cited above is unimportant. The point to emphasize is that numerous works published prior to Hume's *Enquiry* contain versions of the argument (which Hume tried to make his own) that uniform experience trumps human testimony to a miracle. Wollaston (1725), whom we know Hume had read, is surely one source for this argument.[31] Unlike Hume, however, Wollaston doesn't dismiss miracle reports out of hand. For example, in reaction to Herodotus' report of an Egyptian account of two occasions on which the sun rose in the west and set in the east, Wollaston says: "That this account may be false is very consistent with the humor and circumstances of mankind: but that it should be true is very inconsistent with the laws, by which the motions of the celestial bodies seem to be regulated. . . . It is therefore *in nature* much more probable, that this account be false. The odds are on the other side" (57). Peter Annet comes much closer to Hume's flat-out rejection of miracle stories:

> Any romantic story said to be seen, and heard, may be called a *plain manifest case, discernible by the senses of man; of which they are therefore qualified to be good Witnesses*. Things asserted, which are contrary to experience, and reason of all mankind; *and to what they know of the law and usual course of nature*, are, to the common sense and understanding of men, utterly impossible; because such assertions contradict all men's notions of those laws, that are known by common experience. Therefore they cannot admit the facts asserted on *any* evidence; because *they in their own nature exclude all evidence*; as all impossibilities must consequently do. (*RJC* 74; 135)

Turning to another aspect of Hume's essay, there were so many discussions of variants of Locke's king of Siam example that Hume could not have failed to encounter one of them (see section 14). And Hume's contrary miracles argument (see section 23) had many antecedents. All in all, as Wootton (1990) has remarked, "it is harder to identify what is original in Hume's essay than it is to find sources for, and parallels to, his argument" (223).[12]

What I find striking about Hume's skeptical predecessors is the contrast between their ability to bring out the improbabilities involved in particular miracle stories and their inability to frame general philosophical issues in a perspicuous manner. Take, for example, Peter Annet's efforts. On the resurrection of Jesus, he was trenchant and persuasive. Here is a brief sample that gives a taste of the flavor of his argument:

> Is it probable, that an extraordinary action done for an extraordinary end, and highly necessary to be known to mankind, should be so secretly done, that no man saw it! That so great an action should be done in so improper a way! That Jesus should require the men to believe his Disciples, rather than their own senses, in an affair where reason can be of no assistance! (*RJC* 59; 133)

> That he [Jesus] appeared in such a manner to his Disciples, which scarce convinced themselves; yet sent them to convince the world! . . . That Jesus rose again from the dead, staid forty days afterwards, no body knows where, and purposely avoided the most rational method of its being certainly known to the world, viz. by avoiding to appear to the world! (*RJC* 60; 133)

But when he shifts to general considerations, the result is a muddle. In response to the Locke/Sherlock ice example, he writes: "In this case here's all the evidence of sense to prove the thing [i.e. a solid form of water] where it is; and of this there are places and witnesses enow. He that cannot believe, may go and have sensible conviction" (*RJC* 73; 134). This dictum avoids the issue of what to do when firsthand observation is not possible and we must rely on eyewitness testimony. But suppose that firsthand observation is possible. Annet tells us that "If [referring to Sherlock] a stone appeared to roll up a hill of its own accord to my sight, I should think I had reason to doubt the veracity of my eye sight, or of the object. Therefore, I cannot admit the like fact on the evidence of others: Because pretended facts, which are contrary to nature, can have no natural evidence" (*RJC* 74; 135). But, of course, the issue is precisely what is and is not contrary to nature and how inductive evidence bears on the question. Here is Annet's position:

> As we know by experience that all men must die, and rise no more, therefore we conclude, for a dead man to rise to life again, is contrary to the uniform and settled course of nature. Yet if we argue, that it is not contrary nor repugnant to the real laws thereof, as the Gentleman

[Sherlock] insinuates, we make the uniform and settled course, and the real laws of nature, two different things. Thus, we argue without foundation, either from sense or reason; all of which informs us, that it is impossible for a dead body to live again: To believe it possible contradicts this maxim, *That nature is steady and uniform in her operations*. (*RJC* 75; 135–36)

Annet seems to be saying that either naive induction by enumeration works, or nothing does. Hume's view, as we will see below, is not much more sophisticated.


# 8

## *The Structure of Hume's Essay*

---

I defy the reader to give a short, simple, and accurate summary of the argumentation in "Of Miracles." What on first reading appears to be a seamless argument is actually a collection of considerations that sometimes mesh and sometimes don't. It will take much work to tease out the components of Hume's argument and to evaluate the soundness of individual components and the effectiveness of the entire package. But it would be useful to have at the outset a rough and ready sketch of the structure of Hume's case against miracles. Unfortunately, commentators cannot even agree on this much, and we will soon see why.

Hume opens Part 1 of his essay by representing Tillotson's argument against transubstantiation as a contest: scripture and tradition (which inform us that the bread has turned to flesh and the wine has become blood) vs. the evidence of our senses (which inform us that the bread is just bread and the wine is just wine). But the former "carry not such evidence with them as sense; when they are considered merely as external evidences, and are not brought home to everyone's breast, by the immediate operation of the Holy Spirit" (*E* 109; 140). Thus, the contest is really no contest at all since "[A] weaker evidence can never destroy a stronger; and therefore, were the doctrine of the real presence ever so clearly revealed in scripture, it were directly contrary to the rules of just reasoning to give our assent to it" (*E* 109; 140).[33] Hume also represents his argument against miracles as a contest: here it is a "contest of two opposite experiences; of which the one destroys the other, as far as its force goes, and the superior can only operate on the mind by the force, which remains" (*E* 113; 143). On one side, there is uniform experience against the occurrence of the miraculous. On the other, there is testimony, which itself derives its force from experience:

It will be sufficient to observe that our assurance in any argument of this kind [i.e., one based on testimony] is derived from no other principle than our observation of the veracity of human testimony, and of the usual conformity of the facts to the reports of witnesses. (*E* 111; 142)

The reason, why we place any credit in witnesses and historians, is not derived from any *connexion*, which we perceive *a priori*, between testimony and reality, but because we are accustomed to find a conformity between them. (*E* 113; 142–43)

To many commentators it is clear what Hume took to be the upshot of this contest. Here, for example, is C. D. Broad's summary:

So Hume's argument comes to this. Against belief in any alleged miracle we have, by definition of the word miracle, an absolute uniform experience. For believing in the miracle we have only our experience as to the trustworthiness of testimony. And this is not an absolutely uniform experience, however trustworthy we suppose the witness to be. Therefore we have never the right to believe in any alleged miracle however strong the testimony for it may be. (1916–17, 80)

Broad's reading is not a twentieth-century invention; it was in fact put forward by contemporaries of Hume such as Richard Price (1767), who took Hume to be saying that to believe in a miracle on the authority of human testimony is to "prefer a weaker proof to a stronger" (*FD* 385; 158). Price may have had an ulterior motive for this attribution since he thought it led to a a quick refutation of Hume. The regard we give to testimony is not, Price contended, based solely or even largely on data about the frequency with which it delivers the truth. "One action, or one conversation with a man, may convince us of his integrity and induce us to believe his testimony, though we had never, in a single instance, experienced his veracity. His manner of telling the story, its being corroborated by other testimony, and various particulars on the nature and circumstances of it, may satisfy us that it must be true" (*FD* 399; 161).

There certainly are passages, if taken in isolation, that suggest the Price-Broad reading. In the case where the event related is marvelous rather than miraculous, Hume says that the contest of opposing experiences results in a "counterpoise, and mutual destruction of belief and authority" (*E* 113; 143). But by "counterpoize" and "destruction," Hume cannot mean that stories of marvelous events are never to be credited since he allows that, under appropriate conditions, historians can be correct in accepting such stories. When the event related is not just marvelous but really miraculous, Hume invites us to suppose that "the testimony considered apart and in itself, amounts to an entire proof." In that case, he says, "there is proof against proof, of which the strongest must prevail, but with a diminution of its force, in proportion to that of its antagonist" (*E* 114; 143). But Hume does not say explicitly that what is left after the clash of proofs is never sufficient to ground the credibility of a miracle, and, indeed, he nowhere explicitly states the argument attributed to him by Price and Broad.[34] Nor is it plausible that the Price-Broad reading is what Hume thought, even if it is not what he explicitly says. For one thing, this reading would make it hard to understand the function of the famous Maxim which Hume enunciates at the close of Part 1 (see section 15). That Maxim sets the conditions under which testimony is sufficient to establish the credibility of a miracle; but if Price and Broad are right, Hume is saying that there are no such conditions and, hence, no role for the Maxim. For another thing, Part 2 would be puzzling since there Hume allows that especially good testimony can establish the credibility of some secular miracles. Thus, I will assume, contra Price and Broad, that in Part 1 Hume did not mean to foreclose the issue of whether testimony could establish the credibility of a miracle, although I acknowledge that the text is ambiguous enough to allow the Price-Broad reading.[35]

In Part 2 Hume takes back his overgenerous assumption that the falsehood of the testimony to a miracle "would be a real prodigy" (E 116; 144). He enumerates various factors which contribute to the unreliability of eyewitness testimony and gives a cursory review of various Catholic and profane miracle stories. Then he suddenly announces—in the first edition of the *Enquiry*—that no testimony "for any kind of miracle can ever possibly amount to a Probability much less to a Proof." From 1768 onward the "can ever" is softened to a "has ever." And even this latter claim is further qualified to apply only to religious miracles, although initially this qualification was put in a footnote and only after 1768 was it moved into the main text. There is a disturbing slipperiness to Hume's aims and conclusions, which I will address in section 16. But the first order of business is to take up Hume's argument that experience provides a "proof" against miracles.

# 9

## *Hume's Straight Rule of Induction and His "Proof" against Miracles*

In Part 1 of "Of Miracles" Hume writes that "A miracle is a violation of the laws of nature; and as a firm and unalterable experience has established these laws, the proof against a miracle, from the very nature of the fact, is as entire as any argument from experience can possibly be imagined" (E 114; 143). If the argument Hume gives for this assertion is correct, then it is irrelevant that the alleged miracle has a divine or supernatural origin.

To understand the structure of Hume's argument, it is helpful to try to specify the form that Hume thinks inductive reasoning follows. As a starting point, recall Reichenbach's *straight rule of induction*: If n As have been examined and m have been found to be Bs, then the probability that the next A examined will be a B is m/n.[36] Corollary: If m = n, then the probability that the next A will be a B is 1. Hume also thought that induction proceeds by a straight rule which is not easy to formulate in general[37] but which takes on a simple form in the case of uniform experience. As a first cut, we can try to state the corollary as: If n As have been examined, all of which were found to be Bs, then if n is sufficiently large, the probability that all As are Bs is 1. How large "sufficiently large" needs to be is presumably a matter to be settled by psychological investigations.

The evidence for attributing this straight rule to Hume comes from passages such as: (1) "All probability, then, supposes an opposition of experiments and observations, where the one side is found to overbalance the other, and to produce a degree of evidence, proportioned to the superiority" (E 111; 141). (2) The evidence of testimony is "regarded either as a *proof* or a *probability*, according as the conjunction between any particular kind of report and any kind of object has been found to be constant or variable" (E 112; 142). (3) "Why is it more than probable, that all men must die; that lead cannot, of itself, remain suspended in the air; that fire consumes wood, and is extinguished by water; unless it be, that these events are found agreeable to the laws of nature?" (E 114–115; 143). (4) "There must, therefore, be a uniform experience against every miraculous event, otherwise the event would not merit that appellation. And as uniform experience amounts to a proof, there is here a direct and full *proof*, from the very nature of the fact, against the existence of any miracle" (E 115; 143–44). Additional evidence comes from Hume's letter of 1761 to Hugh Blair: "The proof against a miracle, as it is founded on invariable experience, is of that *species* or *kind* of proof which is full and certain when taken alone, because it implies no doubt, as is the case with all probabilities" (L, Vol. 1, 350).

In these passages Hume is saying that when experience is uniform—when sufficiently many As have been examined and all have been found to be Bs—then we have a "proof" that all As are Bs.[38] In the section of the *Enquiry* entitled "Of Probabilities," Hume divides arguments into demonstrations, proofs, and probabilities. Proofs are defined as "such arguments from experience as leave no room for doubt or opposition." In the probabilistic language I will adopt in coming sections, this seems to imply that when experience provides a proof, the conditional probability of the conclusion, given the evidence of experience, is 1. Only when experience is variable—some As have been found to be Bs while other are been found to be non-Bs—is there room for doubt and the probability is less than 1. What Hume meant by "demonstration" is not of direct concern here, but roughly the idea is that a demonstration shows the absolute impossibility of the contrary.

So here in a nutshell is Hume's first argument against miracles. A (Hume) miracle is a violation of a presumptive law of nature. By Hume's straight rule of induction, experience confers a probability of 1 on a presumptive law. Hence, the probability of a miracle is flatly zero. Very simple. And very crude. This "proof" works not only against resurrections but against, say, the "miracle" of a violation of the presumptive law of conservation of energy. Little wonder then that those of Hume's contemporaries who had a less crude view of how induction works found no merit in Hume's "proof." It is now time to meet two of those contemporaries, Bayes and Price.[39]

## 10

### *Hume, Bayes, and Price*

The name of Richard Price is largely unknown to modern readers. But in learned circles in eighteenth century Britain, Price's notoriety was not much below that of Hume, and in the American colonies he was certainly better known than Hume—his *Observations on the Nature of Civil Liberty* (1776) skewered George III and served as an inspiration for the leaders of the American Revolution. A man of many parts, Price was a nonconformist minister; the author of *Observations on Reversionary Payments* (1771), a seminal work in actuarial science; and a persistent but cordial critic of Hume. Hume and Price became acquaintances after Price published his *Review of the Principal Questions and Difficulties in Morals* (1758), which criticized Hume's ethical views.[40] Dissertation IV ("The Importance of Christianity, the Nature of Historical Evidence, and Miracles") of Prices' *Four Dissertations* (1767) is an attack on Hume's "Of Miracles." Price was evidently worried that he might have given offense to Hume, but his concern was groundless. Indeed, Hume was almost effusive in thanking Price for the "civility with which you have treated me":

> [I]t is but too rare to find a literary Controversy conducted with such proper Decency and Good Manners. . . . But you like a true Philosopher, while you overwhelm me with the Weight of your Arguments, give me encouragement by the Mildness of your expressions: and instead of *Rogue, Rascal and Blockhead,* the illiberal Language of the Bishop of Glouster [Warburton] and his School, you address me as a man mistaken, but capable of Reason and conviction. (*NL* 233–234)

Price returned the compliment by praising Hume in the second edition of *Four Dissertations* as "a writer whose genius and abilities are so distinguished, as to be above any of *my* commendations" (*FD* 382). In a more substantive vein, Hume admitted: "I own to you, that the Light, in which you have put this Controversy, is new and plausible and ingenious, and perhaps solid. But I must have some more time to weigh it, before I can pronounce this Judgment with satisfaction to myself" (*NL* 234). Unfortunately, nothing is known about whether Hume ultimately found Price's arguments solid,[41] but later I will offer a conjecture about how Price's criticisms may have induced Hume to make a change in "Of Miracles" (see section 16).

Like Price, Thomas Bayes was a nonconformist minister and a man of many parts. He was made a Fellow of the Royal Society, presumably because he was the author of an anonymous pamphlet defending Newton's calculus against Bishop Berkeley's onslaught in the *Analyst*.[42] Although we know very little about the relationship between Bayes and Price, they must have been much more than causal acquaintances since Bayes's will left Price £100,[43] which at the time was a tidy sum. And it was Price who arranged for the posthumous publication of Bayes' manuscript, given the title "An Essay towards Solving a Problem in the Doctrine of Chances" (1763). It was on this essay, and on an Appendix which Price himself authored, that Price drew in fashioning his critique of Hume's "Of Miracles." In *Four Dissertations*, Price gives a reference to Bayes' paper. But it is doubtful that Hume read the paper, and even if he had it is even more doubtful that Hume would have understood it because he was unfamiliar with the technical developments in the probability calculus.[44]

Is it then fair to use this apparatus as part of a critique of Hume's argument against miracles? My answer is an unqualified yes. In the Abstract to the *Treatise*, Hume endorses Leibniz's complaint that various authors, including Locke, are "too concise when they treat of probabilities, and those other measures of evidence on which life and action intirely depend, and which are our guides even in most of our philosophical speculations." The Abstract announces that "The author of *the treatise of human nature* seems to have been sensible of this defect in these philosophers, and has endeavoured, as much as he can, to supply it" (*T* 647). Of course, by "probabilities" Hume did not have in mind reasoning that proceeds by proving and applying theorems of the probability calculus. But ignorance of the apparatus is no excuse since, for example, before the end of the seventeenth century, there were published attempts to apply the probability calculus to some of the questions at issue in Hume's essay, such as the effect of multiple witnesses (see section 18). A number of Hume's contemporaries, such as Price, understood Hume's claims as being about quantifiable degrees of belief or credibility, the quantification being subject to the constraints of the probability calculus. I have no doubt that Hume would have agreed with this much, and I have little doubt that, whether or not he would have accepted the morals to be drawn in the coming sections, he would have agreed that the probabilistic form of analysis is wholly appropriate when discussing the credibility of testimony.[45] Naysayers will have a hard time explaining away the above quoted letter from Hume to Price, where Hume is implicitly accepting the probabilistic form into which Price cast Hume's argument.

In a brilliant analysis of the sources of Hume's essay, Wootton (1990) has identified two preconditions for the emergence of unbelief, or at least of skepticism with respect to religious doctrines. The first is the conviction that unbelievers and skeptics can be of good moral character (see Wootton 1983). The second precondition

> lay in the new concepts of evidence and probability . . . which made possible a new approach to problems of historical testimony, including those presented in the Gospel story. The "emergence of probability" made it possible to ask, in place of "Can the truth of Christianity be demonstrated?", or "Is it supported by authority?", questions such as "Is it likely that the Gospel narrative is accurate?" and "How good is the evidence for God's existence?" Modern irreligion may be said to be born with these new questions. (1990, 193)

I agree that the seventeenth and eighteenth centuries saw a decisive turn from the first to the second set of questions. But I also see a double irony in the facts that the most subtle and interesting arguments offered by theists of this era relied on the emergence of probability and that the irreligion promoted by Hume's attempts to answer the second set of questions is, in a word, sophomoric when examined under the lens of Bayesianism.

## 11

## *Bayes and Bayesianism*

---

There are many forms of Bayesianism, perhaps more forms than there are practicing Bayesians. But all of the adherents of this persuasion share two central tenets, and many subscribe to a third. First, epistemology is most fruitfully discussed not in terms of all-or-nothing belief but in terms of degrees of belief. Second, rational degrees of belief should be regimented according to the probability calculus.[46] Bayes' (1763) essay contains a nascent form of what has come to be known as the Dutch book argument for this tenet, the idea being that if an agent's degrees of belief violate an axiom of probability, then she can be bilked in the sense that she can be presented with a finite set of bets, each of which she judges as fair, but with the net effect that she is guaranteed to lose money come what may.[47] Third, when an agent has a learning experience and the content of the experience is fully captured by a proposition E, then the agent's degree of belief function $Pr_{new}$ after the learning experience is related to her degree of belief function $Pr_{old}$ before the learning experience by the rule of conditionalization: $Pr_{new}(\cdot) = Pr_{old}(\cdot/E)$, where the conditional probability $Pr(Y/X)$ is defined by $Pr(Y\&X)/Pr(X)$ when $Pr(X) \neq 0$.[48] If $Pr_{old}$ reflects previously acquired knowledge K, that is, $Pr_{old}(\cdot) = Pr_{oldold}(\cdot/K)$, then $Pr_{new}(\cdot) = Pr_{oldold}(\cdot/K\&E)$. From here on I will drop the temporal subscripts on probabilities. The temporal aspect continues to be reflected in the evidence statements that appear to the right of the slash in the conditional probability. Although the rule of condi-tionalization is not looked upon by all Bayesians of being on a par with the probability axioms as a condition sine qua non for rationality, it seems to me fair to apply it to Hume.[49]

What is now called Bayes' theorem shows how the acquisition of new knowledge impacts on the agent's degrees of belief:

$$\Pr(H/E\&K) = \frac{\Pr(H/K) \times \Pr(E/K\&H)}{\Pr(E/K)} \qquad (1)$$

Given the definition of conditional probability, (1) is a trivial consequence, but one with profound implications. In applications, it is helpful to think of H as the hypothesis at issue, K the background knowledge, and E as the new evidence. $\Pr(H/K\&E)$ and $\Pr(H/K)$ are called, respectively, the *posterior* and *prior probability* of H.[50] $\Pr(E/K\&H)$ is called the *likelihood* of H; it is a measure of how well H explains E. $\Pr(E/K)$ is variously called the *prior likelihood* or the *expectancy* of E; it is a measure of how surprising the new evidence E is. Using the principle of total probability (see Appendix), (1) can be recast in a form that is useful in many applications:

$$\Pr(H/E\&K) = \frac{\Pr(H/K) \times \Pr(E/K\&H)}{\Pr(H/K) \times \Pr(E/K\&H) + \Pr(\neg H/K) \times (E/\neg H\&K)} \qquad (2)$$

$$= \frac{1}{1 + \left[\dfrac{1 - \Pr(H/K)}{\Pr(H/K)}\right] \left\{\dfrac{\Pr(E/\neg H\&K)}{\Pr(E/H\&K)}\right\}}$$

For Bayesians, the explanation of the truisms of confirmation and in-duction are most often to be traced back to an application of (1) and (2).[51]

Even if Hume had read Bayes' essay, he would not have found Bayes' theorem there, for the theorem that bears Bayes' name was the invention of later writers. What Hume would have found was the recognition of the importance of prior probabilities for inductive reasoning. And here we reach a divide in Bayesianism: the *subjectivists*, who take the position that there are no constraints on priors, other than the axioms of prob-ability vs. the *objectivists* who hold that there are additional constraints. Bayes belonged to the latter camp, at least for the particular type of inductive inference studied in his essay.

Consider a repeatable process (such as coin flipping) that is character-ized by a fixed objective chance p, $0 \le p \le 1$, of yielding an outcome with a property B on each trial. (The set up corresponds to what modern statisticians call independent and identically distributed [IID] trials. To match up with the previous discussion, take the property A to be that of being an outcome of this IID process.) The problem Bayes set himself then is this: Given that in n trials m of the outcomes are B (denote this evidence by E(m, n)), what is the rational degree of belief that p lies between given limits? The answer is fixed if, and only if, the prior (degree of belief) probability distribution over the objective chance parameter p is given. Bayes supplied an ingenious argument for the conclusion that in the absence of any further background information about the process, other than that it yields IID trials (K), the prior distribution over p should be uniform. The answer to Bayes question is then

$$\Pr(p_1 \leq p \leq p_2/E(m, n)\&K) = \frac{(n + 1)!}{m!(n - m)!} \int_{p_1}^{p_2} \Theta^m(1 - \Theta)^{n-m} d\Theta \qquad (3)$$

The reader who is unfamiliar with the integral calculus should not be dismayed because what will concern us here is not (3) itself but an application.

This application is reached by asking another question. Suppose that n trials are run, all of which yield B outcomes (E(n, n)). What is the probability that the next r trials will all yield B outcomes (H(r)), given the evidence of the previous outcomes? It follows from (3) that

$$\Pr(H(r)/E(n, n)\&K) = \frac{n + 1}{n + r + 1} \qquad (4)$$

which is commonly called Laplace's rule of succession. Neither Bayes nor Price derived (4). But in his Appendix to Bayes' essay, Price did work out an instance of (3) that was surely intended to be a response to Hume's skeptical attack on induction.

Here is Price's description of the problem and his solution:

> Let us imagine to ourselves the case of a person just brought forth into this world, and left to collect from his observations of the order and course of events what powers and causes take place in it. The Sun would, probably, be the first object that would engage his attention; but after losing it the first night he would be entirely ignorant whether he would ever see it again. He would therefore be in the condition of a person making a first experiment about an event entirely unknown to him. But let him see a second appearance or one *return* of the Sun, and an expectation would be raised in him of a second return, and he might know that there was an odds of 3 to 1 for *some* probability of this. (Bayes 1763, 312–313)

On Price's way of analyzing this situation, there is only one relevant trial (m = n = 1) since the first observation is needed to acquaint the observer with the sun. If we take "*some* probability" to mean that p ≥ 0.5, then (3) yields the value of ¾ or, as Price said, odds of 3 to 1.

Bayes' prior probability assignment is open to challenges, but I will not be concerned with them here.[52] What I do want to call attention to is the curious blend of inductivism and anti-inductivism that flows from Bayes' analysis. From (4) it follows that if all of the first n trials have yielded Bs, then the probability that the next trial will also yield a B is (n + 1)/(n + 2). So as n → ∞, the probability that the next instance will be a B approaches 1—inductivism at work. But, as will be seen in the next section, it follows from Bayes' assignment of priors that the probability that *all* future trials will yield Bs remains flatly o no matter how large n becomes—anti-inductivism at work.

As can be seen from formula (3), Bayes was prepared to assign probabilities (in the sense of degrees of belief) to hypotheses about states of affairs that are not directly observable—what in Hume's parlance would be called the hidden springs of nature. Modern Bayesians are eager to apply Bayes' theorem (1)-(2) to the most far flung hypotheses, including entire scientific theories. Whether or not such far flung applications are warranted, there is surely a need to be able to treat inductive inferences that go beyond the crabbed context that Hume took to be paradigmatic of induction: observe instances of As and record how many are Bs; on the basis of this evidence make an inductive posit as to whether the next A observed will be a B or, more boldly, a posit about all unobserved As. Hume, of course, mentions forms of ampliative reasoning that burst this mold, but he offered little by way of analysis other than the dictum that all inductive reasoning proceeds by way of analogy, a safe but unenlightening bromide.

12

## *The Bayes-Price Rejection of Hume's Straight Rule*

Hume is often billed as the arch inductive skeptic. But Hume's straight rule of induction reveals that what his description of inductive practice expresses is more wide-eyed hope than skepticism. The resolution of this superficial paradox is that Hume's notorious skepticism attaches not to the form of inductive practice but to the possibility of providing a non-question-begging justification for this or any other inductive practice. For Bayes and for Price, the situation looked rather different. For them, rationality considerations dictate that degrees of belief should conform to the axioms of probability and that, for the set up considered in Bayes' essay, the prior probability distribution should have a prescribed form. These results in turn entail a rule of induction that is more skeptical, or at least more cautious, than Reichenbach's straight rule and infinitely more skeptical than Hume's straight rule.

In *Four Dissertations* Price writes, in direct opposition to Hume's straight rule, that if a solid turns the same face in a million tosses, there is "only a probability, not a *certainty*" that the solid will turn the same face in the next trial—a probability of $1,000,001/1,000,002$ according to the Bayes-Laplace rule. But Price also makes a stronger claim: "It must, however, be remembered, that the greatest uniformity and frequency of experience will not offer a proper *proof*, that an event will happen in a future trial, or even render it so much as probable, that it will *always* happen in all future trials" (*FD* 392–393; 160). Does Price really mean to affirm the staunchly skeptical position that no finite number of positive instances, no matter how large, can render a lawlike generalization of the form H: "All As are Bs" probable? Yes! For it follows from Bayes' prior probability assignment that $\Pr(H/K) = 0$ in the case where K specifies that an infinite number of instances are involved. So no matter how many positive instances are recorded in the evidence E, $\Pr(H/E\&K) = 0$. To understand why this is so, suppose that there are an infinite number of individuals, named by $a_1, a_2, \ldots$, all of which are As. It can be shown[53] that if the prior probability assignment is such that $\Pr(H/K) > 0$, then a strong form of instance induction must hold in that as the number n of positive instances piles up, the probability that the next r instances will also be positive approaches 1, that is,

$$\lim_{r,n\to\infty}\Pr(Ba_{n+1}\&Ba_{n+2}\& \ldots \&Ba_{n+r}/Ba_1\& \ldots \&Ba_n\&K) = 1 \qquad (5)$$

But first taking the limit $r \to \infty$ in the Bayes-Laplace rule (4) gives 0, in contradiction to (5). As in Carnap's (1950, 1952) systems of inductive logic, universal generalizations in a universe with an infinite number of individuals cannot be probabilified if Bayes' prior probability assignment is accepted, although the probability that the "next instance" will conform to the generalization can approach certainty as the number of positive instances builds up. It is important to note that the probability calculus itself does not dictate this result. If in the set up studied by Bayes the prior distribution over the objective chance parameter p assigns a positive probability mass to $p = 1$, then (5) does hold, as does the stronger result that the probability of the universal generalization approaches 1 as the number of positive instances increases without bound.

It is amusing to note in passing that the Bayes rule for assigning prior probabilities makes the existence of Hume miracles a certainty. If the lawlike generalization L that all As are Bs is supported by invariable experience E, then the assertion of the existence of an exception to L, $(\exists i)(Aa_i\&\neg Ba_i)$, is the assertion of the existence of a Hume miracle. By Bayes rule, $\Pr((\exists i)(Aa_i\&\neg Ba_i)/E\&K) = 1$.

## 13

## *Hume's Stultification of Scientific Inquiry*

Hume was right that no satisfactory justification of inductive practice can be given, if by a justification is meant a noncircular argument that offers a guarantee of success. It does not follow, however, that all inductive procedures are equally rational. Any procedure that proportions degrees of belief in violation of the probability axioms or that dictates a belief change that is in violation of the rule of conditionalization is irrational—or at least there are arguments of some persuasiveness in favor of such a position. But like subjective Bayesians, I don't think that the constraints of rationality extend any further than this, and thus I think that attempts to identify via rationality considerations a unique prior probability distribution à la Bayes and Price are bound to fail. It is therefore rationally open and, in some contexts, useful to adopt a nonzero prior for a universal generalization, permitting—contra Bayes, Price, and Carnap—a universal generalization to be probabilified by its positive instances.

Hume's sin—which goes in the other direction—was much worse. His straight rule of induction is both descriptively inadequate to actual scientific practice, and it is stultifying to scientific inquiry. Among the zillions of protons observed by particle physicists, none has been verified to decay. But particle physicists do not assign a probability of 1 to the proposition that the next proton to be observed will not decay, and they certainly do not think that they have adequate inductive grounds for probabilistic certainty with respect to the general proposition that no proton ever decays—otherwise the expenditure of time and money on experiments to detect proton decay would be inexplicable on the standard expected utility model of decision making. The general situation is this. If constant and uniform experience E speaks in favor of the lawlike generalization L, then by Hume's straight rule $Pr(L/E\&K) = 1$. Thus, if M express an exception to L, $Pr(M/E\&K) = 0$. It follows that for any further evidence E', eyewitness or other, that intuitively should count in favor of M, either $Pr(M/E'\&E\&K) = 0$ or else $Pr(M/E'\&E\&K)$ is not defined, in which case $Pr(E'/E\&K) = 0$. In either case further inquiry into events that would undermine L is useless,[54] for any potential positive evidence against L would either be rejected as probabilistically impossible or else would not help to raise the credibility of an exception to L above zero.[55]

Is this a result that Hume intended? Strictly speaking, the question is meaningless since Hume does not explicitly use the language of conditional probability. Nevertheless, there is both positive and negative evidence about whether Hume intended a consequence like this one. On the positive side, there is Hume's discussion in Part 2 of "Of Miracles" of the hypothetical story of Queen Elizabeth's resurrection (see section 18), Cardinal de Retz's story of the recovery of a leg by rubbing holy water on it, and of the Jansenist miracle stories. Hume praises Cardinal de Retz for giving no credence to the story he related:

> He considered justly, that it was not requisite, in order to reject a fact of this nature, to be able accurately to disprove the testimony, and to trace its falsehood, through all of the circumstances of knavery and credulity that produced it. . . . He therefore concluded, like a just reasoner, that such evidence carried falsehood on the very face of it, and that a miracle supported by any human testimony, was more properly a subject of derision than of argument. (*E* 124; 149)

And about numerous corroborative witnesses to the Jansenist miracles, he writes: "And what have we to oppose to such clouds of witnesses, but the absolute impossibility or miraculous nature of the events, which they relate? And this surely, in the eyes of all reasonable people, will alone be regarded as a sufficient refutation" (*E* 125; 149).

On the negative side, there is the fact that maintaining such a position appears dogmatic. And not surprisingly, Hume does try to distance himself from such dogmatism. When uniform experience supports a law statement L that is contradicted by testimony, Hume speaks of putting "proof against proof, of which the strongest must prevail, but still with a diminution of its force, in proportion to that of its antagonist" (*E* 114; 143). This idea is reiterated in the letter to Blair quoted above in section 9. After claiming to provide a proof against miracles that "implies no doubt," he adds: "[B]ut there are degrees of this species [of proof], and when a weaker proof is opposed to a stronger, it is overcome" (*L*, Vol. 1, 350). But if the weighing of proof against proof is to be done within the ambit of the probability calculus and the rule of conditionalization,[56] then Hume's straight rule has to be dropped—his proof in favor of L by uniform experience cannot be taken to mean probability 1 but at most a high probability that is short of 1. Consequently, uniform experience does *not* furnish a proof against a miracle in the sense of making the conditional probability of its occurrence flatly zero, although this probability may be very, very tiny. Such a concession is far from tiny since it would mean that the distinction between a (Hume) miracle and a marvel is a matter of degree rather than of kind. And once the concession is granted, it is natural to wonder how it can be that testimonial evidence can ground belief in marvels but not in (Hume) miracles.

One response to this challenge involves a partial retreat: grant that for a miracle statement M, $Pr(M/E\&K)$ can be greater than zero and that testimonial evidence t(M) to M can suffice to make $Pr(M/t(M)\&E\&K) > 0.5$, at least for some cases of secular (Hume) miracles; but maintain that, because of the special features of cases of (Hume) miracles with alleged religious significance, testimonial evidence can never suffice to make $Pr(M/t(M)\&E\&K) > 0.5$. In section 16, I will present the evidence that Hume opted for this position in Part 2 of his essay. But before turning to that matter, it is worth examining a case that many of Hume's critics have taken as a vivid illustration of how the account of induction underlying Hume's "proof" against miracles serves to stultify empirical enquiry. I refer to the Indian prince.

# 14

## The Indian Prince

Hume's critics have found innumerable ways to underscore Richard Price's point (see *FD* 405ff; 163) that unless testimonial evidence is allowed to overcome prior improbabilities, there is no way to underwrite the sorts of inferences made in everyday life and in science. We would not give much credence to a newspaper report of the number of the winning ticket in a fair lottery with odds of millions to one; we would not, as Richard Whately noted in his delightful satire "Historical Doubts Relative to Napoleon Bonaparte" (1819), give credence to the reality of a figure whose career is marked by so many fantastical adventures, etc. Hume apologists tend to respond by citing the miracle vs. marvel distinction and by claiming that there is no problem here since the examples in question fall on the marvel side of the cut. That is fair enough. In his *History of England* (1754–1762) Hume wrote: "It is the business of history to distinguish between the *miraculous* and the *marvelous*; to reject the first in all narrations merely profane and human; to doubt the second; and when obliged by unquestionable testimony . . . to admit something extraordinary, to receive as little of it as is consistent with the known facts and circumstances" (128). What is not fair is the hocus pocus that apologists and Hume himself have used in an attempt to deal with examples that certainly appear to fall on the (Hume) miracle side of the cut. Just such a case arises for the Indian prince.

Hume's Indian prince, who had never experienced a cold climate and refused to believe reports of the effects of frost, is undoubtedly an indirect reference to Locke's story of the king of Siam.[57] But the example and the point it raises is hardly original to Locke. A good part of St. Thomas More's *Dialogue Concerning Heresies* (1557) is devoted to combating the notion that reports of miracles are to be dismissed because they seem to be contrary to nature and reason.[58] Not surprisingly, India turns up in one of his illustrations:

> If there were a man of Inde yᵗ neuer cam out of his country nor neuer had sene any whyte man or woman in his lyfe & syth he seeth innumerable peple blak he mygt wene that it were agaynst the nature of man to be whyte. Nowe yf he shall bycause nature semeth to shewe hym so byleue therfor that all the worlde lyed yf they wolde say the contrary who were in the wronge he that byleueth his reason and nature or they yᵗ agaynst his of reason and nature shall tell hym as it is of trouthe? (65)

Here then is the challenge for Hume: if there is a principled objection to allowing testimony to count in favor of a resurrection, will not the same objection also lead to the (absurd?) result that the Indian prince was rational in not allowing testimony to count in favor of the claim that water can become so hard as to bear up the weight of an elephant? Since the challenge is so obvious and since there were so many variants in the literature of the time, it is surprising that Hume did not take it up in the first edition of the *Enquiry*.[59] Hume's silence in the face of this well-known challenge was criticized by implication in Skelton's *Ophiomaches* (1749), which Hume had read in manuscript form.[60] Thus, it can hardly be a coincidence that in the 1750 edition of the *Enquiry* Hume's Indian prince makes an appearance. Hume obviously did not think that the extra paragraph he added to the 1750 edition sufficed because he later penned a note that was printed on the last page of the new edition along with the explanation that "The distance of the Author from the Press is the Cause, why the following Passage arriv'd not in time to be inserted in its proper place." In subsequent editions this note is printed as a footnote. It is difficult to tell whether haste or deliberate obfuscation was responsible for the resulting mess.

Hume begins by saying that the prince, "who refused to believe the first relations [i.e., reports] concerning the effects of frost, reasoned justly" (*E* 113; 143). How so? The prince was right to be suspicious of reports of a solid form of water. But Hume's account of induction seems to imply not just suspicion but outright rejection. Hume does say that "it naturally required very strong testimony to engage his [i.e., the prince's] assent to facts, that arose from a state of nature, with which he was unacquainted, and which bore so little analogy to events, of which he had constant and uniform experience" (*E* 113–114; 143). How Hume thinks that further testimony can justly win the assent of the Indian prince but cannot justly win assent in cases of religious miracles will be discussed in due course. Here I am concerned with Hume's attempt to muddy the waters of the Indian prince.

Hume's first move is to distance himself from Locke, on whose analysis the Dutch ambassador related facts that were "contrary" to the experience of the king of Siam (recall section 7). Hume says that the similar facts related to the Indian prince, "though they were not contrary to his experience, they were not conformable to it" (*E* 114; 143). This is a distinction which many commentators from Campbell (1762) on down have found sophistical. And understandably so: Why isn't the passing of water from a liquid to a solid state just as contrary to the prince's experience as the springing to life of a dead man? The footnote which Hume later added shifts ground in suggesting that what matters in the example is not just the *prince's* experience but *all* past experience. The transformation of water to a solid state, he writes,

> may be denominated *extraordinary*, and requires a pretty strong testimony, to render it credible to people in a warm climate: But still it is not *miraculous*, nor contrary to uniform experience of the course of nature in cases where all the circumstances are the same. The inhabitants of

Sumatra have always seen water fluid in their own climate, and the freezing of their rivers ought to be deemed a prodigy: But they never saw water in Muscovy during the winter; and therefore cannot reasonably be positive what would there be the consequence. (*E* fn 114; 154)

The most straightforward reading of the quoted passage is to take Hume to be saying that the solid form of water is not miraculous because a miracle is to be defined as a violation of a *strongly presumptive law statement*, i.e. a lawlike generalization such that the total collective experience of all mankind provides many positive instances and no negative instances. This reading fits with Hume's declaration that a resurrection is a miracle because it "has never been observed in any age or country" and with his rejection of Locke's subjectivist conception of miracles that relativizes the concept to a particular observer.

So far so good. But granted that the passing of water from a liquid to a solid state is not a miracle in this new sense, how does Hume escape the consequence that his rule of induction which produces a "proof" against a resurrection also leads to a proof against ice? Hume's footnote seems to be suggesting that the inhabitants of Sumatra erred because they did not subscribe to a collectivist version of the straight rule where the "examined instances" of a generalization encompass the instances examined by all mankind in all ages and countries. Such a construal is at odds with Hume's approach to reasoning about matters of fact in terms of individualistic psychology. And apart from the issue of whether it is properly Humean, the collectivist straight rule is, by Hume's own lights, useless. No individual agent can use it if all she has to go on are her own direct, firsthand experiences. Nor can Hume allow her to access, through the medium of testimony, to the experiences of others. For his strategy is to construct an argument from "experience" against miracles and then to set that argument against testimony for miracles; thus, in the context of Hume's polemic, "experience" can only mean direct, nontestimonial experience. This segregation of personal experience and derived experience based on testimony (to use Campbell's [1762] terminology) is wholly artificial since most of inductive inferences are based on a mixture of the two.[61] Hume offers no positive account of how the two are to be integrated; his focus is on the case where the two are in conflict, and all he has to offer for such cases is an undefined "subtraction" procedure by which the one supposedly destroys the force of the other. It is not too strong to say that the founding members of the Royal Society, a number of whom were staunch defenders of miracles, would have found an antiscientific tinge in Hume stance against miracles. For they emphasized the communal character of scientific knowledge, for which testimony is crucial and which, contra Hume, can take precedence over personal experience (see Burns 1981 and section 21 below).

But to end the quibbling, note that even if we were to agree to Hume's parsing of "experience" and to the collectivist view of inductive inference, the problem posed by the Indian prince arises again for a slightly altered example. If, as we now think, *homo sapiens* arose in the hot climate of Africa, there was a stage in human history where the total collective experience of the species coincided in relevant respects with that of the Indian prince. In these circumstances the collectivist version of Hume's straight rule then dictates a conditional probability of 0 for the solid state of water and, thus, a dismissal of a report of such a state of affairs.

Hume still has an out. In his footnote on the Indian prince, Hume says that frozen water is not to be counted as miraculous because it is not "contrary to uniform experience of the course of nature *in cases where all the circumstances are the same*" (emphasis added). This suggests a more sophisticated version of Hume's straight rule: namely, if n As have been examined in circumstances C, and all of them have been found to be Bs, then if n is sufficiently large, the probability that in circumstances C all As are Bs is 1. Perhaps then Hume's suggestion is that since the circumstances are not the same in Muscovy as in Sumatra, the Sumatrans are not correct in inferring, on the basis of their experience, that rivers do not freeze in Muscovy. The trouble with such a suggestion starts with the observation that if "circumstances" may include any facet of the state of the world, then, since in all likelihood the circumstances are never exactly the same in any two instances, the more sophisticated straight rule is rendered inoperative. The commonsense reaction is that not just any facet of the state of the world counts as a *relevant* circumstance. But then the sophisticated straight rule is rendered inoperative until the relevant circumstances are specified. No a priori specification will be forthcoming since it is part of inductive investigations to uncover what these circumstances are. Any well formulated law statement will itself specify what it takes to be the relevant circumstances, which is to say that it can be put in the form "All $\hat{A}$s are Bs" where $\hat{A} = A \& X_1 \& X_2 \& \ldots \& X_n$ and the $X_i$ are specifications of the factors that characterize what are taken to be the relevant circumstances.[62] On Hume's account of induction, what is the warrant for such a well formulated law statement, if not the original straight rule?

Perhaps we are being unfair to Hume. The Indian prince was operating with an hypothesis that says, in effect, that temperature is not a relevant circumstance; that is, whatever the ambient temperature, water never assumes a solid form. The prince's own experience is restricted to a limited temperature range, as Hume remarks: "No Indian, it is evident, could have experience that water did not freeze in cold climates. This is placing nature in a situation quite unknown to him; and it is impossible for him to tell *a priori* what will result from it. It is making a new experiment, the consequence of which is always uncertain" (*E* fn 114; 153). If Hume's suggestion is that the prince's inductive leap is fallacious because it moves from experiences in one temperature range to a conclusion about an unexperienced temperature range, then it must be explained why the suggestion doesn't undermine all inductive reasoning. For *all* induction involves a leap from an observed range to an unobserved range, whether the range involves space, time, or a parameter such as temperature. A more sensible suggestion is that the inductive leap should be made less daring by modifying the original straight rule to require not only that the number of instances be sufficiently large but also that they come from a variety of circumstances and/or that they constitute a representative sample of the entire reference class. That would indeed be an improvement, but improvements of this kind do not avoid the Indian prince embarrassment. That embarrassment will always resurface in more complicated examples as long as the rule of induction yields a probability-one conclusion for a universal generalization from finite data. On the other hand, if Hume's straight rule of induction is modified so as to escape this embarrassment by assigning a probability less than 1, then Hume no longer has a "proof" against miracles, nor a principled distinction between miracles and marvels, and the way is opened for testimonies to establish the credibility of resurrections and the like.

Commentators seem unable to appreciate this basic point. A good example is found in John Stuart Mill's attempted rescue of Hume in *System of Logic* (Bk. III, ch. 25) from the Indian prince embarrassment. When Hume says that the stories the Indian prince found marvelous were "not contrary to his experience," Mill takes him to mean that the facts related are not contrary to any "law of causation" known to the prince. Mill himself employs a straight rule of induction for establishing that A causes B. To be sure, his rule is more complicated than Hume's since the uniform experience needed to instantiate Mill's rule must support the generalizations that correspond to Mill's Methods of Agreement, Difference, Residues, and Concomitant Variation. But when the uniform experience in favor of these generalizations is weighty enough, Mill speaks of a "complete induction" for the law of causation, and any alleged fact that contradicts a (presumptive) law of causation supported by a complete induction is "to be disbelieved totally" (*System of Logic*, 439). This is the same stultifying result that flows from Hume's less sophisticated straight rule. Mill did not succeed in showing how Hume's straight rule of induction can be jiggled so as to exclude the kinds of miracles Hume wanted to banish while also allowing for scientific progress.

Finally, it is worth reflecting on what Hume says about analogy. In the paragraph added to the main text of the 1750 edition, Hume seems to be saying that frozen water bears some positive analogy to the states of nature with which the prince is acquainted, although the analogy is very weak. However, the appended note seems to say that there is no positive analogy:

One may sometimes conjecture from analogy what may follow; but still this is conjecture. And it must be confessed, that, in the present case of freezing, the event follows contrary to the rules of analogy, and is such that a rational Indian would not look for. The operations of cold upon water are not gradual, according to the degrees of cold; but whenever it comes to the freezing point, the water passes in a moment, from the utmost liquidity to perfect hardness. (*E* fn 114; 153–54)

The notion of analogy is vague enough to allow such seemingly contradictory intuitions. But it seems to me that the most sensible reaction is that unless the prince was completely hidebound, he must have had experiences that furnish a positive analogy. I refer to phase changes. In India, as elsewhere, water vapor condenses as the temperature falls, and molten metal solidifies as it cools. If F is the hypothesis that water solidifies at low temperatures, E records the prince's past experiences in which water never freezes, and K records the experiences of the just mentioned phase changes, then the positive analogy suggests that $Pr(F/E\&K)$ be set above 0. If the analogy here is regarded as weak, then $Pr(F/E\&K)$ should not be set much above 0 so that, as Hume says, very strong testimony would be needed to boost the probability of F to a respectable level.

All of this is interesting, but how does it help Hume? He could modify his straight rule so as to confer a probability of 1 on a presumptive (or strongly presumptive) law if and only if there is no positive analogy in favor of an exception. Call such a presumptive law a *presumptive hard law*, and call a violation of such a law a *hard Hume miracle*. Hume could then maintain that testimony to hard miracles is to be rejected while allowing that testimony may overcome doubts about the softer variety of miracles. And further, he could hold that the miracles scientists are willing to entertain—violations of conservation of energy, say—are soft miracles, whereas miracles that lie at the heart of religions—the raising of a dead man, the turning of water into wine, etc.—are hard miracles. I must admit that I find a certain appeal to this line. But I am dubious that it can lead to the kind of "proof" against religious miracles that Hume wanted. The notion of analogy is so elastic that in any moderately complex situation one can always find positive and negative analogies. If one sees a positive analogy for a solid form of water in other phase changes, why not see a positive analogy for resurrection in near death experiences, catatonic states, and the like?

## 15

## *Hume's Maxim*

Toward the end of Part 1, Hume announces a "general maxim":

> That no testimony is sufficient to establish a miracle, unless the testimony be of such a kind, that its falsehood would be more miraculous, than the fact, which it endeavours to establish; and even in that case there is a mutual destruction of arguments, and the superior only gives us an assurance suitable to that degree of force, which remains, after deducting the inferior. (E 115–116; 144)

Hume's Maxim begs to be made precise by translating it into the language of probability theory. There should be no surprise, however, in finding that a number of inequivalent translations are possible since seemingly transparent English statements about the credibility of events turn out to be hiding ambiguities about conditional probabilities.[63] But while there may be no single 'correct' translation of Hume's Maxim, some seem to me, for both technical and contextual reasons, to be preferable to others. At the start, I stipulate that I am mainly interested in translations that take "establish a miracle" to mean make credible rather than to make certain. The opposite reading has, as we will shortly see, certain advantages for Hume, but it also carries the major drawback of making the Maxim useless against opponents, of which there were many in the eighteenth century, who are willing to eschew certainty in favor of reasonable belief. Before dealing with modern translation attempts, it is well to see what Hume's contemporaries thought.

In *Four Dissertations*, Price paraphrased the first part of Hume's Maxim as: "[T]hat no testimony should engage our belief, except the improbability in the falsehood of it is greater than that in the event which it attests" (*FD* 405; 163). In the language of conditional probability Price apparently took this paraphrase to mean either that

$$Pr(M/E\&K) > Pr(\neg M/t(M)\&E\&K) \qquad (P)$$

or else that

$$Pr(M/E\&K) > Pr(t(M)/\neg M\&E\&K) \qquad (P')$$

That Price thought that the conditional probability of M, $Pr(M/E\&K)$, prior to testimony belongs on the left-hand side of the inequality, is clear:

> Let it be remembered, that the improbability of the event here mentioned, must mean the improbability which we should have seen there was of its happening independently of any evidence for it, or, previously to the evidence of testimony informing us that it *has* happened. No other improbability can be meant, because the whole dispute is about the improbability that remains after the evidence of testimony given for the event. (*FD* fn 405; 174–75)

But what he thought belongs on the right-hand side is less clear, although (P) fits best with the text. He posits as an example that the "testimony informed us rightly ten times to one in which it deceived us," and asserts that under this supposition there would be a "probability of ten to one for the reality of every fact supported by testimony" (*FD* 406–407; 163). A plausible reading of this passage is that Price is using frequency data to justify setting $Pr(\neg M/t(M)\&E\&K) = 1/11$. He then goes on to claim that this case provides a counterexample to Hume's Maxim, which would make sense if (P) is taken as the translation. For assuming that $Pr(M/$

E&K) is low—say, one in a million—(P) fails although the testimony renders the miracle credible since in this case $Pr(M/t(M)\&E\&K) = 10/11$.

The reader can easily supply an example to show that (P') likewise fails as a necessary condition for testimony to establish the credibility of a miracle.((P') does come close to being a necessary condition for testimony to establish the credibility of a miracle since $Pr(M/t(M)\&E\&K) > 0.5$ implies that $Pr(M/E\&K) > Pr(t(M)/\neg M\&E\&K) \times Pr(\neg M/E\&K)$ and since $Pr(\neg M/E\&K) = 1 - Pr(M/E\&K)$ will be close to 1 if M is a miracle statement.) However, it is worth noting that (P') *is* a necessary condition for $Pr(M/t(M)\&E\&K) = 1$,[64] so that if, contrary to my stipulation, Hume takes "establish" in this context to mean render certain rather than render credible, then (P') would seem to be a sensible reading of the Maxim. However, we may safely assume that $Pr(M/E\&K) < 1$—otherwise M would already be rendered certain by the background evidence so that it hardly qualifies as a miracle and needs no testimonial evidence for its support. Then a necessary condition for $Pr(M/t(M)\&E\&K) = 1$ is that $Pr(t(M)/\neg M\&E\&K) = 0$, so that (P') holds, so to speak, by default. If "establish" means render certain and if the probability of the falsity of the testimony is translated as $Pr(t(M)/\neg M\&E\&K)$, then the most straightforward maxim would not be the one Hume announced but the alternative maxim that no testimony is sufficient to establish the certainty of a miracle unless the testimony to the miracle be of such a kind that the falsity of the testimony has zero credibility. I doubt that Hume's contemporaries would have been much impressed by this piece of wisdom.

Is there another probabilistic reading of Hume's Maxim on which it fares better? Gillies (1991) and Sobel (1991) read Hume's Maxim by moving the t(M) in (P) (or the ¬M in (P')) to the left hand side of the slash:

$$Pr(M/E\&K) > Pr(\neg M\&t(M)/E\&K) \qquad\qquad (GS)$$

This is certainly nearer the mark, for a little manipulation shows that (GS) is a necessary condition for the credibility of the miracle statement M in the sense that $Pr(M/t(M)\&E\&K) > 0.5$ entails (GS). But there are two things to be said against (GS). First, although (GS) is a necessary condition for the credibility of a miracle, it is not sufficient—(GS) does not entail that $Pr(M/t(M)\&E\&K) > 0.5$. Now the use of "unless" in the first part of Hume's Maxim may seem to indicate that he intended to give only a necessary condition. However, at the end of the paragraph in which the Maxim is stated, Hume writes: "If the falsehood of his testimony would be more miraculous, than the event which he relates; then, and not till then, can he pretend to commend my belief or opinion" (*E* 116; 144). Here Hume seems to propose his test as sufficient as well as necessary. Second, $Pr(\neg M\&t(M)/E\&K)$ does not seem to properly capture the probability of the "falsehood of the testimony." $Pr(\neg M/t(M)\&E\&K)$ and $Pr(t(M)/\neg M\&E\&K)$ are both plausible candidates for that role, an indication of the plausibility being that frequentists would seek to estimate the probability of the falsehood of the testimony either in terms of the percentage of cases where no miracle occurs on occasions when the witness testifies to a miracle, or else in terms of the percentage of cases where the witness testifies to miracles on occasions when no miracle occurs. Now $Pr(\neg M\&t(M)/E\&K) = Pr(t(M)/E\&K) \times Pr(\neg M/t(M)\&E\&K) = Pr(\neg M/E\&K) \times Pr(t(M)/\neg M\&E\&K)$. The latter two products involve the plausible candidate probabilities in question. But they also involve the prior probability of testimony, $Pr(t(M)/E\&K)$, and the prior improbability of the miracle, $Pr(\neg M/E\&K)$, both of which seem irrelevant to the probability of the falsehood of testimony.

Sobel (1996) has proposed reading the first part of Hume's Maxim as:

$$Pr(M\&t(M)/E\&K) > Pr(\neg M\&t(M)/E\&K) \tag{S}$$

But it seems very implausible to take the left-hand side of this inequality to represent the probability of the event the testimony endeavors to establish. The only plausible candidates for that role are the prior probability $Pr(M/E\&K)$ of M and the posterior probability $Pr(M/t(M)\&E\&K)$ of M.

My proposal[65] starts from the fact that Hume describes a situation in which it is known that the witness has testified to the occurrence of a miraculous event. Thus, we should be working with probabilities conditioned on t(M), as well as on the evidence of experience and the other background knowledge K. In such a setting, the probability of the event the testimony endeavors to establish is $Pr(M/t(M)\&E\&K)$. And the probability of the falsehood of the testimony is $Pr(\neg M/t(M)\&E\&K)$. To say that the falsehood of the testimony is more miraculous than the event it endeavors to establish is just to say that the former probability is smaller than the latter, that is,

$$Pr(M/t(M)\&E\&K) > Pr(\neg M/t(M)\&E\&K) \tag{E}$$

Applying the negation principle to (E), it is seen that (E) is equivalent to

$$Pr(M/t(M)\&E\&K) > 0.5 \tag{C}$$

which is just the assertion that the miracle statement is made credible by the testimony. Note that on the assumption that $Pr(t(M)/E\&K) \neq 0$, (S) and (E) are equivalent. But the fact that they are equivalent does not make then equally good reading of Hume's Maxim.[66]

If we have arrived at a correct way of viewing the first part of Hume's Maxim through the lens of probability, then that part of the Maxim is unexceptionable. But at the same time, Price's complaint reasserts itself: "[T]he whole dispute is about the improbability that remains after the evidence of testimony given for the event." The first part of Hume's Maxim is just the unhelpful tautology that no testimony is sufficient to establish the credibility of a miracle unless it is sufficient to make the occurrence more probable than not. Another of Hume's contemporaries, George Campbell, took an equally harsh view of Hume's Maxim:

What then shall be said of the conclusion which he [Hume] gives as the sum quintessence of the first part of the Essay? The best thing, for aught I know, that can be said is, that it contains a most certain truth, though at the same time the least significant, that ever perhaps was ushered into the world with such solemnity. . . . If any reader think himself instructed by this discovery, I should be loth to envy him the pleasure he may derive from it. (*CDM*, 55; 193)

In sum, I conclude that those commentators who have been impressed by the first half of Hume's Maxim have been impressed not by content but by the nice ring of the language of Hume's formulation. Hume apologists are apt to respond that there is a useful moral that can be extracted from Hume's discussion of his Maxim: extraordinary claims require extraordinary proofs. The moral was hardly original to Hume. Thus, for example, Annet wrote: "A history of an extraordinary uncommon kind should have more than common proof. That is, the proofs given should be equal to the things to be proved. And the more momentous the affair is, or is esteem'd, so much more plain, and certain, should be the evidence" (*RJC* 63; 134). But it is risible to attribute to either Hume or Annet some deep insight. All of the parties on the opposite side from Hume in the eighteenth-century debate on miracles knew that miracle claims could not be established without the help of very strong evidence. In some cases they thought they had produced the required evidence. Perhaps they were wrong. But to show that they were wrong takes more than solemnly uttered platitudes.

What additional principles or facts did Hume need to move from the platitude that forms the first part of Hume's Maxim to the conclusion that it is impossible or even difficult to establish the credibility of a miracle? That the prior $\Pr(M/E\&K)$ is zero would sufficient, but I have already rejected this move. That $\Pr(M/E\&K)$ is nonzero but very small does not seem sufficient, as Price himself was quick to argue. He pointed to the

degree of [prior] improbability which there is against almost all the most common facts, independently of the evidence of testimony against them. In many cases of particular histories which are immediately believed upon the slightest testimony, there would have appeared to us previously to this testimony, an improbability of almost infinity to one against their reality. . . . It is then very common for the slightest testimony to overcome an almost infinite [prior] improbability. (*FD* 406; 163)

Hume has two options here. He could challenge Price's claim in general. And in effect Hume does this with his own claim that the probative value of the evidence of testimony to an event is diminished by prior improbability of the event (see section 17). Or he could counter that although Price's claim is correct for some cases, it fails in cases of miracles with alleged religious significance because of the special features of these cases (see section 16). But before turning to these matters a few words should be said about the second half of Hume's Maxim.

The first half of the Maxim admits a probabilistic reading that makes this part of the Maxim into a correct though nearly tautologous principle. But then the second half of the Maxim appears to be nonsensical. Recall that it says that *"even in that case* there is a mutual destruction of arguments, and the superior only gives an assurance suitable to the degree of force, which remains, after deducting the inferior." The italicized phrase suggests that even when the testimony is of such a kind that its falsehood would be more miraculous than the fact which it endeavours to establish there is still a *further* destruction of arguments. Such talk appears to involve an illicit double counting: the weighing up of the countervailing factors in t(M) and in E&K has already been done, and if the result is that Pr(M/t(M)&E&K) > 0.5, then that's the way it is, and no further subtraction is called for. Hume uses the idea of a "destruction of arguments" and the need to "deduct" or "subtract" the force of the one from the other throughout his essay. My contention is that such talk is out of place in the Maxim. It turns up again in Part 2 of the miracles essay, first, in the claim that in the case of popular religions the subtraction "amounts to an entire annihilation" (see section 16) and, second, in his contrary miracles argument (see section 23). In these instances, my contention is that the idea is appropriately but crudely applied. Commentators from Campbell (1762) onward have complained about the crudity. The only precise way to evaluate the complaints is to turn the handle on Bayes's theorem and crank out the posterior probability on the total evidence. The result is not always what Hume wants it to be.[67]

## 16

### *What Is Hume's Thesis?*

At this juncture, readers may be puzzled about what Hume's thesis is, especially if they are operating under the principle of charity which presumes that such an acute philosopher as Hume must have had some claim in mind that is interesting but not glaringly false. I am all for charity, but in this instance charity requires a real stretch.

We have seen that in Part 1 of "Of Miracles" Hume claims to offer a proof against miracles that is "as entire as any argument from experience can possibly be imagined." The proof, such as it is, applies to all miracles whether of a religious or a secular nature. Why doesn't Hume's essay end there? Why did Hume need to add a Part 2 that is twice as long as Part 1? Because the proof from experience is not the final word since it may be opposed by a proof from testimony. Part 2 is concerned with how this contest of opposing arguments plays itself out, especially in cases of alleged miracles deemed to have religious significance. What is Hume's thesis about the outcome of such contests? Throughout Part 2, Hume bobs and weaves, shifting among several different claims against the possibility of establishing the credibility of a miracle. This shiftiness is, I think, symptomatic both of Hume's uncertainty about what he wanted to prove and also of his (perhaps unconscious) doubts about what his arguments establish. I can put my charge sharply, if somewhat unfairly, by posing a dilemma for Hume. There is a weak version of his thesis that is surely correct, but it amounts to no more than a collection of platitudes that hardly require a philosophical dissertation for support. There is a very strong version of his thesis that is far from platitudinous; indeed, it is patently false. Part 2 contains attempts to escape between the horns of platitude and patent falsity. The way is narrow. I will eventually take a path that Hume would not have found uncongenial (see section 20). But unlike Hume, I do not think that this path leads to a philosophical high ground that justifies the self-congratulatory remarks at the beginning of Hume's essay.

To begin, we can read Part 2 on one level as a cautionary sermonette. Reflect, oh gentle reader, on mankind's passion for surprise and wonder; reflect on our susceptibility to deception and self-deception, which is heightened when religious enthusiasm is present; reflect on the fact that the religiously converted may be tempted to use deception to promote a holy cause; and finally, reflect on the fact that miracles abound chiefly "among ignorant and barbarous nations" (E 119; 146). Such reflections should make us think twice before accepting reports of miracles and thrice when the alleged events are thought to have religious significance. Platitudes have their uses, and it doesn't hurt to repeat this one. But Hume's repetition of it does not serve to advance the eighteenth century discussion of miracles since all parties to the debate would have readily agreed to it—indeed, even the proponents of religious miracles enunciate versions of it.

The platitude under discussion can be given various useful forms by means of the probability calculus. For example, the probabilistic translation (C) of the condition for testimony to establish the credibility of a miracle can be shown to be equivalent to

$$\Pr(M/E\&K) > \Pr(t(M)/\neg M\&E\&K) \times \left[ \frac{1 - \Pr(M/E\&K)}{\Pr(t(M)/M\&E\&K)} \right] \quad (C')$$

The Humean sermonette based on (C') goes as follows. Suppose that uniform experience as codified in E is very strongly in favor of a presumptive law of which M states an exception. So as not to stultify the Bayesian version of enquiry, assume that $\Pr(M/E\&K)$ is greater than 0 but very small (e.g., $10^{-20}$). Suppose further as part of the background knowledge K that the witness is a religious enthusiast who takes the alleged miracle in question to have religious significance. Such a person can be expected to shout it to the world if he actually observed the miraculous event, so that if the background knowledge K indicates that the witness is in a favorable position to observe the event if it occurs, then $\Pr(t(M)/M\&E\&K)$

should be very close to 1. Thus, the factor [ ] in (C') will be close to unity. As a consequence, (C') will surely fail if $Pr(t(M)/\neg M\&E\&K)$ is substantially greater than $Pr(M/E\&K)$ $(=10^{-20})$. And $Pr(t(M)/\neg M\&E\&K)$ will be non-negligible for religious enthusiasts who have a tendency to testify to the miraculous event when it doesn't occur, either because they have been deceived or because they resort to the use of deceit to win over the unconverted. Having said all of this, we still haven't escaped the realm of the platitudinous, although the platitude has been given a useful quantitative form. Nor has anything been said to raise disagreement from Hume's opponents. For the probability calculus is perfectly compatible with values for the relevant probabilities for which (C') does hold; and, of course, Hume's opponents will claim that the details of some actual cases of reported religious miracles makes these values reasonable.

Hume certainly escaped the platitudinous when he made the very strong claim, in editions of the *Enquiry* prior to 1768, that "no Testimony for any kind of miracle can ever possibly amount to a Probability, much less to a Proof; and that even supposing it amounted to a Proof, 'twould be opposed by another Proof, deriv'd from the very Nature of the Fact, which it would endeavour to establish" (1748, 198–199). In this context the element of divine intervention in Hume's second definition of 'miracle' is irrelevant since Hume is talking about naturalistically characterized events, such as the return to life of a dead man. Under this reading Hume's very strong claim is false, or so I have argued. In the 1768 edition Hume substituted "has ever amounted to" for "can ever possibly amount to." Was the recognition of a need for a retreat occasioned by Price's *Four Dissertations* (1767) and Hume's conversations with Price? The timing and Hume's complimentary remarks about Price (see section 10) might seem to suggest a positive answer. However, the situation is unclear, for, as will be seen presently, even in the original 1748 edition Hume qualified the absurdly strong thesis just quoted; but perhaps significantly, only after 1768 is that qualification, which was originally stuck in a footnote, moved into the main text.

Between the platitudes and the absurdly strong thesis there is the substantial and important claim that in no actually recorded case is the testimonial evidence strong enough to establish the credibility of a miracle. In one respect Hume's support for this thesis is disappointing. All we get in Part 2 is a cursory review of some of the then famous Catholic and profane miracles. No attempt is made in any of these cases to give a detailed presentation of all the circumstances and all the evidence, eyewitness and otherwise, that would allow one to make an informed judgment as to the credibility of the alleged miracle. Most glaring of all is the omission of any discussion of the case that was the centerpiece of the eighteenth century debate—the resurrection of Jesus. As noted in section 7, this debate was galvanized by Woolston's charge of palpable imposture and by Annet's reiteration of the charge. There were many responses—Sherlock (1728), Pearce (1729), Chandler (1744), Jackson (1744), and West (1747), to name only a few—which claimed to weigh up the evidence in all its rich detail and which found the balance to favor the reality of the resurrection. If Hume had really aspired to be a miracle debunker in the mode of Woolston and Annet, he should have entered the fray.

No doubt prudence suggested that he not enter this particular fray. But there are also strong indications that Hume thought that he could remain above the fray. For Hume, the class of actually reported miracles is co-extensive with the class of miracles that are supposed to have religious significance. As he wrote to Blair in 1761: "I never read of a miracle in my life, that was not meant to establish some new point of religion" (*L*, Vol. 1, 350). Furthermore, the change made in the 1768 edition does not negate the evidence that Hume intended to maintain the strong thesis that testimony cannot establish the credibility of miracles deemed to have religious significance. And without a thesis of this sort, there is little to distinguish Hume's essay—save its forceful rhetoric—from other anti-miracle tracts of the period, and no excuse for Hume not to enter the fray and attempt to answer the detailed arguments of Sherlock and others.

My grounds for attributing this strong thesis to Hume lie in the paragraph containing the change in the 1768 edition and the three paragraphs that follow it. When experience supporting a presumptive law collides with testimony

> we have nothing to do but to subtract the one from the other, and embrace an opinion, either on one side or the other, with that assurance which arises from the remainder. But according to the principle explained, this subtraction with regard to all popular religions, amounts to an entire annihilation; and therefore we may establish it as a maxim, that no human testimony can have such a force as to prove a miracle, and make it a just foundation for any such system of religion. (*E* 127; 150–51)

The following paragraph (originally printed as a footnote and later moved into the main text) emphasizes limitations Hume has added to his strong thesis: "I beg the limitations here made may be remarked, when I say, that a miracle can never be proved, so as to be the foundation of a system of religion. For I own, that otherwise, there may possibly be miracles, or violations of the usual course of nature, of such a kind as to admit proof from human testimony; though, perhaps, it will be impossible to find any such in all the records of history" (*E* 127; 151). Hume then gives two hypothetical examples to help illustrate what the limitations are.

In the first example, Hume considers testimony to the occurrence of eight days of total darkness around the world. Evidently such events are to be regarded as miraculous on Hume's first definition of miracle since readers are led to presume that they are to hypothesize that such an occurrence has never before been experienced in any age or country.[68]

However, his announced limitation applies to this example since the miraculous darkness is not supposed to serve as a foundation for a system of religion, and as a result Hume grants that the testimony could establish the credibility of the events if it is "very extensive and uniform" (*E* 128; 151). In his second hypothetical example Hume imagines that it is reported that Queen Elizabeth died and "after being interred a month, she again appeared, resumed the throne and governed England for three years." Hume response to this example is uncompromising. "I should not doubt of her pretended death, and of those other public circumstances that followed it: I should only assert it to have been pretended, and that it neither was, nor possibly could be real" (*E* 128; 151). This is followed by an instance of Hume's strong thesis: "But should this miracle be ascribed to any new system of religion; men, in all ages, have been so much imposed on by ridiculous stories of that kind, that this very circumstance would be a full proof of cheat, and sufficient, with all men of sense, not only to make them reject the fact, but even reject it without farther examination" (*E* 128–129; 151–52).

The reasoning behind Hume's strong thesis is, to repeat, that in the case of an alleged religious miracle, the subtraction of the weight of uniform experience from the weight of testimony "amounts to an entire annihilation." Viewed through the lens of Bayes' theorem, Hume's subtraction procedure amounts to more than a simple numerical subtraction. The relevant posterior probability can be written as

$$\Pr(M/t(M)\&E\&K) \qquad\qquad (6)$$

$$= \cfrac{1}{1 + \left[\cfrac{1-\Pr(M/E\&K)}{\Pr(M/E\&K)}\right]\left\{\cfrac{\Pr(t(M)/\neg M\&E\&K)}{\Pr(t(M)/M\&E\&K)}\right\}}$$

(This is just an instance of Bayes' theorem (2).) To keep matters simple, let us suppose that the witness is an honest and reliable reporter of what she *thinks* she sees. (Allowance for deliberate deception will be made in coming sections.) But suppose that because she is a religious enthusiast and because the miracle in question has religious significance for her, she is subject to self-deception and the deception of others. Letting D stand for the hypothesis that she is deceived, either into thinking that some particular miracle M occurred when in fact it didn't or into thinking that M did not occur when in fact it did, the principle of total probability can be used to expand the factor { } in (6):

$$\Pr(t(M)/M\&E\&K) = \Pr(t(M)/M\&D\&E\&K)\times\Pr(D/M\&E\&K) \qquad (7)$$
$$+ \Pr(t(M)/M\&\neg D\&E\&K)\times\Pr(\neg D/M\&E\&K)$$

Since $\Pr(t(M)/M\&D\&E\&K) = 0$ and $\Pr(t(M)/M\&\neg D\&E\&K) = 1$, we have that $\Pr(t(M)/M\&E\&K) = \Pr(\neg D/M\&E\&K)$. Similarly, $\Pr(t(M)/\neg M\&E\&K) = \Pr(D/\neg M\&E\&K)$. So under our suppositions, (6) becomes

$$= \frac{1}{1 + \left[ \dfrac{1 - \Pr(M/E\&K)}{\Pr(M/E\&K)} \right] \left\{ \dfrac{\Pr(D/\neg M\&E\&K)}{1 - \Pr(D/M\&E\&K)} \right\}}$$

For (8) to be greater than 0.5, it must be that [ ]{ } < 1. But since M contradicts a presumptive law, Pr(M/E&K) will be very small and, thus, [ ] will be huge. So to make [ ]{ } < 1, { } must be tiny. But in typical cases, Pr(D/M&E&K) is small (e.g., our religious enthusiast is not apt to be deceived into thinking that there is no walking on water when actually presented with such a phenomenon), so that the denominator of { } is close to 1. So unless Pr(D/¬M&E&K) is small enough to balance off the hugeness of [ ], Pr(M/t(M)&E&K) will not be greater than 0.5.

Hume can be read as declaring that his personal probabilities are such that Pr(D/¬M&E&K) is significantly different from zero in every case of the kind in question. He is entitled to his opinion, but then so are others who, in some cases at least, assign Pr(D/¬M&E&K) a small enough value that Pr(M/t(M)&E&K) > 0.5. The subjectivist form of Bayesianism offers no adjudication since it appears that both assignments are consistent with the probability axioms and the rule of conditionalization. The objectivists can hold out hope of a resolution by demanding a conformity of degrees of belief to frequency data, where available. Hume's review of miracle stories in Part 2 can be seen as an attempt to gather such data; but if so, the attempt is crude since not enough information is given to determine whether or not the witnesses were in fact deceived. And as with all frequency data, the reference class is crucial. It would not be very surprising to find, in concert with Hume's cynicism, that the relative frequency with which religious enthusiasts in general have been deceived into thinking that a miracle occurred when it did not is high. But the relevant reference class may be narrower than this. Imagine, for example, that K specifies that the witnesses in question hold that religious conviction should be based on faith or prudential considerations rather than miracles, and that they are determined to make sure that false miracles do not pollute the canon. It would not be surprising to find that the frequency with which this class of witnesses is deceived into thinking that a miracle has occurred when in fact it hasn't is quite low. I will have more to say on these issues in section 20, where I indicate a rare point of agreement with Hume.

The best way to summarize this section is with a challenge. Commentators who wish to credit Hume with some deep insight must point to some thesis which is both philosophically interesting and which Hume has made plausible. I don't think that they will succeed. Hume has generated the illusion of deep insight by sliding back and forth between various theses, no one of which avoids both the Scylla of banality and the Charybdis of implausibility or outright falsehood.

# 17

# Hume's Diminution Principle

I have argued at some length that Hume's blunderbuss arguments against miracles are ineffective and that his ambition to provide a "proof" against miracles is based on an impoverished conception of inductive inference. But "Of Miracles" is dotted with a number of smaller arguments and less ambitious goals that are of considerable interest both in their own right as well as for their implications for their miracles debate.

When testimony is offered in favor of a marvelous or a miraculous event, Hume speaks of a "contest of two opposite experiences; of which the one destroys the other as far as its force goes" (E 113; 143). The contest is supposed to be guided by what I will call Hume's *diminution principle*: "the evidence, resulting from the testimony, admits of a diminution, greater or less, in proportion as the fact is more or less unusual" (E 113; 142). The corollary we are invited to draw is that in the case of a miraculous event, the diminution is so great that the probative value of the testimonial evidence is lost: "*I should not believe such a story were it told me by Cato*: was a proverbial saying in Rome, even during the lifetime of that philosophical patriot. The incredibility of a fact, it was allowed, might invalidate so great an authority" (E 113; 143).

It might seem that Hume's diminution principle is a consequence of Bayesianism. Bayes theorem shows that $Pr(M/t(M)\&E\&K) = Pr(M/E\&K) \times X$—that is, the posterior probability of the miracle after testimony is directly proportional to its prior probability. If $Pr(M/E\&K)$ were flatly zero, Hume's desired corollary would follow immediately, but that possibility has already been dismissed because of its unpalatable consequences. Leaving aside the intended corollary, what of the diminution principle itself? If $Pr(M/E\&K)$ is not zero, it is surely very small—just by definition of a miracle or a marvel—and since the posterior probability of M is proportional to $Pr(M/E\&K)$, does it not follow that the force of the testimonial evidence $t(M)$ is diminished in proportion as the event reported in M is unusual? No. Nevertheless there is something correct about Hume's diminution principle. But the valid core depends not just on the prior improbability of M but also on those factors that tend to make eyewitness testimony unreliable.

A good place to begin the discussion is with Price's attempt in his *Four Dissertations* to refute the diminution principle. Price's counterclaims are that "improbabilities *as such* do not lessen the capacity of testimony to report the truth" and that "the only causes of falsehood in testimony are the intention to deceive, and the danger of being deceived" (FD 413; 165). In cases where the former is absent, Price claims that the testimony "communicates its own probability" to the event, whatever its prior probability

(*FD* 414; oo). So for instance, if past experience shows that the witness is apt to be wrong only one times in ten, then (Price contends) the posterior probability of the event, given the testimony and the background knowledge, is 0.9, no matter how small the (nonzero) prior probability of the event. The type of case Price had in mind is that of a lottery, a case that was thoroughly analyzed by Pierre Simon, the Marquis de Laplace in his *Philosophical Essay on Probabilities* (1814).

Tickets numbered 1 to N are put in a box, and a random mechanism is used to select one of the tickets, which is then replaced and mixed with the other tickets. After each draw, a witness reports on the number drawn. It is found that in the long run she is wrong one time in ten. Let $P_n$ be the proposition that ticket #n was drawn on some particular occasion. Suppose that on this occasion the witness announces that #79 was the winning ticket. Our job is to calculate $Pr(P_{79}/t(P_{79})\&K)$. Using a by now familiar form of Bayes' theorem and setting $Pr(P_{79}/K) = 1/N$, we have

$$Pr(P_{79}/t(P_{79})\&K) = \cfrac{1}{1 + (N-1)\left[\cfrac{Pr(t(P_{79})/\neg P_{79}\&K)}{Pr(t(P_{79})/P_{79}\&K)}\right]} \tag{9}$$

If we want our degrees of belief to reflect the relevant frequency data, we should set $Pr(t(P_{79})/P_{79}\&K) = 0.9$. The sticking point is the numerator of the [ ] term in (9). Using the principle of total probability, we find that

$$Pr(t(P_{79})/\neg P_{79}\&K) = (1/(N-1)) \sum_{n \neq 79}^{N} Pr(t(P_{79})/P_n\&K) \tag{10}$$

So (9) becomes

$$Pr(P_{79}/t(P_{79})\&K) = \cfrac{1}{1 + \sum_{n \neq 79}^{N} Pr(t(P_{79})/P_n\&K)/.9} \tag{11}$$

Here we are stuck until we are given further information about the witness's tendencies in cases where she misreports. If we suppose that when she misreports, there is no tendency to report any one number among the $N - 1$ false numbers rather than another, then for any $n \neq 79$, $Pr(t(P_{79})/P_n\&K) = .1/(N-1)$, which is the probability of misrepresenting equally divided among the $N - 1$ false possibilities.[69] Putting this value in (11) results in $Pr(P_{79}/t(P_{79})\&K) = 0.9$, and just as Price claimed, the testimony "communicates its own probability" to the event. This result is independent of the prior probability of $P_{79}$, $Pr(P_{79}/K) = 1/N$, which can be made as small as you like by making N large enough. Thus, Hume's diminution principle fails in this case.

However, this result does not hold if the witness has, to use Laplace's phrase, "some interest in choosing 79 among the numbers not drawn" (*PEP* 111; 195). If, for example, the witness made a side bet on 79 and is tempted to collect the stakes of the bet by falsely announcing 79, then the posterior probability of $P_{79}$ can be considerably reduced. Price was aware of this pitfall—recall that he was careful to specify that his claim is conditional on the assumption that, although the witness may herself be deceived, she has no motive to deceive others.

To further study the interaction of misperception, deceit, and prior probability, with an aim to evaluating Hume's diminution principle, it is helpful to switch to a second case also mentioned by Price and analyzed by Laplace—a balls-in-an-urn model. The background evidence K specifies that the urn contains one white ball and $N - 1$ black balls. A ball is drawn at random from the urn and the witness provides a color report. Suppose that the witness reports that the color is white (W) rather than black (B). Given K and t(W), what credibility should be assigned to W? The search for an answer is best conducted in terms of cases.

*Case 1.* Assume that any error in testimony results from a misperception of the color, not from any deceit on the part of the witness. Letting $H_c$ be the hypothesis that the color of the ball drawn was erroneously perceived, we can use the principle of total probability to arrive at $\Pr(t(W)/W\&K) = \Pr(\neg H_c/W\&K)$ and $\Pr(t(W)/\neg W\&K) = \Pr(t(W)/B\&K) = \Pr(H_c/B\&K)$. Plugging these values into Bayes' theorem and using the abbreviations $p_c \equiv \Pr(H_c/W\&K)$ and $p'_c \equiv \Pr(H_c/B\&K)$, we have

$$\Pr(W/t(W)\&K) = \frac{1}{1 + (N - 1)\left(\dfrac{p'_c}{1 - p_c}\right)} \tag{12}$$

For sake of illustration, suppose that $p_c = p'_c = 0.1$. If $N = 2$, $\Pr(W/t(W)\&K) = 0.9$, and as Price would have it, the reliability for the witness is communicated to the event testified to. If, however, $N = 1,000$, $\Pr(W/t(W)\&K) = 1/112$, and the posterior probability of the event is greatly diminished. And in general, for fixed values of $p_c$ and $p'_c$ the diminution effect sets in for increasing $N$, that is, for decreasing prior probability. So Price was wrong: his conclusion that, when deceit is absent, improbabilities as such do lessen the capacity of testimony to report the truth is not true in general.

*Case 2.* Next suppose that the witness never makes an error of color perception but may lie about what she sees. Then

$$\Pr(W/t(W)\&K) = \frac{1}{1 + (N - 1)\left(\dfrac{p'_\ell}{1 - p_\ell}\right)} \tag{13}$$

where $p_\ell \equiv \Pr(H_\ell/W\&K)$ and $p'_\ell \equiv \Pr(H_\ell/B\&K)$ and $H_\ell$ is the hypothesis that the witness lies. Again the diminution effect sets in.

*Case 3.* I now allow for both error in color perception and for deceit on the part of the witness, but for sake of simplicity, I assume that error and deceit are probabilistically independent. (I leave it to the reader to make the adjustment for the case that they are not.) Then

$$Pr(W/t(W)\&K) = \cfrac{1}{1 + (N-1)\left(\cfrac{p'_\ell(1 - p_c) + (1 - p'_\ell)p'_c}{p_c p_\ell + (1 - p_c)(1 - p_\ell)}\right)} \tag{14}$$

It follows that as long as there is any positive probability for the witness to perceive a black ball as white or to falsely testify that a ball correctly perceived as black is white, the posterior probability does decrease as the number of black balls is increased, corresponding to a decreased prior probability of W.

Clearly then, the diminution effect operates in some cases but not in others. If he had had the benefit of Laplace's analysis, Hume's claim would have had to have been that cases of religious miracles are less like the lottery case, where the diminution effect is not operative, and more like the balls-in-the-urn case, where the effect is at work. In the balls-in-the-urn case, the diminution effect is operative because the factor

$$\left[\frac{1 - Pr(W/K)}{Pr(W/K)}\right] \times \left\{\frac{Pr(t(W)/\neg W\&K)}{Pr(t(W)/W\&K)}\right\} \text{ increases as the prior probability}$$

$Pr(W/K)$ of drawing a white ball is decreased by increasing the number of back balls in the urn, and this happens because the [ ] factor increases while the factor { } remains the same. $Pr(t(W)/\neg W\&K)$ remains the same because $\neg W$ always denotes the outcome of a black ball being drawn, and, hence, if $\neg W$ is true, the visual stimulus the observer receives is the same no matter how many possibilities correspond to $\neg W$. Now let W be a proposition asserting the occurrence of some typical religious miracle, say, that a man walks unassisted across the surface of a lake. This case can be made to resemble the balls-in-the-urn case by supposing, first, that $\neg W$ always denotes the outcome, say, of the lake having an empty surface and, second, by decreasing the prior probability of W by increasing the number of ways the surface can be empty while still presenting the same visual stimulus our observer. But the case can be made to resemble the lottery case by supposing that $\neg W$ is comprised of different possibilities that present different visual stimuli (empty lake surface; man, with imperceptible wires attached to a balloon, walking across the lake). etc.). Thus, there is no uniform answer to the question of whether the diminution effect applies to cases of religious miracles: it all depends on the details of the case.

But suppose for the sake of argument that the balls-in-the-urn case serves as good analogy for religious miracles and ask what morals can be drawn. From the above analysis of the ball-in-the-urn case, it follows that for any witness who may misperceive or lie, we can chose the number N of black balls large enough that the witness's testimony to the drawing of a white ball would fail to make the event more likely than not and, indeed, would fail to make the event more probable than any chosen tiny $\varepsilon > 0$. Thus, for this set up, the moral Hume wanted to draw in citing the saying that "I should not believe such a story were it told me by Cato" is correct *if* it is understood to have the form: For any given witness (who may misperceive or lie) there is a story which should not be held to be more likely than not if told by that witness. But just as clearly the moral is wrong if it is taken to mean: There is a story so a priori improbable that there is no possible witness such that the story is made more likely than not by the testimony of the witness. For whatever the choice of N, as long as it is finite, there are values of $p'_e$ and $p'_\ell$ different from o but sufficiently small that $Pr(W/t(W)\&E\&K) > 0.5$. On Hume's behalf it can be replied that mathematically possible witnesses are beside the point and that, in actual fact, the psychological profiles of religious enthusiasts make them incapable of reducing the probabilities of error and deceit to low enough values so as to balance the diminution effect and to ground the credibility of religious miracles. Hume clearly believed some proposition in the neighborhood of this one, and his recitation of the checkered history of attested miracles is supposed to provide some inductive evidence in its favor. But "Of Miracles" will be searched in vain for a convincing general argument for it.[70]

For the sake of completeness, I should mention an entirely different sort of diminution effect taken up by Hume in the *Treatise*. If testimony is transmitted down a chain of witnesses and if the force of the testimony is diminished with each successive link, then the original testimony "must in the end lose all of its force and evidence" (*T* 145) if the chain is long enough.[71] Here Hume represents himself as defending the Christian religion against a "celebrated argument," his counterargument being that the evidential value of the Gospel stories is not fatally compromised since in this instance the links in the chain are "all the same kind, and depend on the fidelity of Printers and Copyists" (*T* 146). It is not unlikely that Hume was willing to put up this defense in order to ward off what he saw as a greater danger. John Craig (1699) had used an estimate of the rate of diminution of successive links to calculate a date for the Second coming, his assumption being that Christ would appear again before the evidential value of the Gospel stories is extinguished. Hume's defense undercuts Craig's basis for expecting a Second Coming.[72]

18

*Multiple Witnessing*

One way in which the diminution effect can be countered is by piling up the number of witnesses. Attempts to quantify the effects of multiple witnesses started very early. An especially interesting example is contained in an anonymous essay entitled "A Calculation of the Credibility of Human Testimony" published in the 1699 volume of the *Philosophical Transactions of the Royal Society (London)*.[73] Suppose that each of N "concurrent reporters" gives an assurance of *a* of the arrival of a ship or a gift to me of £1200. It is asserted that together the witnesses give an "assurance" (probability) of $1 - (1 - a)^N$. For (the reasoning goes), the first gives an expectation of $a \cdot £1200$, leaving $(1 - a) \cdot £1200$ unassured. Of what is left unassured, the second witness gives an assurance of $a(1 - a) \cdot £1200$, leaving $(1 - a)(1 - a) \cdot £1200$ unassured, etc. In the end, $£1200 - (1 - a)^N \cdot £1200$ remains unassured. Dividing this expectation by £1220 gives a probability of $1 - (1 - a)^N$. On this analysis, multiple witnessing is very powerful indeed; for no matter how small $a$ is, as long as it is greater than $0$, $1 - (1 - a)^N$ can be made as close to $1$ as you like by making N large enough.

Karl Pearson (1978, 467–468) approved of this result, but stated that it can be obtained more simply in the following way. Suppose for simplicity that the witnesses never misperceive but may lie. Then the event in question fails to occur just in case every one of the N witnesses lies. If the witnesses are independent, the probability of such mass cretinism is said to be $(1 - a)^N$, and thus, by the negation principle, the probability of the event is $1 - (1 - a)^N$. This reasoning is seductive but potentially misleading. That each witness gives an assurance of $a$ for the gift G presumably means that $\Pr(G/t_i(G)\&E\&K) = a$ for $i = 1, 2, \ldots, N$, where $t_i$ stands for the testimony of witness i. If the independence of witnesses meant that $\Pr(\neg G/t_1(G)\& \ldots \&t_N(G)\&E\&K) = \Pr(\neg G/t_1(G)\&E\&K)x \ldots xPr(\neg G/t_N(G)\&E\&K)$, then Pearson's result would be secured. But this is an implausible way to express the assumption that the witnesses testify independently of one another. Why not say in the same spirit that the independence means that $\Pr(G/t_1(G)\& \ldots \&t_N(G)\&E\&K) = \Pr(G/t_1(G)\&E\&K)x \ldots xPr(G/t_N(G)\&E\&K)$, reaching the contrary result that the posterior probability of G is equal to $a^N$? There are some special circumstances under which Pearson's result holds, and Bayesianism reveals what they are. But I will leave it to the reader to reach the revelation by turning the crank on Bayes' theorem, for there is another route to revealing the power of independent witnessing that does not rely on such specialized assumptions.

The effects of multiple testimonies to the same event were given a systematic Bayesian analysis by Charles Babbage in his *Ninth Bridgewater Treatise* (1838). The claimed upshot of his discussion is this: "[I]f independent witnesses can be found, who speak the truth more frequently than falsehood, *it is ALWAYS possible to assign a number of independent witnesses, the improbability of the falsehood of whose concurring testimonies shall be greater than that of the improbability of the miracle itself*" (NBT 202; 212). Here Babbage is accepting Hume's Maxim (see section 15) and using it against him. I take the form of Babbage's claim to be this. Suppose that $\Pr(M/E\&K) = \varepsilon > 0$, and suppose that the witnesses are independent and that each one's testimony is more likely to be true than false. Then no matter how small $\varepsilon$ is (as long as it is positive), there is an $N(\varepsilon)$ such that $\Pr(M/t_1(M)\&t_2(M)\& \ldots \&t_N(M)\&E\&K) > 0.5$. And, in fact, $N(\varepsilon)$ can be chosen so that the posterior probability is as close to $1$ as is desired.

This claim is still vague until the suppositions of independence and reliability of the witnesses are given precise probabilistic form.

I will suppose that on the relevant occasion each of the witnesses testifies, either to the occurrence or the nonoccurrence of the event in question so that $\neg t_i(M)$ is equivalent to $t_i(\neg M)$. I then take the independence of the testimonies to mean that

$$\Pr(\pm t_1(M)\& \ldots \& \pm t_N(M)/\pm M\&E\&K) \tag{I}$$
$$= \Pr(\pm t_1(M)/\pm M\&E\&K)\times \ldots \times\Pr(\pm t_N(M)/\pm M\&E\&K)$$

where $\pm\Phi$ stands for the choice of $\Phi$ or its negation, the understanding being that the same choices must be made uniformly on the left- and right-hand sides of the equality. (Note that (I) is much weaker than the generally implausible principle that, on the basis of E&K alone, the testimonies are uncorrelated, that is, $\Pr(\pm t_1(M)\& \ldots \& \pm t_N(M)/E\&K) = \Pr(\pm t_1(M)/E\&K)x \ldots xPr(\pm t_N(M)/E\&K).$) For sake of simplicity I also assume that all the witnesses are equally reliable (or unreliable) in that for all i, $\Pr(t_i(M)/M\&E\&K) = p$ and $\Pr(t_i(M)/\neg M\&E\&K) = q$. Bayes' theorem then gives the posterior probability of the miracle, conditional on the testimony of the cloud of witnesses:

$$\Pr(M/t_1(M)\& \ldots \& t_N(M)\&E\&K) = \cfrac{\text{I}}{\text{I} + \left[\dfrac{\Pr(\neg M/E\&K)}{\Pr(M/E\&K)}\right]\left(\dfrac{q}{p}\right)^N} \tag{15}$$

The implications of (15) are best discussed in cases. *Case (a)*. p = q. Then for any value of N, $\Pr(M/t_1(M)\& \ldots \& t_N(M)\&E\&K) = \Pr(M/E\&K)$. Thus, no matter how large the cloud of witnesses, their collective testimony has no probative value. *Case (b)*. q > p. Then as $N \to \infty$, $(q/p)^N \to \infty$ and $\Pr(M/t_1(M)\& \ldots \& t_N(M)\&E\&K) \to 0$. Piling one unreliable witness on another only serves to reduce the credibility of the event. *Case (c)*. p > q. Then as $N \to \infty$, $(q/p)^N \to 0$ and $\Pr(M/t_1(M)\& \ldots \& t_N(M)\&E\&K) \to 1$. Here the power of independent witnessing comes into its own. What is remarkable about this power in the above set up is that the witnesses do not have to be reliable in any absolute sense; for example, it could be that they are *unreliable* in the absolute sense that $\Pr(t_i(M)/\neg M\&E\&K) > 0.5$ for each i. All that is required is that they are minimally reliable in the comparative sense that $\Pr(t_i(M)/M\&E\&K) > \Pr(t_i(M)/\neg M\&E\&K)$.

In the case where the witnesses are not equally reliable, (15) has to be replaced by

$$\Pr(M/t_1(M)\& \ldots \& t_N(M)\&E\&K \tag{16}$$
$$= \cfrac{\text{I}}{\text{I} + \left(\dfrac{\Pr(\neg M/E\&K)}{\Pr(M/E\&K)}\right)\left(\dfrac{q_1 q_2 \ldots q_N}{p_1 p_2 \ldots p_N}\right)}$$

where $p_i = \Pr(t_i(M)/M\&E\&K)$ and $q_i = \Pr(t_i(M)/\neg M\&E\&K)$. Now in order to assure that the posterior probability goes to 1 as $N \to \infty$ it is not sufficient to assume that each witness is minimally reliable in the comparative sense that $p_i > q_i$. It is also necessary that the ratio $q_i/p_i$ does not approach 1 too rapidly as N increases.

In the *Théorie Analytique des Probabilités* (1812, 463) Laplace derived a formula similar to (16). However, he seems to have assumed that $q_i = 1 - p_i$. Specializing back to the case where the $p_i$ are all equal to p, we see that under Laplace's analysis the power of multiple independent witnesses does not materialize unless the witnesses are reliable in the absolute sense that $p > 0.5$. If one is not careful, it is easy to fall in with Laplace's assumption, which may help to explain why there has been a general lack of recognition of the power of independent multiple witnessing.

Hume made a nod to the power of independent witnessing. In the case of the hypothetical miracle of eight days of total darkness, he writes:

> [S]uppose, all authors, in all languages, agree, that, from the first of January 1600, there was total darkness over the whole earth for eight days: Suppose that the tradition of this extraordinary event is still strong and lively among the people: that all travellers, who return from foreign countries, bring us accounts of the same tradition without the least variation or contradiction: It is evident, that our present philosophers, instead of doubting the fact, ought to receive it as certain. (E 127–128; 151)

But in the hypothetical case of the death and subsequent resurrection of Queen Elizabeth, he proclaimed that he would be unmoved by the supposition that her physicians, the whole court, and all of parliament proclaim the events: "I must confess that I should be surprised at the occurrence of so many odd circumstances, but I should not have the least inclination to believe so miraculous an event" (E 128; 151).

Assuming that Hume could be made to accept the form of Babbage's result derived above, would he be able to maintain his intransigence against believing in a resurrection? I will return to this matter in section 20. But first there is more to be said about multiple witnessing.


## 19

## *More Multiple Witnessing*

The multiple witnessing discussed in the preceding section involved many witnesses to the same event. Cases where the multiple witnesses testify to the occurrence of different events requires a separate and more complicated treatment, which perhaps accounts for the fact the power of multiple witnessing in these cases has been the subject of conflicting claims.[74] While no definitive resolution is to be expected, the present section aims to establish some simple but revealing results about the power of independent witnessing of different events.

Extending the previous notation, let $t_i(M_i)$ stand for the testimony of witness #i to the miracle $M_i$. The first and most basic task is to find the conditions under which two witnessings are better than one in the sense that $Pr(M_1 \vee M_2/t_1(M_1)\&t_2(M_2)\&K)$ is greater than either of $Pr(M_1/t_1(M_1)\&K)$ or $Pr(M_2/t_2(M_2)\&K)$, assuming that neither of the latter is equal to 1. The second task is to show that the result generalizes, that is, $Pr(M_1 \vee M_2 \vee M_3/t_1(M_1)\&t_2(M_2)\&t_3(M_3)\&K)$ is greater than any of $Pr(M_1 \vee M_2/t_1(M_1)\&t_2(M_2)\&K)$, $Pr(M_1 \vee M_3/t_1(M_1)\&t_3(M_3)\&K)$, or $Pr(M_2 \vee M_3/t_2(M_2)\&t_3(M_3)\&K)$, assuming that none of the latter is equal to 1, etc., for an arbitrary number of miracles. The third task is to find the conditions under which asymptotic certainty is obtained, that is, $\lim_{n \to \infty} Pr(M_1 \vee M_2 \vee \ldots \vee M_n/t_1(M_1)\&t_2(M_2)\& \ldots \&t_n(M_n)\&K) = 1$.

Turning to the basic task, a positive result will depend, as in section 18, on appropriate conditions of independence and minimal reliability of the witnesses. As in the previous section I will assume that $\neg t_i(M_i)$ is equivalent to $t_i(\neg M_i)$. The needed independence can then be expressed in terms of two screening off conditions. The first requires that

$$Pr(\pm t_1(M_1)/\pm M_1 \& \pm M_2 \& X) = Pr(\pm t_1(M_1)/\pm M_1 \& X)$$
$$Pr(\pm t_2(M_2)/\pm M_1 \& \pm M_2 \& X) = Pr(\pm t_2(M_1)/\pm M_2 \& X) \qquad (S_1)$$
$$\text{for any X such that } Pr(\pm M_1 \& \pm M_2 \& X) \neq 0$$

where again the understanding is that the choice of the formula or its negation is the same on both sides of the equality. Think of $M_1$ and $M_2$ as referring to occurrences in distinct spatiotemporal locations. The witness at any given location is supposed to react only to what happens, or fails to happen, at that location. Note that, consistent with $(S_1)$, $M_1$ can be probabilistically relevant to $t_2(M_2)$ (i.e., $Pr(t_2(M_2)/M_1) \neq Pr(t_2(M_2))$) because, for instance, $M_2$ is positively correlated with $M_1$ and because when $M_2$ occurs witness #2 is very likely to report its occurrence. But if the witnesses are independent in the intended sense, the occurrence (or nonoccurrence) of $M_1$ can bear on $t_2(M_2)$ only through the occurrence or (nonoccurrence) of $M_2$.

The second screening off condition says that

$$Pr(\pm t_2(M_2)/\pm M_{1,2} \& \pm t_1(M_1)\&X) = Pr(\pm t_2(M_2)/\pm M_{1,2}\&X)$$
$$Pr(\pm t_1(M_1)/\pm M_{1,2} \& \pm t_2(M_2)\&X) = Pr(\pm t_1(M_1)/\pm M_{1,2}\&X) \qquad (S_2)$$
$$\text{for any X such that } Pr(\pm M_{1,2}\&t_1(M_1)\&X) \neq 0 \neq$$
$$Pr(\pm M_{1,2}\&t_2(M_2)\&X)$$

Consistent with $(S_2)$, $t_1(M_1)$ and $t_2(M_2)$ can be probabilistically relevant to one another, but if the witnesses are independent in the intended sense, the relevance must go through the occurrence (or nonoccurrence) of $M_1$ and $M_2$.

Note that together $(S_1)$ and $(S_2)$ imply an analogue of the independence condition (I) used in the preceding section; namely,

$$Pr(\pm t_1(M_1) \& \pm t_2(M_2) / \pm M_1 \& \pm M_2 \& K) =$$
$$Pr(\pm t_1(M_1) / \pm M_1 \& K) \times Pr(\pm t_2(M_2) / \pm M_2 \& K) \qquad (I')$$

To find a sufficient condition for the desired basic result, start with the general addition axiom

$$Pr(M_1 \vee M_2 / t_1(M_1) \& t_2(M_2) \& K) = Pr(M_1 / t_1(M_1) \& t_2(M_2) \& K)$$
$$+ Pr(M_2 / t_1(M_1) \& t_2(M_2) \& K) - Pr(M_1 \& M_2 / t_1(M_1) \& t_2(M_2) \& K) \qquad (17)$$

It is a consequence of the probability axioms that

(a) $Pr(M_1 / t_1(M_1) \& t_2(M_2) \& K) \geq Pr(M_1 \& M_2 / t_1(M_1) \& t_2(M_2) \& K)$  $\qquad (18)$
(b) $Pr(M_2 / t_1(M_1) \& t_2(M_2) \& K) \geq Pr(M_1 \& M_2 / t_1(M_1) \& t_2(M_2) \& K)$

Thus, if it could be shown that

(a) $Pr(M_1 / t_1(M_1) \& t_2(M_2) \& K) > Pr(M_1 / t_1(M_1) \& K)$  $\qquad (19)$
(b) $Pr(M_2 / t_1(M_1) \& t_2(M_2) \& K) > Pr(M_2 / t_2(M_2) \& K)$

then it would follow, as desired, that $Pr(M_1 \vee M_2 / t_1(M_1) \& t_2(M_2) \& K)$ is greater than either of $Pr(M_1 / t_1(M_1) \& K)$ or $Pr(M_2 / t_2(M_2) \& K)$. A long slog using $(S_1)$, $(S_2)$, and the conditions that $Pr(M_1 / t_1(M_1) \& K) < 1$ and $Pr(M_2 / t_2(M_2) \& K) < 1$, shows that (19a) holds if and only if

$$[Pr(M_2 / M_1 \& K) - Pr(M_2 / \neg M_1 \& K)] \times$$
$$\{Pr(t_2(M_2) / M_2 \& K) - Pr(t_2(M_2) / \neg M_2 \& K)\} > 0 \qquad (20)$$

It is sufficient for (20) to hold that the second witness is minimally reliable (i.e., $Pr(t_2(M_2) / M_2 \& K) > Pr(t_2(M_2) / \neg M_2 \& K)$) and that $M_1$ is positively relevant to $M_2$ (i.e., $Pr(M_2 / M_1 \& K) > Pr(M_2 / \neg M_1 \& K)$). But interestingly enough it is also sufficient that the second witness is not minimally reliable while $M_1$ is negatively relevant to $M_2$. The analysis of (19b) is similar.

The upshot is that for two witnesses to different miracles, the dual testimony of both witnesses makes it more likely that some miracle has occurred than if either of the witnesses alone had testified, provided that the witnesses are independent in the sense of $(S_1)$ and $(S_2)$ and provided that they are both minimally reliable (respectively, not minimally reliable) and the miracles are positively (respectively, negatively) relevant to one another. With some more work, weaker sufficient conditions for the efficacy of dual witnessing can be established, but I leave this exercise in Bayesianism to the reader.

I also leave it to the reader to show that the above result generalizes from two witnesses to an arbitrary finite number, and I turn to the issue of whether asymptotic certainty as to the occurrence of some miracle or other is reached as the number of independent witnesses is increased without bound. What complicates the issue is that we want to rule out the possibility that $\lim_{n \to \infty} Pr(M_1 \vee M_2 \vee \ldots \vee M_n / K) = 1$, for otherwise the asymptotic certainty would have nothing to do with the testimonial evidence. Now $\lim_{n\to\infty}\Pr(M_1 \vee M_2 \vee \ldots \vee M_n/K) = 1 - \lim_{n\to\infty}$ $\Pr(\neg M_1 \& \neg M_2 \& \ldots \& \neg M_n/K)$. Since $\Pr(\neg M_1/K)$, $\Pr(\neg M_1 \& \neg M_2/K)$, $\ldots$ is a monotonically decreasing series and is bounded below, it has a limit $\ell$, which we want to be greater than 0. But $\Pr(\neg M_1 \& \neg M_2 \& \ldots$ $\& \neg M_n/K) = \Pr(\neg M_1/K) \times \Pr(\neg M_2/\neg M_1 \& K) \times \ldots \times \Pr(\neg M_n/\neg M_1 \& \neg M_2 \& \ldots$ $\& \neg M_{n-1} \& K)$. If $\ell$ is to be greater than 0, it must be the case that $\Pr(\neg M_n/$ $\neg M_1 \& \neg M_2 \& \ldots \& \neg M_{n-1} \& K) \to 1$, or equivalently, $\Pr(M_n/\neg M_1 \& \neg M_2 \& \ldots$ $\& \neg M_{n-1} \& K) \to 0$. In this case, we can say that the Ms bear a strong asymptotic analogy to each other. Now assuming that the basic result generalizes to an arbitary finite number of miracles, $\Pr(M_1/t_1(M_1) \& K)$, $\Pr(M_1 \vee M_2/t_1(M_1) \& t_2(M_2) \& K), \ldots$, forms a monotonically increasing series. Since it is bounded from above, the limit $\lim_{n\to\infty} \Pr(M_1 \vee M_2 \vee \ldots \vee$ $M_n/t_1(M_1) \& t_2(M_2) \& \ldots \& t_n(M_n) \& K)$ exists. We would like this limit to be 1, or equivalently $\lim_{n\to\infty}\Pr(\neg M_1 \& \neg M_2 \& \ldots \& \neg M_n/t_1(M_1) \& t_2(M_2) \& \ldots$ $\& t_n(M_n) \& K) = 0$. By similar reasoning to the above, the latter condition holds if $\Pr(\neg M_n/\neg M_1 \& \neg M_2 \& \ldots \& \neg M_{n-1} \& t_1(M_1) \& t_2(M_2) \& \ldots \& t_n(M_n) \& K)$ $\nrightarrow 1$, or equivalently, $\Pr(M_n/\neg M_1 \& \neg M_2 \& \ldots \& \neg M_{n-1} \& t_1(M_1) \& t_2(M_2) \&$ $\ldots \& t_n(M_n) \& K) \nrightarrow 0$. By applying the appropriate generalizations of $(S_1)$ and $(S_2)$, this last condition is seen to be equivalent to $\Pr(M_n/\neg M_1 \& \neg M_2 \& \ldots$ $\& \neg M_{n-1} \& t_n(M_n) \& K) \nrightarrow 0$. In words, asymptotic certainty as to the occurrence of some miracle or other is reached if the testimony of the independent and minimally reliable witnesses to the different miracles is strong enough to overcome the strong asymptotic analogy among the miracles. The qualification of this result makes it much less powerful than the limit result achieved for the case of independent witnesses to the same event.

## 20

## *What Is Right about Hume's Position*

In 1761 Hugh Blair sent Hume a copy of the manuscript of George Campbell's *Dissertation on Miracles*. Hume was clearly annoyed by Campbell's attack, but out of consideration for Blair, his comments were moderate.[75] There is one golden nugget worth quoting from Hume's response to Blair: "Does a man of sense run after every silly tale of witches or hobgoblins or fairies, and canvass particularly the evidence? I never knew any one, that examined and deliberated about nonsense who did not believe it before the end of his inquiries" (L 350). The point Hume is making encompasses religious miracles but applies more generally to "silly tales" of all stripes. Indeed, I venture that if Hume were writing today he would focus not on religious miracles but on such things as UFO abductions and the like. Like Hume, I do not think that a man of sense should give much credence to such tales, although unlike Hume I do not think that there are valid principles of inductive reasoning to show that such tales are never, in principle, to be credited.

But then what am I—and Hume—to do about the results of sections 18 and 19 on the power of multiple witnessing? There is no lack of witnesses to silly tales, e.g. opinion polls show that an alarmingly large percentage of the people in the United States believe that they have been alien abductees. Still I do not—and I presume Hume would not—take alien abduction reports seriously. There are only five ways out.

The first is to point to some defect either in Bayesianism itself or in the Bayesian analysis of multiple witnessing. This is not an option I can choose since, for present purposes, I am a Bayesian,[76] and since I think the Bayesian analysis of multiple witnessing is correct.

The second out is to set the prior probability of UFO abductions (that is the conditional probability of abductions given all of the background evidence prior to receiving eyewitness testimony) to zero. This is not an option I would want to exercise since it precludes any Bayesian learning on the matter. The evidence is mounting that a nontrivial percentage of stars have planets. Presumably some nontrivial percentage of these alien planets have conditions favorable to life, and presumably on some non-trivial percentage of the hospitable planets, the processes of evolution produce higher life forms capable of interplanetary travel. Thus, I think it rash to utterly dismiss the possibly that our planet has been visited by extraterrestrials.

The third out is to set the prior probability above zero but still so low that the testimony of a million witnesses would not push the posterior probability to a respectable level. This is a superficially more attractive option, but its effectiveness is ephemeral. Even if a worldwide opinion poll found hundreds of millions of witnesses to alien abductions, I would still not become a believer. (I am not completely intransigent on this matter. I would, for instance, be swayed by hard physical evidence, such as pieces from a flying saucer.)

The fourth out is to deny the independence assumptions that were crucial to the positive results of sections 18 and 19. This is a much more plausible and effective option. The fact that many self-confessed alien abductees draw similar pictures of their captors and tell similar stories about invasive examinations of their bodies is to me not evidence in favor of alien abductions but rather evidence of the pervasive influence of media stories and television "documentaries." But I would certainly ad-mit—and argue that Hume would have to admit—that there is nothing in principle impossible about arranging circumstances where the requi-site independence conditions are satisfied for witnesses to (alleged) alien abductions or for that matter to (alleged) religious miracles. (It is not hard to imagine how to arrange the external circumstances so as to prevent one witness from directly influencing another and so as to pre-vent the indirect influence though media stories. But it would also be necessary to rule out or take into account the possibility that humans are "hard wired" to have the sorts of experiences that get reported as alien abductions.)

The fifth out is to deny the minimal reliability assumption. Hume would presumably want to follow this route. Recall that in discussing the hypothetical case of the resurrection of Queen Elizabeth he writes: "You would in vain object to me the difficulty, and almost impossibility of deceiving the world in an affair of such consequence. . . . I would still reply, that the knavery and folly of men are such common phenomena, that I should rather believe the most extraordinary events to arise from their concurrence, than to admit so signal a violation of the laws of nature" (E 128; 151). Now again I do not believe that there is any, in principle, unbreachable obstacle to satisfying the minimal reliability condition for witnesses to religious miracles or UFO abductions. But I do believe, in a way that I cannot articulate in detail, that these cases are in fact relevantly similar to the case of faith healing where there is a palpable atmosphere of collective hysteria that renders the participants unable to achieve the minimal reliability condition—indeed, one might even say that a necessary condition for being a sincere participant in a faith healing meeting is the suspension of critical faculties essential to accurate reporting. Here, finally, Hume and I are in partial agreement. But the difference between us is that I am just giving a personal opinion. Moreover, I acknowledge that the opinion is of the kind whose substantiation requires not philosophical argumentation and pompous solemnities about extraordinary claims requiring extraordinary proofs, but rather difficult and delicate empirical investigations both into the general workings of collective hysteria and into the details of particular cases. I could say (with pompous solemnity) that my prior probabilities are such that I am not in much doubt about what such investigations will uncover. Or I could say (less pompously) that I am cynical. But unlike Hume, I do not propose to promote my cynicism to the status of a philosophical doctrine that will "*silence* the most arrogant bigotry and superstition" and "will with the wise and learned, be an everlasting check to all kinds of superstition and delusion."

## 21

## *Fall Back Positions for Hume*

Hume refused to engage the details of the case at the center of the eighteenth-century miracles debate in Britain, the resurrection of Jesus. He rested his case on the inability of eyewitness testimony to establish the credibility of a events satisfying his first definition of 'miracle'—what I have called a Hume miracle—when those events were supposed to have religious significance. I have argued, contra Hume, that there is no in principle difficulty here. Supposing that Hume had been brought to see the errors of his ways, how might he have responded? The question is speculative, but there is plenty of material in Hume's essay to ground and control the speculation.

Hume might have joined forces with Woolston and Annet and argued the particulars of New Testament miracles. But not only was he not inclined to do so, there are various indications that he thought that other avenues were open. In particular, there was available an obvious strategy that would have allowed him to remain above the fray; namely, to point out that even if eyewitness testimony does suffice to establish the resurrection of Jesus, it does not follow that the resurrection serves as a "just foundation for religion"; for that would require, Hume might say, the satisfaction of the second definition of miracle, which demands that the resurrection is the result of a volition of the Deity. Having gotten his opponents on the defensive, there are two ways for Hume to try to produce a rout.

The first is to appeal to the meaning of 'cause.'[77] That c caused e means, on Hume's analysis, that c and e are events that have occurred, that c and e stand in the appropriate relations of temporal precedence and spatiotemporal contiguity, and that events like c are always followed by events like e. But, the objection continues, a volition of the Deity cannot be a cause in this sense since it is not an event that is localizable in the spatiotemporal nexus of the world. Although this tack appears to lead to a quick victory, it is not one that Hume himself sailed, and it is not hard to see why. Theists could cheerfully concede that Hume has correctly analyzed the concept of a naturalistic cause and that volitions of deities cannot be naturalistic causes. But, the response would continue, there remains the possibility that a volition of the Deity is a nonnaturalistic cause in some sense that does not require the divine volition to be part of the spatiotemporal nexus. Alternatively, there is the possibility that the Deity is noncausally responsible for the resurrection. For example, according to Leibniz (1686, 1710), God operates in human affairs not by causally intervening in the course of the world but by actualizing one out of the panoply of possible worlds, each of which admits no exceptions to God's "laws of general order" but which may contain exceptions to the "subordinate maxims" (i.e., laws of nature, or what would be laws of nature if they were exceptionless). Of course, such a response might rest on notions that prove to be incoherent under close scrutiny. (For example, there is obviously a problem in making sense of a volition or decision of a deity if such a thing has to be conceived atemporally.) But to show that would involve Hume in theological disputes of the type he hoped to avoid.

The second tactic open to Hume is to argue that even if it is meaningful to speak of the Deity being causally or noncausally responsible for the miracle event, such a link could never be demonstrated because it would require completion of the impossible task of ruling out all possible naturalistic causes of the event in question. A version of this objection was stated by Mill in his *System of Logic*:

> If we do not already believe in supernatural agencies, no miracle can prove to us their existence. The miracle itself, considered merely as an extraordinary fact, may be satisfactorily certified by our senses or by testimony; but nothing can ever prove that it is a miracle [in the sense of having a supernatural origin]: there is still another possible hypothesis, that of its being the result of some unknown natural cause; and this possibility cannot be so completely shut out as to leave no alternative but that of admitting the existence and intervention of a being superior to nature. (1843, 440)

This formidable sounding objection is trotted out again and again in various forms by admirers of Hume's miracles argument. It rests on the twin assumptions that miracle enthusiasts see the function of miracles as proving or demonstrating theological doctrines and that miracles can only serve this function if the events in question do not admit of a naturalistic explanation. Both assumptions are false in the context of the eighteenth century miracles debate. First, miracles were viewed by Hume's more sophisticated opponents not as proofs or demonstrations of religious doctrines but as grounds for reasonable belief. Second, the events in question can serve this function even if they are the result of some natural cause, as Locke and the Newtonians realized (recall section 5).

To illustrate that the more sophisticated opponents posited in my first claim are far from imaginary, I start from the fact, noted by Burns (1981) and van der Loos (1965), that there was a sizable intersection between liberal Anglicans and the original members of the Royal Society. This group was united in rejecting the Cartesian quest for certitude in favor of the goal of "moral certainty," by which they meant something roughly equivalent to the beyond-a-reasonable-doubt standard of modern criminal trials. They were also clear both that sometimes even this more modest goal was not within reach, in which case one might have to settle for high credibility or even for a preponderance of evidence, and that this is so no less in religion than in science and everyday life. A particularly clear statement of this viewpoint is to be found in *Of the Principles and Duties of Natural Religion* (1699) by John Wilkins, Bishop of Chester and a founder of the Royal Society.

> 'Tis sufficient that matters of Faith and Religion be propounded in such a way, as to render them highly credible, so as an honest and teachable man may willingly and safely assent to them, and according to the rules of Prudence be justified in so doing. Nor is it either *necessary* or *convenient*, that they should be established by such cogent Evidence, as to necessitate consent. Because this would not leave any place for the virtue of *Believing*, or the freedom of our obedience; nor any ground for Reward and Punishment.

It would not be thank-worthy for a man to believe that which of necessity he must believe, and cannot otherwise chuse.[78] (30–31)

Another example is provided by Tillotson, upon whom Hume heaps ironic (?) praise at the opening of "Of Miracles": "And for any man to urge that tho' men in temporal affairs proceed upon moral assurance, yet there is a greater assurance required to make men seek Heaven and avoid Hell, seems to me highly unreasonable" (1728, 23–24). And as a final example, in his discourse on natural religion Samuel Clarke (1705) averred that "such *moral* Evidence, or mixt Proofs from Circumstances and Testimony, as most Matters of Fact are only capable of, and wise and honest Men are always satisfied with, ought to be accounted sufficient for the present Case [the truth of the Christian revelation]" (*ONR* 600). Locke also belonged to this camp, but, in contrast to the figures named above, he was unhappy about giving up the strong sense of knowledge which implies certainty.

Grant then that Hume's more sophisticated opponents were willing to settle for reasonable belief. And grant that testimonial evidence has sufficed to establish the credibility of some New Testament miracle M event, such as a resurrection—in the language of conditional probability, $Pr(M/t(M)\&E\&K) \geq p$, where p is greater than 0.5 and, perhaps, even close to 1. Hume's admirers can still claim that it has not been shown how this credibility can be transferred to some doctrine C of Christianity, that is, $Pr(C/t(M)\&E\&K) > 0.5$. Hume himself does not explicitly pose this challenge, but he does say something relevant toward the end of Part 2 of his essay: "Though the Being to whom the miracle is ascribed, be, in this case, Almighty, it does not, upon that account, become a whit more probable; since it is impossible to know the attributes or actions of such a Being, otherwise than from the experience which we have of his productions, in the usual course of nature" (*E* 129; 152). Grant Hume that it is impossible for us to know from direct experience the attributes of the Almighty Being. By the same token, we cannot know by direct experience the attributes of quarks. But we can form specific hypotheses about the attributes and actions of the Almighty or of quarks, and these hypotheses can make a difference to the conditional probabilities of events we can come to know by direct experience. And because of this, testimonial evidence to these events can make a difference to the confirmation/disconfirmation of the hypotheses about the Almighty or about quarks, or so I will argue in the following section. We have yet another example of how Hume's crabbed view of induction, which he tried to turn against miracles, makes it impossible for modern science to operate.

# 22

# Probabilifying Religious Doctrines

Given some plausible assumptions, the question of how testimony to the occurrence of an event that constitutes a miracle in the sense of Hume's first definition—say, a resurrection—can serve to probabilify a theological doctrine can be divided into two sub-questions: First, how can the testimony probabilify the naturalistically characterized miracle event? And, second, how can such a miracle probabilify the doctrine?[79] Using the principle of total probability, we find that

$$\Pr(C/t(M)\&E\&K) = \Pr(C/M\&t(M)\&E\&K) x \Pr(M/t(M)\&E\&K)$$
$$+ \Pr(C/\neg M\&t(M)\&E\&K) x \Pr(\neg M/t(M)\&E\&K) \quad (21)$$

Assume, as seems plausible, that the testimony $t(M)$ to some New Testament miracle $M$ bears on some tenet $C$ of Christianity only through $M$ in the sense that

$$\Pr(C/\pm M\&t(M)\&E\&K) = \Pr(C/\pm M\&E\&K) \quad (22)$$

Then (21) becomes

$$\Pr(C/t(M)\&E\&K) = \Pr(C/M\&E\&K)\times\Pr(M/t(M)\&E\&K)$$
$$+ \Pr(C/\neg M\&E\&K)\times\Pr(\neg M/t(M)\&E\&K) \quad (23)$$

which provides the promised division.

Let us assume, for the sake of simplicity, that testimony has been very successful in establishing $M$ beyond reasonable doubt, that is, $\Pr(M/t(M)\&E\&K) \approx 1$. Then by (23), $\Pr(C/t(M)\&E\&K) \approx \Pr(C/M\&E\&K)$. The question of how well testimonial evidence to $M$ supports $C$ then devolves to the question of how well $M$ supports $C$. This latter question is not easy to answer, but there is something to be said that might seem to be uncontroversial. It might seem that if $M$ is some New Testament miracle and $C$ comprises the central tenets of Christianity, then Christians and non-Christians alike will agree that

$$\Pr(M/C\&E\&K) > \Pr(M/\neg C\&E\&K) \quad (24)$$

or equivalently

$$\Pr(M/C\&E\&K) > \Pr(M/E\&K) \quad (25)$$

It follows that

$$\Pr(C/M\&E\&K) > \Pr(C/\neg M\&E\&K) \quad (26)$$

or equivalently

$$\Pr(C/M\&E\&K) > \Pr(C/E\&K) \quad (27)$$

So from the seemingly uncontroversial (24), it follows that M incrementally confirms C. In the case where M is a logical consequence of C, we have an instance of hypothetico-deductive confirmation; the fact that such an M incrementally confirms C is then a direct consequence of Bayes' theorem, assuming that neither of Pr(C/E&K) nor Pr(M/E&K) is 0 or 1.

To reach the conclusion that t(M) incrementally confirms C it is not necessary to make the simplifying assumption that testimonial evidence has been so effective in establishing M. Assume that Pr(M/t(M)&E&K) > Pr(M/E&K). Does it follow from (22) and (24) that

$$Pr(C/t(M)\&E\&K) > Pr(C/E\&K) \qquad (?)$$

Applying the principle of total probability to both sides of (?) and using (22) and the negation principle, one finds that (?) holds if and only if

$$Pr(C/M\&E\&K)[Pr(M/t(M)\&E\&K) - Pr(M/E\&K)]$$
$$> Pr(C/\neg M\&E\&K)[Pr(M/t(M)\&E\&K) - Pr(M/E\&K)] \qquad (28)$$

By our starting assumption, the [ ] term is positive, so that (?) holds if and only if Pr(C/M&E&K) > Pr(C/¬M&E&K), which holds if and only if (24) holds. The (?) is discharged.

This has been so easy that one suspects that there must be a catch. Could the catch lie in the seemingly innocuous (24)? Suppose, for sake of illustration, that ¬C consists of the disjunction of Zoroastrianism (Z) and Buddhism (B). Then Pr(M/¬C&E&K) = [Pr(M/Z&E&K)×Pr(Z/E&K) + Pr(M/B&E&K)×Pr(B/E&K)]/[Pr(Z/E&K) + Pr(B/E&K)]. To simplify, assume that Pr(M/Z&E&K) = Pr(M/B&E&K) = v. Then Pr(M/¬C&E&K) = v, which for a New Testament miracle M is presumably much less than Pr(M/C&E&K), so that (24) holds. But now suppose that ¬C includes the possibility of a nasty deceiver god (N) who abolishes heaven and hell but arranges for the occurrence of M in order to lure the unsuspecting into lives of fruitless religious observance. Setting Pr(M/N&E&K) = 1, we now have Pr(M/¬C&E&K) > Pr(N/E&K)/[Pr(Z/E&K) + Pr(B/E&K) + Pr(N/E&K)]. The right-hand side of this inequality may be greater than or equal to Pr(M/C&E&K) if Pr(N/E&K) is very large in comparison with (Pr(Z/E&K) + Pr(B/E&K)) and Pr(M/C&E&K) < 1, in which case (24) fails. This result may be somewhat discouraging to theists because it shows that whether or not miracles are seen as confirming a particular form of theism depends on the prior probabilities assigned to this and to the alternative forms of theism. But it should not be absolutely discouraging since, in general, the bearing of evidence on a scientific theory also depends on the available alternative theories and their prior probabilities.

The results of this section concern incremental confirmation. Mere incremental confirmation may not be what theists want for their doctrines, but it is a start. And once the start is made, there does not seem to be any principled road block to achieving a substantial degree of confirmation. For example, testimonies to a number of New Testament miracles can each give bits of incremental confirmation to C that together add up to substantial confirmation. Or the evidence of miracles can combine with the evidence of prophecy and design to provide grounds for the credibility or even moral certainty of religious doctrines.

In sum, the evidentiary function of miracles, which I am urging and which I claim was envisioned by Hume's more able eighteenth-century opponents, is more sophisticated than is allowed by many modern commentators on Hume's essay. The weak point in the envisioned evidentiary function lies in the fact that even after the miraculous event has been probabilified, there is still work to be done in assessing the support it gives to some religious doctrine. There are delicate issues involved in such an assessment, and there is no guarantee that theists can successfully negotiate them. Spinoza for one was convinced that God cannot be known from miracles. He remarked, with undisguised sarcasm, that "[T]he Isreaelites, from all their miracles, were unable to form a sound conception of God, as their experience testified: for when they had persuaded themselves that Moses had departed from among them, they petitioned Aaron to give them visible gods; and the idea of God they had formed as the result of all their miracles was—a calf!" (*TPT* 88; 112). Some of Hume's contemporaries were more sanguine. Thomas Chubb (1741), for example, thought that the circumstances attending miracles can, in some cases, "make it *more likely* and *probable* that *God* is the agent producing those effects, rather than *any other* invisible being" (71). I do not presume to say how these issues are to be resolved. I insist only that, first, they are paralleled by similar issues in the assessment of how, say, low probability events in a cloud chamber serve to probabilify theoretical hypotheses in elementary particle physics and, second, that there are no in principle obstacles to a positive outcome in either science or religion.

23

## Hume's Contrary Miracles Argument

Hume, as if realizing that his main arguments are wanting, prepared a defense-in-depth. Concede that it is possible in principle for testimonial evidence to establish the credibility of a Hume miracle, such as a resurrection. Is that concession really fatal, as urged in the last section, or is there a way to block the transfer of credibility of a Hume miracle to the credibility of religious tenets? The most effective block would be to prevent the wheels of the Bayesian machinery from even beginning to turn. And one way to do that is to refuse to assign probabilities to religious doctrines on the grounds that they lack cognitive significance. Such a logical positivist ploy was not Hume's way. For him, theistic hypotheses are meaningful and open to rational discussion, and thus he has no way to prevent the Bayesian machinery from grinding away. Is there reason to think that there is some additional grist that has been neglected so far and will prevent the grinding of the Bayesian machinery from producing support for a particular system of religion? Hume's contrary miracles argument can be construed as an attempt to provide the grist.[80] As with other parts of Hume's argumentation, the considerations involved here were not original to Hume but were widely discussed by Hume's contemporaries, Annet (1747) and Chubb (1741) being but two examples. The gist of the argument goes back to Locke, who wrote "And if the opinions and persuasions of others, whom we know and think well of, be a ground of assent, men have reason to be Heathens in Japan, Mahometans in Turkey, Papists in Spain, Protestants in England, and Lutherans in Sweden" (*ECHU* 368; 99).

Hume's version of the argument begins with the observation that the various religions of the world have incompatible doctrines at their cores ("in matters of religion, whatever is different is contrary" [*E* 121; 147]). Each religion claims to be supported by miracles.[81] But, Hume maintains, the miracles that support one religion undermine the others, and the testimonies to the miracles of different religions undermine each other.[82]

> Every miracle, therefore, pretended to have been wrought in any of these religions (and all of them abound in miracles), as its direct scope is to establish the particular system to which it is attributed; so has it the same force, though more indirectly, to overthrow every other system. In destroying a rival system, it likewise destroys the credit of those miracles, on which that system was established; so that all the prodigies of different religions are to be regarded as contrary facts, and the evidences of these prodigies, whether weak or strong, as opposite to each other. (*E* 121–122; 147)

Hume seems to be presupposing the following connection between religions and miracles. Let $R_1$, $R_2$, . . . be systems of religion, and let $M_1$, $M_2$, . . . be corresponding miracle statements. Then $M_i$ could not be true unless $R_i$ is true. If we take this to mean that $M_i$ entails $R_i$, then since $R_i$ is incompatible with $R_j$ for $j \neq i$, $M_i$ entails $\neg R_j$. And since $M_j$ entails $R_j$, $M_i$ entails $\neg M_j$. Thus, a miracle for any one system of religion does, quite literally, destroy rival systems and their corresponding miracles.

In the preceding section, I have rejected the view of the relation between miracles and religious doctrines on which Hume's contrary miracles argument rests. I proposed that instead of furnishing proofs or demonstrations of religious doctrines, miracles provide partial confirmation of these doctrines. This fits with the view point of one strain of Christian apologetics that holds that it is theologically undesirable for miracles to entail the truth of Christianity since God should not be seen as coercing belief.[83] Given this more liberal conception of the relation between miracles and systems of religion, what general principle of confirmation would Hume need in order to secure the conclusion that miracles for one religion disconfirm rival systems of religions and the miracles on which they rest? Here is one try:

(P₁) Let $H_1, H_2, \ldots, H_n$ be pairwise incompatible hypotheses. Suppose that $E_i$, i = 1, 2, . . . , n, gives positive support to $H_i$ for each i, that is, $\Pr(H_i/E_i\&K) > \Pr(H_i/K)$. Then $E_i$ gives negative support to the other hypotheses, that is, $\Pr(H_j/E_i\&K) < \Pr(H_j/K)$ for j ≠ i, and the other evidence statements, that is, $\Pr(E_j/E_i\&K)$ $\Pr(E_j/K)$ for j ≠ i.

This principle is false in general. For instance, even though the $H_i$ are incompatible with one another, it can happen that $H_i\&K$ entails E for each i. Then if the prior probabilities of E and the $H_i$ are all strictly between 0 and 1, it is a simple exercise using Bayes' theorem to show that E incrementally confirms each of the $H_i$.

Consider another try.

(P₂) Let $H_1, H_2, \ldots, H_n$ be pairwise incompatible, and let $E_i$, i = 1, 2, . . . , n be such that (a) $\Pr(E_i/H_i\&K) > \Pr(E_i/\neg H_i\&K)$, but $\Pr(E_i/H_j\&K) < \Pr(E_i/\neg H_j\&K)$ for j ≠ i. Then it follows that (b) $\Pr(H_i/E_i\&K) > \Pr(H_i/K)$ but $\Pr(H_j/E_i\&K) < \Pr(H_j/K)$ for j ≠ i, and (c) $\Pr(E_j/E_i\&K) < \Pr(E_j/K)$ for j ≠ i. Further, if $t_i(E_i)$ is the testimony of witness #i to the truth of $E_i$ and if (d) $\Pr(E_i/t_i(E_i)\&K) > \Pr(E_i/K)$ then (e) $\Pr(t_i(E_i)/t_j(E_j)\&K) < \Pr(t_i(E_i)/K)$ for j ≠ i.

Assumption (a) is plausible when the $H_i$ are contrary religious doctrines and the $E_i$ are miracle statements appropriate to the corresponding religions. (But recall the discussion of the preceding section.) Then (b) does follow so that the miracles of one religion do undermine the other religions in the sense of incremental disconfirmation. However, it does not follow without further assumptions that (c) holds for this application (i.e., that the miracles of one religion undermine the miracles of the others). The implication does hold if it is further assumed that (f) $\Pr(E_i/H_i\&E_j\&K)$ = $\Pr(E_i/H_i\&K)$ for j ≠ i, and (g) $\Pr(E_i/\neg H_i\&E_j\&K) = \Pr(E_i/\neg H_i\&K)$ for j ≠ i. The assumption (f) strikes me as plausible for its intended applications; but (g) strikes me as dubious. Similarly, (e) follows from (d) only with the help of further dubious assumptions.

But grant for the sake of argument that (P₂) does hold for the intended application to religious doctrines. What moral is Hume entitled to draw? Hume thinks that the answer is clear: "This argument may appear over subtle and refined; but it is not really different from the reasoning of a judge, who supposes, that the credit of two witnesses, maintaining a crime against any one, is destroyed by the testimony of two others, who affirm him to have been two hundred leagues distant, at the same instant when the crime is said to have been committed" (E 122; 148). But, of course, judges and juries are not always at a loss when presented with testimonies that are directly or indirectly in conflict, for they may have good reason to give high credibility to the testimony of some witnesses and low credibility to the testimonies of others. What Hume needs to underwrite the claim of the last quotation is not $(P_2)$ but

(P$_3$)   Let $H_1$, $H_2$, . . . , $H_n$ be pairwise incompatible hypotheses, and suppose that $E_i$, i = 1, 2, . . . , n, are such that (a) each $E_i$ gives positive support to $H_i$ and negative support to $H_j$, for j ≠ i, and (perhaps also) (b) the $E_i$ are pairwise incompatible or at least are probabilistically negatively relevant to one another, then it cannot be rational to assign probabilities such that $Pr(H_k/t_1(E_1)\&t_2(E_2)\& . . . \&t_n(E_n)\&K)$ is much greater for some $H_k$ than any competing $H_j$, j ≠ k.

$(P_3)$ is clearly false in general. And Hume has given no reason to think that it is true for the special case where the $H_i$ are competing religious doctrines and the $t_i(E_i)$ are testimonies to their corresponding miracles.

In sum, Hume's contrary miracles argument has some effect against those who take miracles to be proofs of religious doctrines. But against those who take miracles only as providing confirmation of religious doctrines, Hume's argument is not vouchsafed by any valid principles of confirmation—at least not of the Bayesian variety. Hume is thus forced to leave the high ground and descend into the trenches where, as he must have been aware, there were opponents who had considered the contrary miracles argument and were prepared to argue on the basis of contextual details for the superiority of the New Testament miracle stories over heathen miracle stories. These opponents may or may not have been right. But Hume had no good reason for avoiding an engagement with them.

## 24

## *Conclusion*

In "Of Miracles," Hume pretends to stand on philosophical high ground, hurling down thunderbolts against miracle stories. The thunderbolts are supposed to issue from general principles about inductive inference and the credibility of eyewitness testimony. But when these principles are made explicit and examined under the lens of Bayesianism, they are found to be either vapid, specious, or at variance with actual scientific practice. When Hume leaves the philosophical high ground to evaluate particular miracle stories, his discussion is superficial and certainly does not do justice to the extensive and vigorous debate about miracles that had been raging for several decades in Britain. He was able to create the illusion of a powerful argument by maintaining ambiguities in his claims against miracles, by the use of forceful prose and confident pronouncements, and by liberal doses of sarcasm and irony. Early in Part 2, Hume warns us that "Eloquence, when at its highest pitch, leaves little room for reason and reflection; but addressing itself entirely to the fancy or the affections, captivates the willing hearers, and subdues their understanding" (E 118; 145).

I find it ironic that so many readers of Hume's essay have been subdued by its eloquence. And I find it astonishing how well posterity has treated "Of Miracles," given how completely the confection collapses under a little probing. No doubt this generous treatment stems in part from the natural assumption that someone of Hume's genius must have produced a powerful set of considerations. But I suspect that in more than a few cases it also involves the all too familiar phenomenon of endorsing an argument because the conclusion is liked. There is also the understandable, if deplorable, desire to sneer at the foibles of the less enlightened— and how more pleasurable the sneering if it is sanctioned by a set of philosophical principles!

Having denigrated Hume's essay, I want to praise the man. An unmistakable mark of greatness in philosophy is the ability to identify important problems and to pose them in interesting and provocative forms. That Hume succeeded in this regard for the issue of how eyewitness testimony bears on the credibility of miracles is evident not only from the contrast with the efforts of his contemporaries (e.g., Conyers Middleton's antimiracles tract *Free Inquiry* [1749] is, by the standards Hume set, philosophically uninteresting and boring reading)[84] but also from that fact that his essay continues to provoke a lively debate. However, his own responses to the issues he so provocatively posed were bound to fall short, driven as he was by a deep set animus toward organized religion and hampered by his own inadequate account of inductive inference and by his unfamiliarity with the probabilistic tools his contemporaries were developing. But Hume undoubtedly provoked others to produce useful quantitative analyses of the role of deception and self-deception in diminishing the force of testimony, the power of independent multiple witnesses, and so forth.

How much comfort can theists take from the failure of Hume's project? Considerable comfort can be found not so much in the failure of Hume's arguments—for there could conceivably be better arguments waiting in the wings—but in the manner of their failure. Let me begin explaining what I mean by reminding the reader of a key difference between logical positivism and logical empiricism. As a representative of the latter camp, Hans Reichenbach rejected the verifiability and falsifiability criteria of meaningfulness, which would have relegated not only religion but large portions of science as well to the limbo reserved for gibberish. Instead, he opted for a confirmability criterion which required cognitively meaningful hypotheses to admit of probabilification by the evidence of observation and experiment. As a would-be realist about the unobservable entities postulated by modern science, Reichenbach saw a need for a criterion with an "overreaching" character: "The probability theory of meaning . . . allows us to maintain propositions as meaningful which concern facts outside the domain of immediately given verifiable facts; it allows us to pass beyond the domain of given facts. This *overreaching* character of probability inferences is the basic method of the knowledge of nature" (1961, 127). I am in agreement here with Reichenbach, although I would substitute the degrees of belief interpretation of probability for his favored frequency interpretation. And I would note that the overreaching character of Bayesian epistemology stretches much further than Reichenbach himself might have wanted; indeed, it seems to me to extend into the religious realm. Belief formation in natural religion can proceed inductively as it does in science and everyday life on the basis of observation and eyewitness testimony. And the resulting degrees of belief are to be deemed rational as long as they satisfy the strictures of Bayesianism.

Rationality of belief is one thing, objectivity quite another. There are two ways in which the latter can be achieved in natural religion. First, we saw that given some mild assumptions, which can be made plausible or at least can be motivated, results about the incremental confirmation of hypotheses about miracles and religious doctrines proper can be proved as theorems of probability. Second, given minimal assumptions about the reliability of witnesses, convergence to certainty, as the number of witnesses increases, about the occurrence of miraculous events can be proven, again as theorems of probability. Thus, if evidence driven consensus is the mark of objectivity of opinion, then objectivity can be achieved in some circumstances in natural religion as well as in science and everyday life. Unfortunately, the scope of the 'some' does not extend very far, and certainly not to the crucial cases. Richard Swinburne, a modern pioneer of the use of Bayesianism in theology, has argued that the available empirical evidence lends strong inductive support to the existence of the Christian God (see Swinburne 1979). I accept that his position can be given a consistent Bayesian underpinning. But I also insist that there are degrees of belief functions (mine, for instance) that satisfy the Bayesian strictures but assign a low probability to the existence of the Christian God on the basis of the same evidence Swinburne marshals. But before inferring that disputes over matters religious are to be dismissed as merely subjective, it is well to ask whether we are any better off in science. There are in fact precious few results about evidence-driven merger of opinion for all equally dogmatic Bayesian agents (that is, agents whose prior probability assignments give zero to the same sentences) that apply to the hypotheses and theories of the advanced sciences[85]—in this respect quarks are no better off than Gods. One response is to cast around for more modest results. Alan Franklin (1990) has argued that merger of opinion with respect to certain theories in elementary particle physics can be achieved if the members of the relevant scientific community start with probability functions that are not too divergent. This is surely true, but it would seem equally true that members of a religious community will reach consensus if their prior probabilities are not too dissimilar. Another response is that atheism and agnosticism are no less merited in science than in religion; and indeed, instrumentalism (atheism) and agnosticism (constructive empiricism) are currently popular attitudes toward scientific theories that postulate unobservable entities. Yet another reaction is that because Bayesianism implies a parallel between science and religion, it is at best an incomplete account of ampliative inference. For those who share this reaction, the challenge is to provide an alternative account.

To return to Hume's essay, one can hope that future historical research will deepen our understanding of its origins, composition, and interpretation. But while the essay will endure as an important historical artifact and as a signpost to interesting philosophical issues, those philosophers who try to mine it for nuggets of wisdom are bound to be disappointed—it is a confection of rhetoric and *schein Geld.*

# Appendix on Probability

The interpretation of probability used here is degree of belief. Thus, in the treatment below, probabilities are assigned to sentences. It is assumed that the sentences belong to a formalized language that is closed under the usual truth functional connectives—and (&), or (v), not ($\neg$), etc. A notion of allowed model (or possible world) is presupposed, which in turn gives rise to a notion of a valid sentence: $\models$ A (A is valid) means that A is true in all allowed models. $\models$ A might variously mean that A is valid in first order predicate logic, or that A is a theorem in your favorite scientific theory, or ... There are three basic axioms of probability.

$$Pr(A) \geq 0 \tag{A1}$$

$$Pr(A) = 1 \text{ if } \models A \tag{A2}$$

$$Pr(A \text{ v } B) = Pr(A) + Pr(B) \text{ if } \models \neg(A\&B) \tag{A3}$$

The following are consequences of (A1)–(A3). Pr *respects logical equivalence*[86]:

$$Pr(A) = Pr(B) \text{ if } \models A \leftrightarrow B \tag{A4}$$

The *upper bound rule*:

$$Pr(A) \leq 1 \tag{A5}$$

The *negation rule*:

$$Pr(\neg A) = 1 - Pr(A) \tag{A6}$$

The *general addition rule*:

$$Pr(A \text{ v } B) = Pr(A) + Pr(B) - Pr(A\&B) \tag{A7}$$

The *weakening rule*:

$$Pr(A) \leq Pr(B) \text{ if } \models A \rightarrow B \tag{A8}$$

The *principle of total probability*:

$$Pr(A) = \sum_{i=1}^{n} Pr(A\&B_i) \text{ if } B_1, B_2, \dots, B_n \text{ are such that}$$

$$\models \neg(B_j\&B_k) \text{ for } j \neq k, \text{ and } \models B_1 \text{ v } B_2 \text{ v} \dots \text{ v } B_n \tag{A9}$$

Defining conditional probability by $Pr(Y/X) \equiv Pr(Y\&X)/Pr(X)$ when $Pr(X) \neq 0$, another form of total probability states that:

$$Pr(A/C) = \sum_{i=1}^{n} Pr(A/C\&B_i) \times Pr(B_i/C), \text{ where the } B_i \text{ are as in (A9)} \quad (A10)$$

*Exercise for readers*: show that (A4)–(A10) follow from (A1)–(A3).

In some applications (A1)–(A3) need to be strengthened by the principle of *countable additivity*:

If $A_i$, i = 1, 2, 3, . . . , are such that $A_{i+1} \vDash A_i$ for all i,

and $\{A_1, A_2, . . . \}$ is consistent, then $\lim_{n \to \infty} Pr(A_n) = 0$.[87] $\quad$ (A11)

Suppose that in intended models universal quantification ranges over a countably infinite domain in which the individuals are named by $a_1, a_2,$ . . . Then $(\forall i)Pa_i \vDash Pa_1 \& . . . \& Pa_n$, for all n. So $Pr((\forall i)Pa_i) \leq \lim_{n \to \infty} Pr(Pa_1 \& . . . \& Pa_n)$. With countable additivity, the $\leq$ becomes $=$.

# Notes

1. Originally published in 1748 as *Philosophical Essays Concerning Human Understanding*. For simplicity, I will refer to it throughout as the *Enquiry*. The version reproduced in Part II is from Hume (1898); it marks the changes and additions Hume made to "Of Miracles" as the *Enquiry* went through various editions. Hume commentators have generally neglected the clues to Hume's intentions offered by these changes.
2. For a recounting of this history, see Hempel (1965) and Laudan (1983).
3. It is clear that many of the claims made in pseudo-scientific disciplines are genuine claims; that is, in the logical positivists' jargon, they do have cognitive and empirical significance.
4. Here I am in complete agreement with Laudan (1983).
5. Some commentators assume that Hume's apparently admiring reference to Tillotson was intended to be ironic or mocking. I do not see why the reference must be read this way even though, of course, Hume thought that he had disposed of the miracles on which Tillotson partly rested his own religious convictions. For an account of Tillotson's argument against transubstantiation, see Levine (1988). Tillotson also offers prudential arguments for believing in the existence of God in his "The Wisdom of Being Religious" (1664). Jordan (1991) suggests that this sermon is one of Hume's main targets in Dialogue XII of *Dialogues Concerning Natural Religion*.
6. Two especially good books are Gasking (1978) and Yandell (1990).
7. See Burns (1981). In 1751 Hume sent Gilbert Elliot a sample of his *Dialogues Concerning Natural Religion*:

   You wou'd perceive . . . that I make Cleanthes the Hero of the Dialogues. Whatever you can think of, to strengthen that Side of the Argument, will be most acceptable to me. Any Propensity you imagine I have to the other Side, crept in upon me against my Will: and tis not long ago that I burn'd an old manuscript Book, wrote before I was twenty. . . . It began with an anxious Search after Arguments, to confirm the common Opinion: Doubts stole in, dissipated, return'd, were again dissipated, return'd again; and it was a perpetual Struggle of a restless Imagination against Inclination, perhaps against Reason. (*L*, Vol. I, 154)

8. Philo states the matter in the conditional mode: "If it affords no inference that affects human life" (1776, 227). But it is clear from the context that Philo (Hume?) thinks that the antecedent holds.

9. See Jordan (1991) for documentation of this two-pronged strategy in the natural religion of the eighteenth century.

10. As Robert Meyers (1997) has noted, the *Treatise* contains proto versions of some of the arguments that later appeared in "Of Miracles." For example, in Bk II, Pt. 3, sec. 1, Hume writes:

> Shou'd a traveller, returning from a far country, tell us, that he has seen a climate in the fiftieth degree of northern latitude, where all the fruits ripen and come to perfection in the winter, and decay in the summer, after the same manner as in *England* they are produc'd and decay in the contrary seasons, he wou'd find few so credulous as to believe him. I am apt to think a traveller wou'd met with as little credit, who shou'd inform us of people exactly of the same character with those in *Plato's Republic* on the one hand, or those in *Hobbes's Leviathan* on the other. There is a general course of nature in human actions, as well as in the operations of the sun and climate. There are also characters peculiar to different nations and particular persons, as well as common to mankind. The knowledge of these characters is founded on the observation of an uniformity in actions, that flow from them; and this uniformity forms the very essence of necessity. (*T* 402–403)

11. The editors of *New Letters of David Hume* hypothesize that this is William Hamilton, Jacobite poet and friend of Hume.

12. Commentators differ on the most likely place to have inserted "Of Miracles" in the *Treatise*; see for example, Nelson (1986) and Wootton (1990). The most likely answer seems to me to be that Hume would have inserted it in a place that corresponds to its thematic location in the *Enquiry*— that is, after the discussion of knowledge and probability and before the discussion of skeptical philosophy.

13. For a different explanation of why Hume decided to publish the miracles essay, see Nelson (1986).

14. This view is repeated in the *Ethics*: "Nothing happens in nature which could be attributed to any defect in it, for nature is always and everywhere one and the same. Its virtue and its power of acting are the same—that is, the laws and rules of nature, according to which all things happen and are changed from one form to another, are always and everywhere the same" (III pref, II: 138; quoted in Curley 1969, 49).

15. Alan Donegan (1996) has noted that Spinoza's views lead to a position on eyewitness testimony which, in principle, is distinct from Hume's. Unlike Hume, Spinoza was not committed to a reflexive skepticism regarding testimony to events that apparently go against the order of nature; rather, Spinoza is committed only to the existence of a naturalistic explanation, whether or not the testimony is correct. In practice, however, Spinoza's interpretation of scripture is such that Hume could have found little with which to quarrel. For example, as regards the miracle reported in Joshua 10: 12–14, Spinoza reads the passage "the sun stood still, and the moon stayed" metaphorically—not that the sun and moon literally stopped in their tracks but only that the day was, or seemed, longer than usual, (*TPT* 93). As for resurrections, Spinoza held that the revival by Elisha of a boy believed to be dead (II Kings iv: 34–35) was not a genuine resurrection but merely a case of a comatose boy revived by the warmth of Elisha's body (*TPT* 91; 113). The alleged resurrection of Jesus is treated

the opposite way: Spinoza believed the testimony that Jesus died on the cross but not the testimony that he returned from the dead (Ep 75; Shirley 1995, 337–339). More generally, I know of no instance in which Spinoza accepts testimony to an event that contravenes the order of nature in the sense of an inductively well confirmed lawlike regularity.

16. See Harrison (1995) for references to and analyses of relevant Newtonian texts.

17. Holland (1965) offers the modern version of the coincidence conception of miracles. Locke's brief for miracles relies less on coincidence and more on what Burns (1981) dubs the "principle of context," according to which it is reasonable to take an event as having religious significance if the circumstances are such as to make the event a suitable vehicle for revealing God's purposes and character; see Locke's *Discourse of Miracles*, reproduced in Pt. II. A similar view is found in Chubb (1741).

18. The message is spelled out in both English and French over Canada.

19. From the perspective of modern science, the paradigm example of miracle in the eighteenth century debate—a resurrection—is on a par with the Emuh example, at least assuming that the laws of biology must supervene on the laws of physics. For the motions of the elementary particles in the body of a dead person needed to bring her back to life would not seem to contravene any of the fundamental laws of physics, although such motions presumably have a very low probability on a par with the improbability of the motions of the water vapor molecules that spelled out the messages in the Emuh case. But I do not see that learning elementary particle physics automatically undermines the evidentiary value for Christianity of the resurrection of Jesus. Admittedly, this way of looking at miracles does not fit well with Hume's rather simplistic conception of laws of nature (see sections 6 and 9). So much the worse for Hume I say.

20. The issue of what constitutes a lawlike regularity is subject to continuing controversy in philosophy. The details of this issue will not directly affect the current discussion.

21. This is a simplification that can lead to incorrect results. To take Reichenbach's example, "All spheres of pure gold have a mass of less than 10 million kg" is a lawlike generalization. But even if it holds for all space and all time, it would not express a law of nature. The reason why is explained by David Lewis's (1973) best systems analysis on which laws are identified by the axioms or theorems of the deductive system (= axiomatizable set of true sentences) that achieves the best compromise between strength and simplicity. The simplification considered here is intended to do justice to Hume's naive conception of laws.

22. Annet (1744a) made the point. Modern commentators return to it again and again; see, for example, Flew (1966), Everitt (1987), and Curd (1996). In *The Concept of Miracle*, Swinburne (1970) held that "All As are Bs" can express a law even if it admits an unrepeatable counterinstance. But he seems to have given up this view in the later *The Existence of God* (1979).

23. Read $\boxed{N}L$ as "it is nomologically necessary that L." See Sobel (1996) for a discussion of Hume's views on this matter.

24. C. D. Broad read Hume this way. He went on to complain that on Hume's definition of miracle, only one token of a type of miracle can occur. "It

seems that Hume would have to say that, if anybody has ever been raised from the dead, it was a miracle on the first occasion, because it contradicted all previous experience; but that, if it ever happened again, the second case would not be a miracle, because it did not contradict *all* previous experience" (1916–17, 86). But Broad thought that, intuitively speaking, there could be several resurrection miracles.

25. For good overviews of the eighteenth century miracles debate, see Burns (1981), Wootton (1990), and Stewart (1994).

26. Hume also refers to Locke by name in the *Enquiry*. Owen (1994) has made the case for viewing Locke as the target of Hume's skeptical doubts about probabilistic reasoning.

27. Credit is due to Gasking (1978) for making apparent the importance of this work, or rather of the reactions to it.

28. Leslie Stephen (1962) goes so far as to question Woolston's mental stability.

29. Woolston may have been a buffoon, but he undoubtedly achieved notoriety and his views were widely discussed. Burns (1981, 10) relates that 30,000 copies of his *Six Discourses* were printed and that Swift recorded that

Here is Woolston's tracts, the twelfth edition
'Tis read by every politician:
The country members when in town
To all their boroughs send them down:
You never met a thing so smart;
The courtiers have them all by heart.

30. According to Leslie Stephen (1962, Vol. 1, 208). Stephen reports that Annet was "ruined by the scandal . . . and edifying stoires were told of his being driven to accept charity at the hands of the benevolent Archbishop Secker."

31. See *T*, note p. 461. Hume refers to "a late author." The editor, Selby-Bigge, added the name Wollaston.

32. This was also a theme of Burns (1981). Wootton's special contribution is the identification of possible French sources for Hume's essay. I remain unconvinced that Hume's miracles essay was influenced in any philosophically significant way by French writers. What is abundantly clear, however, is that Hume had read widely about alleged Catholic miracles performed in France and had concluded that they were all obvious frauds; see the three page footnote which Hume added to the 1750 edition (printed on pp. 344–346 of Hume [1975]). Wootton proposes that Hume's original contribution lies in his famous Maxim which provides a "clear procedure" for deciding when testimony establishes the credibility of a miracle. If my analysis of the Maxim is correct (see section 15), then Hume's contribution comes to naught.

33. It is questionable whether or not this is an accurate rendering of Tillotson's argument. A perhaps better way of making his point is to say that a belief in transubstantiation involves an epistemological inconsistency. The evidence for or against the doctrine comes from our senses; but since our senses tell us that the bread is just bread and the wine is just wine, they could provide evidence for the doctrine only if they were deceiving

us, in which case they are unreliable and cannot be used to ground justified belief.

34. Commentators continue to be at odds over this matter; see, for example, Fogelin (1990) vs. Slupik (1995).

35. There is a compromise position. Burns (1981) hypothesizes that the original 1730s version of Hume's essay consisted mainly of the "proof" of Part 1, a "proof" that Hume intended "as demonstrating the absolute inconceivability of rational belief in miracles" (154). But (on Burn's hypothesis) at some later time Hume decided to proceed more cautiously and present himself as arguing only that "exceptionally high-quality testimony was necessary to render miracle stories credible." Thus, the additional considerations of Part. 2 needed to buttress the modified Part 1. I find this reconstruction not implausible.

36. Here I am slurring over the fact that Reichenbach was mainly concerned with inferring limiting relative frequencies from finite sample data. He then had to face the problem of the single case; i.e., how is limiting frequency supposed to serve as guide to expectations about particular instances? See Reichenbach (1971). This and other versions of the straight rule of induction run into problems with Goodman's "grue," but I will ignore these problems in the present context since things are already complicated enough. However, I claim that these problems provide further ammunition for the Bayesian analysis of inductive inference that will be used below (see Earman 1992).

37. In the *Treatise* Hume writes: "Suppose . . . I have found by long observation, that of twenty ships which go to sea, only nineteen return. Suppose I see at present twenty ships that leave the port: I transfer my past experience to the future, and represent to myself nineteen ships as returning in safety, and one as perishing" (*T* 134). And in the *Enquiry*: "[I]t seems evident, that, when we transfer the past to the future, in order to determine the effect, which will result from any cause, we transfer all the different events, in the same proportion as they have appeared in the past" (*E* 58). So (Hume would say), if n As have been examined and m have been found to be Bs, and if n new As are examined then . . . what? The most probable number of Bs is m? The expected number of Bs is m? The probability is 1 that the number of Bs is m?

38. In Bk. I, sec. 15 of the *Treatise* ("Rules by which to judge of causes and effects"), Hume points to some relatively sophisticated inductive procedures designed to determine cause and effect relations. Here Hume takes a cause to be necessary as well as sufficient for is effect ("The same cause always produces the same effect, and the same effect never arises but from the same cause" [*T* 173]. Thus, care must be taken to weed out the nonnecessary effects:

There is no phaenomenon in nature, but what is compounded and modify'd by so many different circumstances, that in order to arrive at the decisive point, we must carefully separate whatever is superfluous, and enquire by new experiments if every particular circumstance of the first experiment was essential to it. These new experiments are liable to a discussion of the same kind; so that the utmost constancy is requir'd to make us persevere in our enquiry, and the utmost sagacity to choose the right way among so many that present themselves. (*T* 175)

39. Some commentators have expressed puzzlement over the "fact" that Hume deals only with eyewitness testimony to miracles and does not deal with first-hand experience. If my attribution of the straight rule to Hume is correct, this puzzlement rests on a false presupposition.

40. See Klibansky and Mossner (1958, 233)

41. It is known that Hume visited Price at his home in Newington Green. It is reported that on one of these occasions Hume "cordially acknowledged that on one point Mr. Price has succeeded in convincing him that his arguments were inconclusive" (quoted in Thomas 1924, 30). Unfortunately, the subject of this discussion is not recorded.

42. The authorship of *An Introduction to the Doctrine of Fluxions* (1751) has been attributed to Bayes, but Bayes' election as a Fellow came in 1742. Pearson (1978) has attributed another work, *Explanation of Fluxions* (1741), to Bayes, and hypothesizes that this work was responsible for Bayes' election to the Royal Society.

43. More precisely, the will left £200 to be divided between John Boyl and Richard Price; see Barnard (1958).

44. Thus I cannot agree with Raynor's (1980) claim that Hume knew about Bayes's work as early as 1767; and it is certain that Hume did not know about "Bayes's theorem" at this date since this theorem is not in Bayes' paper (see below).

45. Gower (1990, 1991) has argued that Hume's talk of probabilities does not conform to the standard axioms of probability. For a response, see Mura (1998).

46. A brief overview of the relevant part of probability theory is given in the Appendix.

47. The Dutch book construction is not above criticism; see Maher (1993, sec. 5.1).

48. A more sophisticated rule of conditionalization has been developed by Jeffrey (1983) to cover the case of uncertain learning. Dutch book justifications for rules of conditonalizations have also been offered; see Skyrms (1987).

49. For a defense of the view that the axioms of probability, but not the rule of conditionalization, characterize the logic of inductive reasoning, see Howson (1996).

50. The prior probability $Pr(H/K)$ of H—the probability of H prior to getting the new evidence E—need not be thought of as the a priori probability of H—the *tabula rasa* probability of H—since the background knowledge K may be very rich.

51. See Howson and Urbach (1993) and Earman (1992) for relevant examples.

52. Bayes' attempted justification of his prior probability assignment is discussed in Earman (1992, ch. 1). If this justification succeeded, it would provide a solution to the problem of induction.

53. See Earman (1992, ch.4) if you are interested in the proof.

54. Broad complained that "if the testimony of others does not shake my belief in the law, there is no reason for me to think that there is anything that needs explanation or investigation. If scientists had actually proceeded in this way, some of the most important natural laws would never have been discovered" (1916–17, 87).

55. C. D. Broad made the same point without explicitly using the probability apparatus:

> Clearly many propositions have been accounted laws of nature because of invariable experience in their favor, then exceptions have been observed, and finally these propositions have ceased to be regarded as laws of nature. But the first reported exception was, to anyone who had not himself observed it, in precisely the same position as a story of a miracle, if Hume be right. Those, then, to whom the first exception was reported ought to have rejected it, and gone on believing in the alleged law of nature. Yet, if the first report of the first exception makes *no* difference to their belief in the law, their state of belief will be precisely the same when a second exception is reported as it was on the first occasion. . . . So that it would seem on Hume's theory that if, up to a certain time, I and every one else have always observed A to be followed by B, then no amount of testimony from the most trustworthy persons that they observed A not followed by B ought to have the least effect on my belief in the law. (1916–17, 87)

56. There remains the possibility of non-Bayesian learning. E.g., if $Pr(L/E\&K)$ = 1 and if evidence E' in favor of an exception to L is acquired, then Pr is changed by some means different than conditionalization to a new Pr' such that $Pr'(L/E'\&E\&K) < 1$. I will not discuss such possibilities here, except to say that what is sauce for the goose is sauce for the gander: if such a change is allowed in, say, the case of the (presumptive) law of the conservation of energy, why isn't it also allowed in the case of the (presumptive) law that a dead person cannot return to life?

57. See section 7. George Campbell is an example of one of Hume's contemporaries who interpreted the Indian prince this way; see his *Dissertation on Miracles* (CDM 32ff).

58. An unidentified source at Notre Dame called this text to my attention.

59. Versions are to be found in Sherlock (1728); Butler (1736), who speaks of "the prince who has always lived in a warm climate"; and Annet (1744a).

60. As noted by Burns (1981) and Wootton (1994). See Mossner (1954, 232).

61. Campbell (1762) accuses Hume of equivocating between these two senses of "experience." While this charge seems to me to be unfair, I think that there is much merit in Section II ("Mr Hume charged with some fallacies in his way of managing the argument") of Part I of Campbell's *Dissertation on Miracles*.

62. The notion that law statements may contain *ceteris paribus* clauses is criticized in Earman and Roberts (1999).

63. As Colin Howson has kindly reminded me.

64. I am grateful to Colin Howson for bringing this point to my attention.

65. This interpretation was first offered in Earman (1993).

66. It is easy to show that

$$(Pr(t(M)/E\&K) > 0) \rightarrow \{[Pr(M/t(M)\&E\&K) > 0.5]$$
$$\leftrightarrow [Pr(M\&t(M)/E\&K) > Pr(\neg M\&t(M)/E\&K)]\}.$$

Sobel (1996) shows that

$$\{[Pr(t(M)/E\&K) > 0]\&[Pr(M/t(M)\&E\&K) > 0.5]\}$$
$$\leftrightarrow \{Pr(M\&t(M)/E\&K) > Pr(\neg M\&t(M)/E\&K)\}.$$

67. Hambourger (1980) attributes to Hume the following "principle of relative likelihood": "Suppose that someone or, perhaps, a group of people testify to the truth of a proposition P that, considered by itself, is improbable. Then to evaluate the testimony, one must weigh the probability that P is true against the probability that the informants are lying or mistaken. If it is more likely that P is true than that the informants are lying or mistaken, then, on balance, the testimony renders P more likely than not, and it may be reasonable for one to believe that P. However, if it is as likely, or even more likely, that the informants are lying or mistaken than it is that P is true, then, on balance, the testimony does not render P more likely true than false, and it would not be reasonable to believe that P" (590). Exercise for the reader: Let P be the proposition that ticket number so-and-so won the lottery, and let the testimony to P be in the form of report from a newspaper known for its reliable reporting. Does this example provide, as claimed by Hambourger, a counterexample to the principle of relative likelihood? See Hájek (1995).

68. Some commentators have read Hume as presenting the example of eight days of total darkness as an example of a marvel rather than a miracle. This reading does not square well with the text just quoted. Nor does it square with Hume's 1761 letter to Blair:

> There is no contradiction in saying, that all the testimony which ever was really given for any miracle, or ever will be given, is the subject of derision; and yet forming a fiction or supposition for a particular miracle, which might not only merit attention, but amount to a full proof of it. For instance, the absence of sun during 48 hours; but reasonable men would only conclude from this fact, that the machine of the globe was disordered during the time. (L, Vol. 1, 349–350)

69. Here I am following Sobel (1996). See also Schlesinger (1987, 1991).

70. Peter Huber's column "Insights," *Forbes* January 22, 1996, contains the claim that Bayes' theorem implies that "Inherently unlikely events remain unlikely even in the face of reports that they have occurred." His illustration:

> Consider a simple case. When your grandma sees a taxi, her eyesight is good enough to call the color right 80% of the time. If she reports seeing an orange taxi, how likely is it that she's got the color right? The answer is not 80%. It depends, and not on her eyes alone, or even mostly on her eyes, as you might suppose. The answer depends as much on records of the Bureau of Motor Vehicles. If 9 out of 10 taxis in the city are in fact yellow, and the rest orange, granny's orange-taxi call will be wrong 9 times out of 13.

> Exercise to reader: How does Huber get his answer? Is it correct? Extra credit: From whom did Huber steal this example?

71. Compare to Locke: "[I]n traditional truths, each remove weakens the force of the proof: and the more hands the tradition has successively passed through, the less strength and evidence does it receive from them" (*ECHU* 378; 104). When Hume reports Tillotson's argument against transubstan-

tiation, he writes that "Our evidence, then, for the *Christian* religion is less than the evidence for the truth of our senses; because, even in the first authors of our religion it was no greater; and it is evident it must diminish in passing from them to his disciples; nor can any one rest such confidence in their testimony, as in the immediate object of his senses" (*E* 109; 140).

72. Craig was a popular target; for instance, he is attacked by Laplace (*PEP* 126; 202).

73. Dale (1992) has provided persuasive evidence that the author was George Hooper, who became bishop of Bath and Wells in 1704.

74. See, for example, Schlesinger (1987) and Otte (1993). A good recent review is given by Holder (1998).

75. "But as I am not apt to lose my temper, and would still less incline to do so with a friend of yours, I shall calmly communicate to you some remarks on the argument" (*L*, Vol. 1, 349). Grieg, the editor of *Letters of David Hume*, characterizes the Rev. Blair as "a vain, timid, fussy, kindhearted little man that everybody liked" (*L*, Vol. 1, fn 348).

76. In other modes I am a skeptic about Bayesianism; see my (1992).

77. I owe this point to Richard Gale.

78. Does Bayesian make sense of the notion of the "virtue of believing," other than through the unattractive position in which an agent assigns a high degree of belief to the existence of the Christian deity even though Bayesian calculations show that on the basis of the total evidence available to her, she should assign a lower degree of belief?

79. I am ignoring the "problem of old evidence" (see Earman 1992, ch. 5) because it applies equally to the confirmation of theological and non-theological hypotheses alike. But, of course, unless this problem is resolved, Bayesianism cannot be used as a basis for an account of confirmation.

80. It is unfair to view Hume's contrary miracles argument merely as a fallback position. For Hume, it had a much greater importance. As noted above, many theists were committed for other reasons (e.g., the argument from design) to the existence of God, and miracles served for them as an indication of what kind of God exists. The contrary miracles argument is supposed to show that miracles cannot serve this function and cannot support (what Hume would have termed) the superstitions of Christianity or of any particular religion for that matter.

81. Hume's claim that all religions "abound in miracles" is false. Of Confucianism, Annet wrote: "I never read, that it was either given, or confirm'd by miracles; but truth has no need of them" (*RJC* 78; 137).

82. Locke would have argued that Hume is wrong in his reading of history:

The heathen world, amidst an infinite and uncertain jumble of deities, fables, and worships, had no room for a divine attestation of any one against the rest. Those owners of many gods were at liberty in their worship; and no one of their divinities pretending to be the one only true God, no one of them could be supposed in the pagan scheme to make use of miracles to establish his worship alone, or to abolish that of the other; much less was there any use of miracles to confirm any articles of faith, since no one of them had any such to propose as necessary to be believed by their votaries. (*DM* 257; 115)

I leave it to the reader to decide the merits of this claim.

83. As Rodney Holder has mentioned to me. But see note 78.

84. In its day, however, Middleton's work attracted much more notoriety than Hume's *Enquiry*. Hume was miffed. In *My Own Life*, he spoke of the initial reception of the *Enquiry*, which was published while he was in Italy: "[T]his piece was at first little more successful than the Treatise of Human Nature. On my return from Italy, I had the Mortification to find all England in a Ferment on account of Dr. Middleton's Free Inquiry; while my Performance was entirely overlooked and neglected" (*L*, Vol. 1, p. 3). Middleton's advertised targets of attack were the miracles allegedly performed after the time of the Apostles. However, most readers took him to be undermining the New Testament miracles as well.

85. See Earman (1992, ch. 5) for a discussion of these results.

86. The biconditional $\leftrightarrow$ can be introduced by defining $A \leftrightarrow B$ as $(A \rightarrow B)\&(B \rightarrow A)$, and the material conditional $\rightarrow$ can be introduced by defining $A \rightarrow B$ as $\neg A \lor B$.

87. $X \vDash Y$ means that $Y$ is true in every allowed model in which $X$ is true. A set if sentences is consistent just in case it is true in some allowed model.

# Works Cited

Annet, P. 1744a. *The Resurrection of Jesus Considered, In Answer to the Tryal of the Witnesses. By a Moral Philosopher.* 3d ed. London: Printed for M. Cooper.

———— 1744b. *The Resurrection Reconsidered. Being an Answer to Clearer and Others.* London: Printed for the author by M. Cooper.

———— 1745. *The Resurrection Defenders Stript of All Defense.* London: Printed for the Author.

———— 1747. *Supernaturals Examined.* London: F. Page.

———— 1761. *The Free Enquirer.* London: Printed for E. Cabe.

Anonymous (George Hooper?) 1699. "A Calculation of the Credibility of Human Testimony," *Philosophical Transactions of the Royal Society (London)* 21: 359–365.

Armstrong, B. F. 1992. "Hume on Miracles: Begging-the-Question Against Believers," *History of Philosophy Quarterly* 9: 319–328.

Babbage, C. 1838. *The Ninth Bridgewater Treatise.* Page references to the 2d ed. London: Frank Cass, 1967.

Barnard, G. A. 1958. "Thomas Bayes—A Biographical Note," *Biometrika* 45: 293–295.

Bayes, T. 1763. "An Essay towards Solving a Problem in the Doctrine of Chances," *Philosophical Transactions of the Royal Society(London)* 53: 370–418. Reprinted in *Biometrika* 45 (1958): 296–315.

Berlitz, C. 1974. *The Bermuda Triangle.* New York: Avon Books.

Boyle, R. 1686. *A Free Enquiry into the Vulgarly Received Notion of Nature.* London: Printed by H. Clark for J. Taylor.

Broad, C. D. 1916–17. "Hume's Theory of the Credibility of Miracles," *Proceedings of the Aristotelian Society* 17: 77–94.

Burns, R. M. 1981. *The Great Debate on Miracles, From Joseph Glanville to David Hume.* East Brunswick, N.J.: Associated University Presses.

Butler, J. 1736. *The Analogy of Religion.* London: Printed for J. and P. Knapton. Reprinted with an Introduction by E. C. Mosner. New York: Frederick Unger Publishing, 1961.

Campbell, G. 1762. *A Dissertation on Miracles.* 2d ed. Page references to the 1834 edition. London: T. Tegg and Son.

Carnap, R. 1950. *Logical Foundations of Probability.* Chicago: University of Chicago Press.

———— 1952. *The Continuum of Inductive Methods.* Chicago: University of Chicago Press.

Chandler, S. 1744. *Witnesses of the Resurrection of Jesus Christ Reexamined:*

*And their Testimony Proved Entirely Consistent.* London: Printed for J. Noon and R. Hett.

Chubb, T. 1741. *Discourse on Miracles.* London: T. Cox.

Clarke, S. 1705. "A Discourse Concerning the Unalterable Obligations of Natural Religion, and the Truth and Certainty of the Christian Revelation." Page references to *The Works of Samuel Clarke.* Vol. 2, 580–733. New York: Garland Publishing, 1978.

Clarke, S. 1997. "When to Believe in a Miracle," *American Philosophical Quarterly* 34: 95–102.

Craig, J. 1699. "Mathematical Principles of Christian Theology." Reprinted in *History and Theory* 3, Bei. 4: 1–31.

Curd, M. 1996. "Miracles as Violations of Laws of Nature." In *Faith, Freedom, and Rationality,* ed. J. Jordan and D. Howard-Snyder. 171–183. Lanham, Md.: Rowman & Littlefield.

Curley, E. M. 1969. *Spinoza's Metaphysics: An Essay in Interpretation.* Cambridge, Mass.: Harvard University Press.

Dale, A. I. 1992. "On the Authorship of 'A Calculation of the Credibility of Human Testimony'," *Historia Mathematica* 19: 414–417.

Dawid, P., and D. Gillies, 1989. "A Bayesian Analysis of Hume's Argument Concerning Miracles," *Philosophical Quarterly* 39: 57–63.

Donegan, A. 1996. "Spinoza's theology." In *The Cambridge Companion to Spinoza,* ed. D. Garret, 343–364. Cambridge, Cambridge University Press.

Earman, J. 1992. *Bayes or Bust: A Critical Examination of Bayesian Confirmation Theory.* Cambridge, Mass: MIT Press.

——— 1993. "Bayes, Hume, and Miracles," *Faith and Philosophy* 10: 293–310.

Earman, J., and J. Roberts, 1999. "Ceteris Paribus, There are No Provisos," *Synthese* 118: 439–478.

Everitt, N. 1987. "The Impossibility of Miracles," *Religious Studies* 23: 347–349.

Flew, A. 1966. *God and Philosophy.* London: Hutchinson.

Fogelin, R. 1990. "What Hume Actually Said About Miracles," *Hume Studies* 16: 81–86.

Franklin, A. 1990. *The Neglect of Experiment.* Cambridge: Cambridge University Press.

Gasking, J. C. A. 1978. *Hume's Philosophy of Religion.* New York: Barnes and Noble. 2nd ed. Atlantic Highlands N.J.: Humanities Press, 1988.

Gillies, D. 1991. "A Bayesian Proof of a Humean Principle," *British Journal for the Philosophy of Science* 42: 255–256.

Gower, B. 1990. "David Hume and the Probability of Miracles," *Hume Studies* 16: 1–17.

——— 1991. "Hume on Probability," *British Journal for the Philosophy of Science* 42: 1–19.

Greig, J. Y. T. (ed.). 1932. *Letters of David Hume.* 2 vol. Oxford: Oxford University Press.

Hájek, A. 1995. "In Defense of Hume's Balancing of Probabilities in the Miracles Argument," *Southwestern Philosophy Review* 11: 111–118.

Hambourger, R. 1980. "Belief in Miracles and Hume's Essay," *Noûs* 14: 587–604.

Harrison, P. 1995. "Newtonian Science, Miracles, and the Laws of Nature," *Journal of the History of Ideas* 56: 531–553.

Hempel, C. G. 1965. "Empiricist Criteria of Cognitive Significance: Problems and Changes." In *Aspects of Scientific Explanation*, 101–119. New York: Free Press.

Hobbes, T. 1668. *Leviathan*. Page references to R. E. Flathman and D. Johnston (eds.), *Thomas Hobbes: Leviathan*. New York: W. W. Norton & Co.

Holder, R. D. 1998. "Hume on Miracles: Bayesian Interpretation, Multiple Testimony, and the Existence of God," *British Journal for the Philosophy of Science* 49: 49–65.

Holland, R. F. 1965. "The Miraculous," *American Philosophical Quarterly* 2: 43–51.

Howson, C. 1996. "Logic and Probability," *British Journal for the Philosophy of Science* 48: 517–531.

Howson, C., and P. Urbach, 1993. *Scientific Reasoning: The Bayesian Approach*. 2d ed. La Salle, Ill.: Open Court.

Hume, D. 1739–40. *A Treatise of Human Nature*. Page references to L. A. Selby-Bigge (ed.) 2d ed, with revised and variant reading by P. H. Niddich. Oxford: Clarenden Press, 1978.

———— 1748. *Philosophical Essays Concerning Human Understanding*. London: A. Millar.

———— 1754–62. *History of England*. Page references to D. F. Norton and R. H. Popkin (eds.), *David Hume: Philosophical Historian*. Indianapolis, Ind.: Bobbs-Merrill, 1965.

———— 1776. *Dialogues Concerning Natural Religion*. Page references to N. Kemp Smith (ed.), *Hume's Dialogues Concerning Natural Religion*. 2d ed. New York: Social Science Publishers, 1948.

———— 1898. *Essays Moral, Political, and Literary by David Hume*. Vol. 2. T. H. Green and T. H. Grose (eds.), London: Longmans, Green.

———— 1975. *Enquiries Concerning Human Understanding and Concerning the Principles of Morals*. Reprinted from the posthumous edition of 1777. Page references to 3d edition with text revised and notes by P. H. Niddich. Oxford: Clarendon Press, 1975.

Jackson, J. 1744. *An Address to Deists*. London: Printed for J. and P. Knapton.

Jeffrey, R. C. 1983. *The Logic of Decision*. 2d ed. New York: McGraw-Hill.

Jordan, J. 1991. "Hume, Tillotson, and Dialogue XII," *Hume Studies* 17: 125–139.

Kemp Smith, N. (ed.). 1948. *Hume's Dialogues Concerning Natural Religion*. 2d ed. New York: Social Science Publishers.

Klibansky, R., and E. C. Mossner, (eds.). 1954. *New Letters of David Hume*. Oxford: Clarendon Press.

Kusche, L. 1986. *The Mystery of the Bermuda Triangle—Solved*. Buffalo, N.Y.: Prometheus Books.

Laplace, P. S. 1812. *Théorie Analytique des Probabilités*. Page references to the 3d ed. (1820) reprinted in *Oeuvres complètes de Laplace*. Vol. 7. Paris: Gauthier-Villars, 1886.

———— 1814. *Essai philosophique sur les probabilitiés*. Page references to F. W. Truscott and F. L. Emory (trans.), *A Philosophical Essay on Probabilities*. New York: Dover, 1951.

Laudan, L. 1983. "The Demise of the Demarcation Problem." In *Physics, Philosophy and Psychoanalysis*, ed. R. S. Cohen and L. Laudan, 111–127. Dordrecht: D. Reidel.

Leibniz, G. W. 1686. *Discourse on Metaphysics*. English translation in L. E. Loemker (ed.), *G. W. Leibniz: Philosophical Papers and Letters*. 2d ed., 303–330. Dordecht: D. Reidel, 1970.

———— 1710. *Theodicy*. English translation A. Farrer (ed.), *Theodicy*. New Haven, Conn.: Yale University Press, 1952.

Levine, M. P. 1988. "Belief in Miracles: Tillotson's Argument against Transubstantiation as a Model for Hume," *International Journal for Philosophy of Religion* 23: 125–160.

Lewis, D. 1973. *Counterfactuals*. Cambridge, Mass.: Harvard University Press.

Locke, J. 1690. *An Essay Concerning Human Understanding*. Page references to A. C. Fraser (ed.), *An Essay Concerning Human Understanding, by John Locke*. New York: Dover, 1959.

———— 1706. "A Discourse of Miracles." Page references to *The Works of John Locke*. Vol. 9. Germany: Scientia Verlag Aalen.

Maher, P. 1993. *Betting on Theories*. Cambridge: Cambridge University Press.

McKinnon, A. 1967. " 'Miracle' and 'Paradox'," *American Philosophical Quarterly* 4: 308–314.

Meyers, R. 1997. "The Marvelous and the Miraculous in Hume," preprint.

Middleton, C. 1749. *A Free Inquiry into the Miraculous Powers, which Are Supposed to Have Subsisted in the Christian Church, from the Earliest Ages through Several Successive Centuries*. London: Printed for R. Manby and H. S. Cox.

Mill, J. S. 1843. *A System of Logic*. Page references to the 8th ed. New York: Harper and Bros., 1874.

More, St. Thomas 1557. *A Dialogue Concerning Heresies*. Page references to T. M. C. Lawler (ed.), *Complete Works of St. Thomas More*. Vol. 6, Part I. New Haven, Conn: Yale University Press, 1963.

Mossner, E. C. 1954. *Life of David Hume*. Austin, Tex: University of Texas Press.

Mura, A. 1998. "Hume's Inductive Logic," *Synthese* 115: 303–331.

Nelson, J. O. 1986. "The Burial and Resurrection of Hume's Essay 'Of Miracles'," *Hume Studies* 12: 57–76.

Nickell, J. 1993. *Looking for a Miracle*. Buffalo, N.Y.: Prometheus Books.

Otte, R. 1993. "Schlesinger and Miracles," *Faith and Philosophy* 10: 93–98.

Owen, D. 1994. "Hume's Doubts about Probable Reasoning: Was Locke the Target?" In *Hume and Hume's Connexions*, ed. M. A. Stewart and J. P. Wright, 140–159. University Park: Pennsylvania State University Press.

Pearce, Z. 1729. *The Miracles of Jesus Vindicated*. London: Printed for J. Roberts.

Pearson, K. 1978. *The History of Statistics in the 17th and 18th Centuries*. London: Printed for Charles Griffin.

Pegis, A. C. (ed.). 1944. *The Basic Writing of Saint Thomas Aquinas*. Vol. 1. New York: Random House.

Price, R. 1758. *A Review of the Principal Questions and Difficulties in Morals*. London: A. Millar.

———— 1767. *Four Dissertations*. Page references to the 2d ed. 1768. London: A. Millar and T. Cadell.

———— 1771. *Observations on Reversionary Payments*. London: T. Cadell.

———— 1776. *Observations on the Nature of Civil Liberty, the Principles of Government, and the Justice and Policy of the War with America*. London: T. Cadell.

Raynor, D. 1980. "Hume's Knowledge of Bayes's Theorem," *Philosophical Studies* 38: 105–106.

Reichenbach, H. 1961. *Experience and Prediction*. Chicago: University of Chicago Press.

——— 1971. *The Theory of Probability*. 2d ed. Berkeley: University of California Press.

Schlesinger, G. N. 1987. "Miracles and Probabilities," *Noûs* 21: 219–232.

——— 1991. "The Credibility of Extraordinary Events," *Analysis* 51: 120–126.

Sherlock, T. 1728. *Tryal of the Witnesses of the Resurrection of Jesus*. London: J. Roberts. Page references to the 11th ed. London: J. and H. Pembert, 1743.

Shirley, S. (tr.). 1995. *Spinoza. The Letters*. Indianapolis, Ind.: Hackett.

Skelton, P. 1749. *Ophiomaches: Or, Deism Revealed*. London: A. Millar.

Skyrms, B. 1987. "Dynamic Coherence and Probability Kinematics," *Philosophy of Science* 54: 1–20.

Slupik, C. 1995. "A New Interpretation of Hume's 'Of Miracles'," *Religious Studies* 31: 517–536.

Sobel, J. H. 1987. "On the Evidence of Testimony for Miracles: A Bayesian Interpretation of David Hume's Analysis," *Philosophical Quarterly* 37: 166–186.

——— 1991. "Hume's Theorem on Testimony Sufficient to Establish a Miracle," *Philosophical Quarterly* 41: 229–237.

——— 1996. *Logic and Religion*. Forthcoming.

Spinoza, B. 1670. *A Theologico-Political Treatise*. Page references to R. H. M. Elves (ed.), *The Chief Works of Benedict de Spinoza. A Theologico-Political Treatise and A Political Treatise*. Vol. 1. New York: Dover, 1951.

Stephen, L. 1962. *History of English Thought in the Eighteenth Century*. 3d ed. 2 Vols. New York: Harcourt, Brace & World. First published in 1876.

Stewart, M. A. 1994. "Hume's Historical View of Miracles." In *Hume and Hume's Connexions*, ed. M. A. Stewart and J. P. Wright, 171–200. University Park, Pa.: Pennsylvania State University Press.

Swinburne, R. 1970. *The Concept of Miracle*. New York: St. Martin's Press.

——— 1979. *The Existence of God*. Oxford: Clarenden Press.

Thomas, R. 1924. *Richard Price: Philosopher and Apostle of Liberty*. London: Humphrey Milford.

Tillotson, J. 1664. "The Wisdom of Being Religious." Reprinted as Sermon 1 in Tillotson (1728).

——— 1728. *The Works of the Most Reverend Dr. John Tillotson*. London: J. Darby.

Tweyman, S. (ed.). 1996. *Hume on Miracles*. Bristol: Thommes Press.

Van der Loos, H. 1965. *The Miracles of Jesus*. Leiden: E. J. Brill.

West, G. 1747. *Observations on the History and Evidence of the Resurrection of Jesus Christ*. London: Printed for R. Dodsley.

Whately, R. 1819. "Historic Doubts Relative to Napoleon Bonaparte." Reprinted in R. S. Pomeroy (ed.), *Historic Doubts Relative to Napoleon Bonaparte*. Berkeley, Calif.: Scholar Press, 1985.

Whiston, W. 1696. *A New Theory of the Earth*. London: Printed by R. Roberts for B. Tooke.

Wilkins, J. 1699. *Of the Principles and Duties of Natural Religion*. Page references to the 5th ed. London: Printed for R. Chiswell, 1704.

Wollaston, W. 1725. *The Religion of Nature Delineated*. London: S. Palmer.

Woolston, T. 1727–1729. *Six Discourses on the Miracles of Our Savior*. London. Reprinted by Garland Publishing, New York, 1979.

Wootton, D. 1983. "The Fear of God in Early Modern Political Theory," *Historical Papers/Communications Historique*, 56–80.

———— 1990. "Hume's 'Of Miracles': Probability and Irreligion." In *Studies in the Philosophy of the Enlightenment*, ed. M. A. Stewart, 191–229. Oxford: Clarendon Press.

Yandell, K. E. 1990. *Hume's "Inexplicable Mystery": His Views on Religion*. Philadelphia: Temple University Press.

# Additional Bibliography

Armstrong, B. F. 1995. "Hume's Actual Argument against Miracles," *History of Philosophy Quarterly* 12: 65–76.

Basinger, D. 1984. "Miracles as Violations: Some Clarifications," *Southern Journal of Philosophy* 22:1–7.

Beckwith, F. J. 1989. *David Hume's Argument against Miracles. A Critical Analysis*. New York: University Press of America.

Brown, G. 1995. "Miracles in the Best of All Possible Worlds," *History of Philosophy Quarterly* 12: 19–37.

Coady, C. A. J. 1992. *Testimony: A Philosophical Study*. Oxford: Clarendon Press.

Coleman, D. 1988. "Hume, Miracles and Lotteries," *Hume Studies* 14: 328–346.

Ellin, J. 1993. "Again: Hume on Miracles," *Hume Studies* 19: 203–212.

Ferguson, K. G. 1992. "An Intervention into the Flew/Fogelin Debate," *Hume Studies* 17: 105–112.

Fitzgerald, P. 1985. "Miracles," *Philosophical Forum* 17: 48–64.

Flew, A. 1979. "The Red Queen at Subtraction," *Hume Studies* 5: 110–111.

——— 1990. "Fogelin on Hume on Miracles," *Hume Studies* 16: 141–144.

Gasking, J. C. A. 1985. "Contrary Miracles Concluded," *Hume Studies* 1985 Suppl.: 1–14.

Gilman, J. E. 1989. "Reconceiving Miracles," *Religious Studies* 25: 477–487.

Grey, W. 1994. "Philosophy and the Paranormal. Part 2: Skepticism, Miracles, and Kowledge," *Skeptical Inquirer* 18: 288–294.

Hambourger, R. 1987. "Need Miracles Be Extraordinary?" *Philosophy and Phenomenological Research* 47: 435–449.

Houston, J. H. 1994. *Reported Miracles*. Cambridge: Cambridge University Press.

Langtry, B. 1985. "Miracles and Principles of Relative Likelihood," *International Journal for Philosophy of Religion* 18: 123–131.

——— 1990. "Hume, Probability, Lotteries and Miracles," *Hume Studies* 16: 67–74.

Lowe, E. J. 1987. "Miracles and Laws of Nature," *Religious Studies* 23: 263–278.

Merrill, K. R. 1991. "Hume's 'Of Miracles,' Pierce and the Balance of Likelihoods," *Journal of the History of Philosophy* 29: 85–113.

Millican, P. 1993. "'Hume's Theorem' Concerning Miracles," *Philosophical Quarterly* 43: 489–495.

Otte, R. 1996. "Mackie's Treatment of Miracles," *International Journal for Philosophy of Religion* 39: 151–158.

Owen, D. 1987. "Hume Versus Price on Miracles and Prior Probabilities: Testimony and the Bayesian Calculation," *Philosophical Quarterly* 37: 187–202.

Repert, V. 1989. "Miracles and the Case for Theism," *Philosophy of Religion* 25: 35–51.

Root, M. 1989. "Miracles and the Uniformity of Nature," *American Philosophical Quarterly* 26: 333–342.

Ross, I. S. 1995. "Hume's Language of Skepticism," *Hume Studies* 21: 237–254.

Schoen, E. L. 1991. "David Hume and the Mysterious Shroud of Turin," *Religious Studies* 27: 209–222.

Sorenson, R. A. 1983. "Hume's Skepticism Concerning Reports of Miracles," *Analysis* 20: 60.

Swinburne, R. 1983. "Mackie, Induction, and God," *Religious Studies* 19: 385–391.

Ward, K. 1985. "Miracles and Testimony," *Religious Studies* 21: 131–145.

Weintraub, R. 1996. "The Credibility of Miracles," *Philosophical Studies* 82: 359–375.

Williams, T. C. 1990. *The Idea of the Miraculous: The Challenge to Science and Religion.* London: Macmillan.

Wilson, F. 1989. "The Logic of Probabilities in Hume's Argument against Miracles," *Hume Studies* 15: 255–275.

# PART II

## The Documents

## Chapter 15, "Of Probability"

1. As *demonstration* is the showing the agreement or disagreement of two ideas, by the intervention of one or more proofs, which have a constant, immutable, and visible connexion one with another; so *probability* is nothing but the appearance of such an agreement or disagreement, by the intervention of proofs, whose connexion is not constant and immutable, or at least is not perceived to be so, but is, or appears for the most part to be so, and is enough to induce the mind to judge the proposition to be true or false, rather than the contrary. For example: in the demonstration of it a man perceives the certain, immutable connexion there is of equality between the three angles of a triangle, and those intermediate ones which are made use of to show their equality to two right ones; and so, by an intuitive knowledge of the agreement or disagreement of the intermediate ideas in each step of the progress, the whole series is continued with an evidence, which clearly shows the agreement or disagreement of those three angles in equality to two right ones: and thus he has certain knowledge that it is so. But another man, who never took the pains to observe the demonstration, hearing a mathematician, a man of credit, affirm the three angles of a triangle to be equal to two right ones, assents to it, i. e. receives it for true: in which case the foundation of his assent is the probability of the thing; the proof being such as for the most part carries truth with it: the man on whose testimony he receives it, not being wont to affirm anything contrary to or besides his knowledge, especially in matters of this kind: so that that which causes his assent to this proposition, that the three angles of a triangle are equal to two right ones, that which makes him take these ideas to agree, without knowing them to do so, is the wonted veracity of the speaker in other cases, or his supposed veracity in this.

2. Our knowledge, as has been shown, being very narrow, and we not happy enough to find certain truth in everything which we have occasion to consider; most of the propositions we think, reason, discourse—nay, act upon, are such as we cannot have undoubted knowledge of their truth: yet some of them border so near upon certainty, that we make no doubt at all about them; but assent to them as firmly, and act, according to that assent, as resolutely as if they were infallibly demonstrated, and that our knowledge of them was perfect and certain. But there being

degrees herein, from the very neighbourhood of certainty and demonstration, quite down to improbability and unlikeness, even to the confines of impossibility; and also degrees of assent from full assurance and confidence, quite down to conjecture, doubt, and distrust: I shall come now, (having, as I think, found out *the bounds of human knowledge and certainty*,) in the next place, to consider *the several degrees and grounds of probability, and assent or faith.*

3. Probability is likeliness to be true, the very notation of the word signifying such a proposition, for which there be arguments or proofs to make it pass, or be received for true. The entertainment the mind gives this sort of propositions is called *belief, assent*, or *opinion*, which is the admitting or receiving any proposition for true, upon arguments or proofs that are found to persuade us to receive it as true, without certain knowledge that it is so. And herein lies the difference between *probability* and *certainty, faith*, and *knowledge*, that in all the parts of knowledge there is intuition; each immediate idea, each step has its visible and certain connexion: in belief, not so. That which makes me believe, is something extraneous to the thing I believe; something not evidently joined on both sides to, and so not manifestly showing the agreement or disagreement of those ideas that are under consideration.

4. Probability then, being to supply the defect of our knowledge, and to guide us where that fails, is always conversant about propositions whereof we have no certainty, but only some inducements to receive them for true. The grounds of it are, in short, these two following: first, the conformity of anything with our own knowledge, observation, and experience. Secondly, the testimony of others, vouching their observation and experience. In the testimony of others, is to be considered: 1. The number. 2. The integrity. 3. The skill the witnesses. 4. The design of the author, where it is a testimony out of a book cited. 5. The consistency of the parts, and circumstances of the relation. 6. Contrary testimonies.

5. Probability wanting that intuitive evidence which infallibly determines the understanding and produces certain knowledge, the mind, if it *will proceed rationally*, ought to examine all the grounds of probability, and see how they make more or less for or against any proposition, before it assents to or dissents from it; and, upon a due balancing the whole, reject or receive it, with a more or less firm assent, proportionably to the preponderancy of the greater grounds of probability on one side or the other. For example:

If I myself see a man walk on the ice, it is past probability; it is knowledge. But if another tells me he saw a man in England, in the midst of a sharp winter, walk upon water hardened with cold, this has so great conformity with what is usually observed to happen, that I am disposed by the nature of the thing itself to assent to it; unless some manifest suspicion attend the relation of that matter of fact. But if the same thing be told to one born between the tropics, who never saw nor heard of any such thing before, there the whole probability relies on testimony: and as the relators are more in number, and of more credit, and have no interest to speak contrary to the truth, so that matter of fact is like to find more or less belief. Though to a man whose experience has always been quite contrary, and who has never heard of anything like it, the most untainted credit of a witness will scarce be able to find belief. As it happened to a Dutch ambassador, who entertaining the king of Siam with the particularities of Holland, which he was inquisitive after, amongst other things told him, that the water in his country would sometimes, in cold weather, be so hard, that men walked upon it, and that it would bear an elephant, if he were there. To which the king replied, *Hitherto I have believed the strange things you have told me, because I look upon you as a sober fair man, but now I am sure you lie.*

6. Upon these grounds depends the probability of any proposition: and as the conformity of our knowledge, as the certainty of observations, as the frequency and constancy of experience, and the number and credibility of testimonies do more or less agree or disagree with it, so is any proposition in itself more or less probable. There is another, I confess, which, though by itself it be no true ground of probability, yet is often made use of for one, by which men most commonly regulate their assent, and upon which they pin their faith more than anything else, and that is, the opinion of others; though there cannot be a more dangerous thing to rely on, nor more likely to mislead one; since there is much more falsehood and error among men, than truth and knowledge. And if the opinions and persuasions of others, whom we know and think well of, be a ground of assent, men have reason to be Heathens in Japan, Mahometans in Turkey, Papists in Spain, Protestants in England, and Lutherans in Sweden. But of this wrong ground of assent I shall have occasion to speak more at large in another place.

## Chapter 16, "Of the Degrees of Assent"

1. The grounds of probability we have laid down in the foregoing chapter: as they are the foundations on which our *assent* is built, so are they also the measure whereby its several degrees are, or ought to be regulated: only we are to take notice, that, whatever grounds of probability there may be, they yet operate no further on the mind which searches after truth, and endeavours to judge right, than they appear; at least, in the first judgment or search that the mind makes. I confess, in the opinions men have, and firmly stick to in the world, their assent is not always from an actual view of the reasons that at first prevailed with them: it being in many cases almost impossible, and in most, very hard, even for those who have very admirable memories, to retain all the proofs which, upon a due examination, made them embrace that side of the question. It suffices that they have once with care and fairness sifted the matter as far as they could; and that they have searched into all the particulars, that they could imagine to give any light to the question; and, with the best of their skill, cast up the account upon the whole evidence: and thus, having once found on which side the probability appeared to *them*,

after as full and exact an inquiry as they can make, they lay up the conclusion in their memories, as a truth they have discovered; and for the future they remain satisfied with the testimony of their memories, that this is the opinion that, by the proofs they have once seen of it, deserves such a degree of their assent as they afford it.

2. This is all that the greatest part of men are capable of doing, in regulating their opinions and judgments; unless a man will exact of them, either to retain distinctly in their memories all the proofs concerning any probable truth, and that too, in the same order, and regular deduction of consequences in which they have formerly placed or seen them; which sometimes is enough to fill a large volume on one single question: or else they must require a man, for every opinion that he embraces, every day to examine the proofs: both which are impossible. It is unavoidable, therefore, that the *memory* be relied on in the case, and that men be persuaded of several opinions, whereof the proofs are not actually in their thoughts; nay, which perhaps they are not able actually to recall. Without this, the greatest part of men must be either very sceptics; or change every moment, and yield themselves up to whoever, having lately studied the question, offers them arguments, which, for want of memory, they are not able presently to answer.

3. I cannot but own, that men's sticking to their past judgment, and adhering firmly to conclusions formerly made, is often the cause of great obstinacy in error and mistake. But the fault is not that they rely on their memories for what they have before well judged, but because they judged before they had well examined. May we not find a great number (not to say the greatest part) of men that think they have formed right judgments of several matters; and that for no other reason, but because they never thought otherwise? that imagine themselves to have judged right, only because they never questioned, never examined, their own opinions? Which is indeed to think they judged right, because they never judged at all. And yet these, of all men, hold their opinions with the greatest stiffness; those being generally the most fierce and firm in their tenets, who have least examined them. What we once *know*, we are certain is so: and we may be secure, that there are no latent proofs undiscovered, which may overturn our knowledge, or bring it in doubt. But, in matters of *probability*, it is not in every case we can be sure that we have all the particulars before us, that any way concern the question; and that there is no evidence behind, and yet unseen, which may cast the probability on the other side, and outweigh all that at present seems to preponderate with us. Who almost is there that hath the leisure, patience, and means to collect together all the proofs concerning most of the opinions he has, so as safely to conclude that he hath a clear and full view; and that there is no more to be alleged for his better information? And yet we are forced to determine ourselves on the one side or other. The conduct of our lives, and the management of our great concerns, will not bear delay: for those depend, for the most part, on the determination of our judgment in points

wherein we are not capable of certain and demonstrative knowledge, and wherein it is necessary for us to embrace the one side or the other.

4. Since, therefore, it is unavoidable to the greatest part of men, if not all, to have several *opinions*, without certain and indubitable proofs of their truth; and it carries too great an imputation of ignorance, lightness, or folly for men to quit and renounce their former tenets presently upon the offer of an argument which they cannot immediately answer, and show the insufficiency of; it would, methinks, become all men to maintain peace, and the common offices of humanity, and friendship, in the diversity of opinions; since we cannot reasonably expect that any one should readily and obsequiously quit his own opinion, and embrace ours, with a blind resignation to an authority which the understanding of man acknowledges not. For however it may often mistake, it can own no other guide but reason, nor blindly submit to the will and dictates of another. If he you would bring over to your sentiments be one that examines before he assents, you must give him leave at his leisure to go over the account again. And, recalling what is out of his mind, examine all the particulars, to see on which side the advantage lies: and if he will not think our arguments of weight enough to engage him anew in so much pains, it is but what we often do ourselves in the like case; and we should take it amiss if others should prescribe to us what points we should study. And if he be one who takes his opinions upon trust, how can we imagine that he should renounce those tenets which time and custom have so settled in his mind, that he thinks them self-evident, and of an unquestionable certainty; or which he takes to be impressions he has received from God himself, or from men sent by him? How can we expect, I say, that opinions thus settled should be given up to the arguments or authority of a stranger or adversary, especially if there be any suspicion of interest or design, as there never fails to be, where men find themselves ill treated? We should do well to commiserate our mutual ignorance, and endeavour to remove it in all the gentle and fair ways of information; and not instantly treat others ill, as obstinate and perverse, because they will not renounce their own, and receive our opinions, or at least those we would force upon them, when it is more than probable that we are no less obstinate in not embracing some of theirs. For where is the man that has incontestable evidence of the truth of all that he holds, or of the falsehood of all he condemns; or can say that he has examined to the bottom all his own, or other men's opinions? The necessity of believing without knowledge, nay often upon very slight grounds, in this fleeting state of action and blindness we are in, should make us more busy and careful to inform ourselves than constrain others. At least, those who have not thoroughly examined to the bottom all their own tenets, must confess they are unfit to prescribe to others; and are unreasonable in imposing that as truth on other men's belief, which they themselves have not searched into, nor weighed the arguments of probability, on which they should receive or reject it. Those who have fairly and truly

examined, and are thereby got past doubt in all the doctrines they profess and govern themselves by, would have a juster pretence to require others to follow them: but these are so few in number, and find so little reason to be magisterial in their opinions, that nothing insolent and imperious is to be expected from them: and there is reason to think, that, if men were better instructed themselves, they would be less imposing on others.

5. But to return to the grounds of assent, and the several degrees of it, we are to take notice, that the propositions we receive upon inducements of *probability* are of *two sorts*: either concerning some particular existence, or, as it is usually termed, matter of fact, which, falling under observation, is capable of human testimony; or else concerning things, which, being beyond the discovery of our senses, are not capable of any such testimony.

6. Concerning the *first* of these, viz. *particular matter of fact.*

I. Where any particular thing, consonant to the constant observation of ourselves and others in the like case, comes attested by the concurrent reports of all that mention it, we receive it as easily, and build as firmly upon it, as if it were certain knowledge; and we reason and act thereupon with as little doubt as if it were perfect demonstration. Thus, if all Englishmen, who have occasion to mention it, should affirm that it froze in England the last winter, or that there were swallows seen there in the summer, I think a man could almost as little doubt of it as that seven and four are eleven. The first, therefore, and *highest degree of probability*, is, when the general consent of all men, in all ages, as far as it can be known, concurs with a man's constant and never-failing experience in like cases, to confirm the truth of any particular matter of fact attested by fair witnesses: such are all the stated constitutions and properties of bodies, and the regular proceedings of causes and effects in the ordinary course of nature. This we call an argument from the nature of things themselves. For what our own and other men's *constant observation* has found always to be after the same manner, that we with reason conclude to be the effect of steady and regular causes; though they come not within the reach of our knowledge. Thus, That fire warmed a man, made lead fluid, and changed the colour or consistency in wood or charcoal; that iron sunk in water, and swam in quicksilver: these and the like propositions about particular facts, being agreeable to our constant experience, as often as we have to do with these matters; and being generally spoke of (when mentioned by others) as things found constantly to be so, and therefore not so much as controverted by anybody—we are put past doubt that a relation affirming any such thing to have been, or any predication that it will happen again in the same manner, is very true. These *probabilities* rise so near to *certainty*, that they govern our thoughts as absolutely, and influence all our actions as fully, as the most evident demonstration; and in what concerns us we make little or no difference between them and certain knowledge. Our belief, thus grounded, rises to *assurance*.

7. II. The *next degree of probability* is, when I find by my own experience, and the agreement of all others that mention it, a thing to be for the most part so, and that the particular instance of it is attested by many and undoubted witnesses: v.g. history giving us such an account of men in all ages, and my own experience, as far as I had an opportunity to observe, confirming it, that most men prefer their private advantage to the public: if all historians that write of Tiberius, say that Tiberius did so, it is extremely probable. And in this case, our assent has a sufficient foundation to raise itself to a degree which we may call *confidence*.

8. III. In things that happen indifferently, as that a bird should fly this or that way; that it should thunder on a man's right or left hand, &c., when any particular matter of fact is vouched by the concurrent testimony of unsuspected witnesses, there our assent is also *unavoidable*. Thus: that there is such a city in Italy as Rome: that about one thousand seven hundred years ago, there lived in it a man, called Julius Caesar; that he was a general, and that he won a battle against another, called Pompey. This, though in the nature of the thing there be nothing for nor against it, yet being related by historians of credit, and contradicted by no one writer, a man cannot avoid believing it, and can as little doubt of it as he does of the being and actions of his own acquaintance, whereof he himself is a witness.

9. Thus far the matter goes easy enough. Probability upon such grounds carries so much evidence with it, that it naturally determines the judgment, and leaves us as little liberty to believe or disbelieve, as a demonstration does, whether we will know, or be ignorant. The difficulty is, when testimonies contradict common experience, and the reports of history and witnesses clash with the ordinary course of nature, or with one another: there it is, where diligence, attention, and exactness are required, to form a right judgment, and to proportion the assent to the different evidence and probability of the thing: which rises and falls, according as those two foundations of credibility, viz. *common observation in like cases*, and *particular testimonies in that particular instance*, favour or contradict it. These are liable to so great variety of contrary observations, circumstances, reports, different qualifications, tempers, designs, oversights, &c., of the reporters, that it is impossible to reduce to precise rules the various degrees wherein men give their assent. This only may be said in general, That as the arguments and proofs *pro* and *con*, upon due examination, nicely weighing every particular circumstance, shall to any one appear, upon the whole matter, in a greater or less degree to preponderate on either side; so they are fitted to produce in the mind such different entertainments, as we call *belief, conjecture, guess, doubt, wavering, distrust, disbelief,* &c.

10. This is what concerns assent in matters wherein testimony is made use of: concerning which, I think, it may not be amiss to take notice of a rule observed in the law of England; which is, That though the attested copy of a record be good proof, yet the copy of a copy, ever so well

attested, and by ever so credible witnesses, will not be admitted as a proof in judicature. This is so generally approved as reasonable, and suited to the wisdom and caution to be used in our inquiry after material truths, that I never yet heard of any one that blamed it. This practice, if it be allowable in the decisions of right and wrong, carries this observation along with it, viz. *That any testimony, the further off it is from the original truth, the less force and proof it has.* The being and existence of the thing itself, is what I call the original truth. A credible man vouching his knowledge of it is a good proof; but if another equally credible do witness it from his report, the testimony is weaker: and a third that attests the hearsay of an hearsay is yet less considerable. So that in traditional truths, each remove weakens the force of the proof: and the more hands the tradition has successively passed through, the less strength and evidence does it receive from them. This I thought necessary to be taken notice of: because I find amongst some men the quite contrary commonly practised, who look on opinions to gain force by growing older; and what a thousand years since would not, to a rational man contemporary with the first voucher, have appeared at all probable, is now urged as certain beyond all question, only because several have since, from him, said it one after another. Upon this ground propositions, evidently false or doubtful enough in their first beginning, come, by an inverted rule of probability, to pass for authentic truths; and those which found or deserved little credit from the mouths of their first authors, are thought to grow venerable by age, are urged as undeniable.

11. I would not be thought here to lessen the credit and use of *history*: it is all the light we have in many cases, and we receive from it a great part of the useful truths we have, with a convincing evidence. I think nothing more valuable than the records of antiquity: I wish we had more of them, and more uncorrupted. But this truth itself forces me to say, That no probability can rise higher than its first original. What has no other evidence than the single testimony of one only witness must stand or fall by his only testimony, whether good, bad, or indifferent; and though cited afterwards by hundreds of others, one after another, is so far from receiving any strength thereby, that it is only the weaker. Passion, interest, inadvertency, mistake of his meaning, and a thousand odd reasons, or capricios, men's minds are acted by, (impossible to be discovered,) may make one man quote another man's words or meaning wrong. He that has but ever so little examined the citations of writers, cannot doubt how little credit the quotations deserve, where the originals are wanting; and consequently how much less quotations of quotations can be relied on. This is certain, that what in one age was affirmed upon slight grounds, can never after come to be more valid in future ages by being often repeated. But the further still it is from the original, the less valid it is, and has always less force in the mouth or writing of him that last made use of it than in his from whom he received it.

12. [*Secondly*], The probabilities we have hitherto mentioned are only such as concern matter of fact, and such things as are capable of obser-

vation and testimony. There remains that other sort, concerning which men entertain opinions with variety of assent, though *the things be such, that falling not under the reach of our senses, they are not capable of testimony.* Such are, 1. The existence, nature and operations of finite immaterial beings without us; as spirits, angels, devils, &c. Or the existence of material beings which, either for their smallness in themselves or remoteness from us, our senses cannot take notice of—as, whether there be any plants, animals, and intelligent inhabitants in the planets, and other mansions of the vast universe. 2. Concerning the manner of operation in most parts of the works of nature: wherein, though we see the sensible effects, yet their causes are unknown, and we perceive not the ways and manner how they are produced. We see animals are generated, nourished, and move; the loadstone draws iron; and the parts of a candle, successively melting, turn into flame, and give us both light and heat. These and the like effects we see and know: but the causes that operate, and the manner they are produced in, we can only guess and probably conjecture. For these and the like, coming not within the scrutiny of human senses, cannot be examined by them, or be attested by anybody; and therefore can appear more or less probable, only as they more or less agree to truths that are established in our minds, and as they hold proportion to other parts of our knowledge and observation. *Analogy* in these matters is the only help we have, and it is from that alone we draw all our grounds of probability. Thus, observing that the bare rubbing of two bodies violently one upon another, produces heat, and very often fire itself, we have reason to think, that what we call *heat* and *fire* consists in a violent agitation of the imperceptible minute parts of the burning matter. Observing likewise that the different refractions of pellucid bodies produce in our eyes the different appearances of several colours; and also, that the different ranging and laying the superficial parts of several bodies, as of velvet, watered silk, &c., does the like, we think it probable that the *colour* and shining of bodies is in them nothing but the different arrangement and refraction of their minute and insensible parts. Thus, finding in all parts of the creation, that fall under human observation, that there is a *gradual connexion of one with another, without any great or discernible gaps between, in all that great variety of things we see in the world,* which are so closely linked together, that, in the several ranks of beings, it is not easy to discover the bounds betwixt them; we have reason to be persuaded that, *by such gentle steps,* things ascend upwards in degrees of perfection. It is a hard matter to say where sensible and rational begin, and where insensible and irrational end: and who is there quick-sighted enough to determine precisely which is the lowest species of living things, and which the first of those which have no life? Things, as far as we can observe, lessen and augment, as the quantity does in a regular cone; where, though there be a manifest odds betwixt the bigness of the diameter at a remote distance, yet the difference between the upper and under, where they touch one another, is hardly discernible. The difference is exceeding great between some men and some animals: but if we will compare the understanding and abilities of some men and some brutes, we shall find so little difference, that it will be hard to say, that that of the man is either clearer or larger. Observing, I say, such gradual and gentle descents downwards in those parts of the creation that are beneath man, the rule of analogy may make it probable, that it is so also in things above us and our observation; and that there are several ranks of intelligent beings, excelling us in several degrees of perfection, ascending upwards towards the infinite perfection of the Creator, by gentle steps and differences, that are every one at no great distance from the next to it. This sort of probability, which is the best conduct of rational experiments, and the rise of hypothesis, has also its use and influence; and a wary reasoning from analogy leads us often into the discovery of truths and useful productions, which would otherwise lie concealed.

13. Though the common experience and the ordinary course of things have justly a mighty influence on the minds of men, to make them give or refuse credit to anything proposed to their belief; yet there is one case, wherein the strangeness of the fact lessens not the assent to a fair testimony given of it. For where such supernatural events are suitable to ends aimed at by Him who has the power to change the course of nature, there, *under such circumstances*, that may be the fitter to procure belief, by how much the more they are beyond or contrary to ordinary observation. This is the proper case of *miracles*, which, well attested, do not only find credit themselves, but give it also to other truths, which need such confirmation.

14. Besides those we have hitherto mentioned, there is one sort of propositions that challenge the highest degree of our assent, upon bare testimony, whether the thing proposed agree or disagree with common experience, and the ordinary course of things, or no. The reason whereof is, because the testimony is of such an one as cannot deceive nor be deceived: and that is of God himself. This carries with it an assurance, beyond doubt, evidence beyond exception. This is called by a peculiar name, *revelation*, and our assent to it, faith, which [as absolutely determines our minds, and as perfectly excludes all wavering,] as our knowledge itself; and we may as well doubt of our own being, as we can whether any revelation from God be true. So that faith is a settled and sure principle of assent and assurance, and leaves no manner of room for doubt or hesitation. *Only we must be sure that it be a divine revelation and that we understand it right*: else we shall expose ourselves to all the extravagancy of enthusiasm, and all the error of wrong principles, if we have faith and assurance in what is not *divine* revelation. And therefore, in those cases, our assent can be rationally no higher than the evidence of its being a revelation, and that this is the meaning of the expressions it is delivered in. If the evidence of its being a revelation, or that this is its true sense, be only on probable proofs, our assent can reach no higher than an assurance or diffidence, arising from the more or less apparent probability of the proofs. But of *faith*, and the precedency it ought to have

before other arguments of persuasion, I shall speak more hereafter; where I treat of it as it is ordinarily placed, in contradistinction to reason; though in truth it be nothing else but *an assent founded on the highest reason.*

## *Benedict De Spinoza,* A Theologico-Political Treatise *(1670), Chapter 6*

Chapter 6, "Of Miracles"

As men are accustomed to call Divine the knowledge which transcends human understanding, so also do they style Divine, or the work of God, anything of which the cause is not generally known: for the masses think that the power and providence of God are most clearly displayed by events that are extraordinary and contrary to the conception they have formed of nature, especially if such events bring them any profit or convenience: they think that the clearest possible proof of God's existence is afforded when nature, as they suppose, breaks her accustomed order, and consequently they believe that those who explain or endeavour to understand phenomena or miracles through their natural causes are doing away with God and His providence. They suppose, forsooth, that God is inactive so long as nature works in her accustomed order, and *vice versa*, that the power of nature and natural causes are idle so long as God is acting: thus they imagine two powers distinct one from the other, the power of God and the power of nature, though the latter is in a sense determined by God, or (as most people believe now) created by Him. What they mean by either, and what they understand by God and nature they do not know, except that they imagine the power of God to be like that of some royal potentate, and nature's power to consist in force and energy.

The masses then style unusual phenomena "miracles," and partly from piety, partly for the sake of opposing the students of science, prefer to remain in ignorance of natural causes, and only to hear of those things which they know least, and consequently admire most. In fact, the common people can only adore God, and refer all things to His power by removing natural causes, and conceiving things happening out of their due course, and only admires the power of God when the power of nature is conceived of as in subjection to it.

This idea seems to have taken its rise among the early Jews who saw the Gentiles round them worshipping visible gods such as the sun, the moon, the earth, water, air, &c., and in order to inspire the conviction that such divinities were weak and inconstant, or changeable, told how they themselves were under the sway of an invisible God, and narrated their miracles, trying further to show that the God whom they worshipped arranged the whole of nature for their sole benefit: this idea was so pleasing to humanity that men go on to this day imagining miracles, so that they may believe themselves God's favourites, and the final cause for which God created and directs all things.

What pretension will not people in their folly advance! They have no single sound idea concerning either God or nature, they confound God's decrees with human decrees, they conceive nature as so limited that they believe man to be its chief part! I have spent enough space in setting forth these common ideas and prejudices concerning nature and miracles, but in order to afford a regular demonstration I will show—

I. That nature cannot be contravened, but that she preserves a fixed and immutable order, and at the same time I will explain what is meant by a miracle.

II. That God's nature and existence, and consequently His providence cannot be known from miracles, but that they can all be much better perceived from the fixed and immutable order of nature.

III. That by the decrees and volitions, and consequently the providence of God, Scripture (as I will prove by Scriptural examples) means nothing but nature's order following necessarily from her eternal laws.

IV. Lastly, I will treat of the method of interpreting Scriptural miracles, and the chief points to be noted concerning the narratives of them.

Such are the principal subjects which will be discussed in this chapter, and which will serve, I think, not a little to further the object of this treatise.

Our first point is easily proved from what we showed in Chap. IV. about Divine law—namely, that all that God wishes or determines involves eternal necessity and truth, for we demonstrated that God's understanding is identical with His will, and that it is the same thing to say that God wills a thing, as to say that He understands it; hence, as it follows necessarily from the Divine nature and perfection that God understands a thing as it is, it follows no less necessarily that He wills it as it is. Now, as nothing is necessarily true save only by Divine decree, it is plain that the universal laws of nature are decrees of God following from the necessity and perfection of the Divine nature. Hence, any event happening in nature which contravened nature's universal laws, would necessarily also contravene the Divine decree, nature, and understanding; or if anyone asserted that God acts in contravention to the laws of nature, he, *ipso facto*, would be compelled to assert that God acted against His own nature—an evident absurdity. One might easily show from the same premises that the power and efficiency of nature are in themselves the Divine power and efficiency, and that the Divine power is the very essence of God, but this I gladly pass over for the present.

Nothing, then, comes to pass in nature[1] in contravention to her universal laws, nay, everything agrees with them and follows from them, for whatsoever comes to pass, comes to pass by the will and eternal decree of God; that is, as we have just pointed out, whatever comes to pass, comes to pass according to laws and rules which involve eternal necessity and truth; nature, therefore, always observes laws and rules which involve eternal necessity and truth, although they may not all be known to us, and therefore she keeps a fixed and immutable order. Nor is there any sound reason for limiting the power and efficacy of nature, and asserting that her laws are fit for certain purposes, but not for all; for as the efficacy and power of nature, are the very efficacy and power of God, and as the laws and rules of nature are the decrees of God, it is in every way to be believed that the power of nature is infinite, and that her laws are broad enough to embrace everything conceived by the Divine intellect; the only alternative is to assert that God has created nature so weak, and has ordained for her laws so barren, that He is repeatedly compelled to come afresh to her aid if He wishes that she should be preserved, and that things should happen as He desires: a conclusion, in my opinion, very far removed from reason. Further, as nothing happens in nature which does not follow from her laws, and as her laws embrace everything conceived by the Divine intellect, and lastly, as nature preserves a fixed and immutable order; it most clearly follows that miracles are only intelligible as in relation to human opinions, and merely mean events of which the natural cause cannot be explained by a reference to any ordinary occurrence, either by us, or at any rate, by the writer and narrator of the miracle.

We may, in fact, say that a miracle is an event of which the causes cannot be explained by the natural reason through a reference to ascertained workings of nature; but since miracles were wrought according to the understanding of the masses, who are wholly ignorant of the workings of nature, it is certain that the ancients took for a miracle whatever they could not explain by the method adopted by the unlearned in such cases, namely, an appeal to the memory, a recalling of something similar, which is ordinarily regarded without wonder; for most people think they sufficiently understand a thing when they have ceased to wonder at it. The ancients, then, and indeed most men up to the present day, had no other criterion for a miracle; hence we cannot doubt that many things are narrated in Scripture as miracles of which the causes could easily be explained by reference to ascertained workings of nature. We have hinted as much in Chap. II., in speaking of the sun standing still in the time of Joshua, and going backwards in the time of Ahaz; but we shall soon have more to say on the subject when we come to treat of the interpretation of miracles later on in this chapter.

It is now time to pass on to the second point, and show that we cannot gain an understanding of God's essence, existence, or providence by means of miracles, but that these truths are much better perceived through the fixed and immutable order of nature.

I thus proceed with the demonstration. As God's existence is not self-evident, it must necessarily be inferred from ideas so firmly and incontrovertibly true, that no power can be postulated or conceived sufficient to impugn them. They ought certainly so to appear to us when we infer from them God's existence, if we wish to place our conclusion beyond the reach of doubt; for if we could conceive that such ideas could be impugned by any power whatsoever, we should doubt of their truth, we should doubt of our conclusion, namely, of God's existence, and should never be able to be certain of anything. Further, we know that nothing either agrees with or is contrary to nature, unless it agrees with or is contrary to these primary ideas; wherefore if we would conceive that anything could be done in nature by any power whatsoever which would be contrary to the laws of nature, it would also be contrary to our primary ideas, and we should have either to reject it as absurd, or else to cast doubt (as just shown) on our primary ideas, and consequently on the existence of God, and on everything howsoever perceived. Therefore miracles, in the sense of events contrary to the laws of nature, so far from demonstrating to us the existence of God, would, on the contrary, lead us to doubt it, where, otherwise, we might have been absolutely certain of it, as knowing that nature follows a fixed and immutable order.

Let us take miracle as meaning that which cannot be explained through natural causes. This may be interpreted in two senses: either as that which has natural causes, but cannot be examined by the human intellect; or as that which has no cause save God and God's will. But as all things which come to pass through natural causes, come to pass also solely through the will and power of God, it comes to this, that a miracle, whether it has natural causes or not, is a result which cannot be explained by its cause, that is a phenomenon which surpasses human understanding; but from such a phenomenon, and certainly from a result surpassing our understanding, we can gain no knowledge. For whatsoever we understand clearly and distinctly should be plain to us either in itself or by means of something else clearly and distinctly understood; wherefore from a miracle or a phenomenon which we cannot understand, we can gain no knowledge of God's essence, or existence, or indeed anything about God or nature; whereas when we know that all things are ordained and ratified by God, that the operations of nature follow from the essence of God, and that the laws of nature are eternal decrees and volitions of God, we must perforce conclude that our knowledge of God and of God's will increases in proportion to our knowledge and clear understanding of nature, as we see how she depends on her primal cause, and how she works according to eternal law. Wherefore so far as our understanding goes, those phenomena which we clearly and distinctly understand have much better right to be called works of God, and to be referred to the will of God than those about which we are entirely ignorant, although they appeal powerfully to the imagination, and compel men's admiration.

It is only phenomena that we clearly and distinctly understand, which heighten our knowledge of God, and most clearly indicate His will and decrees. Plainly, they are but triflers who, when they cannot explain a thing, run back to the will of God; this is, truly, a ridiculous way of expressing ignorance. Again, even supposing that some conclusion could be drawn from miracles, we could not possibly infer from them the existence of God: for a miracle being an event under limitations is the expression of a fixed and limited power; therefore we could not possibly infer from an effect of this kind the existence of a cause whose power is infinite, but at the utmost only of a cause whose power is greater than that of the said effect. I say at the utmost, for a phenomenon may be the result of many concurrent causes, and its power may be less than the power of the sum of such causes, but far greater than that of any one of them taken individually. On the other hand, the laws of nature, as we have shown, extend over infinity, and are conceived by us as, after a fashion, eternal, and nature works in accordance with them in a fixed and immutable order; therefore, such laws indicate to us in a certain degree the infinity, the eternity, and the immutability of God.

We may conclude, then, that we cannot gain knowledge of the existence and providence of God by means of miracles, but that we can far better infer them from the fixed and immutable order of nature. By miracle, I here mean an event which surpasses, or is thought to surpass, human comprehension: for in so far as it is supposed to destroy or interrupt the order of nature or her laws, it not only can give us no knowledge of God, but, contrariwise, takes away that which we naturally have, and makes us doubt of God and everything else.

Neither do I recognize any difference between an event against the laws of nature and an event beyond the laws of nature (that is, according to some, an event which does not contravene nature, though she is inadequate to produce or effect it)—for a miracle is wrought in, and not beyond nature, though it may be said in itself to be above nature, and, therefore, must necessarily interrupt the order of nature, which otherwise we conceive of as fixed and unchangeable, according to God's decrees. If, therefore, anything should come to pass in nature which does not follow from her laws, it would also be in contravention to the order which God has established in nature for ever through universal natural laws: it would, therefore, be in contravention to God's nature and laws, and, consequently, belief in it would throw doubt upon everything, and lead to Atheism.

I think I have now sufficiently established my second point, so that we can again conclude that a miracle, whether in contravention to, or beyond, nature, is a mere absurdity; and, therefore, that what is meant in Scripture by a miracle can only be a work of nature, which surpasses, or is believed to surpass, human comprehension. Before passing on to my third point, I will adduce Scriptural authority for my assertion that God cannot be known from miracles. Scripture nowhere states the doctrine openly, but it can readily be inferred from several passages. Firstly, that in which Moses commands (Deut. xiii.) that a false prophet should be put to death, even though he work miracles: "If there arise a prophet among you, and giveth thee a sign or wonder, and the sign or wonder come to pass, saying, Let us go after other gods . . . thou shalt not hearken unto the voice of that prophet; for the Lord your God proveth you, and that prophet shall be put to death." From this it clearly follows that miracles could be wrought even by false prophets; and that, unless men are honestly endowed with the true knowledge and love of God, they may be as easily led by miracles to follow false gods as to follow the true God; for these words are added: "For the Lord your God tempts you, that He may know whether you love Him with all your heart and with all your mind."

Further, the Israelites, from all their miracles, were unable to form a sound conception of God, as their experience testified: for when they had persuaded themselves that Moses had departed from among them, they petitioned Aaron to give them visible gods; and the idea of God they had formed as the result of all their miracles was—a calf!

.    .    .    .    .    .    .    .

I now go on to my *third* point, and show from Scripture that the decrees and mandates of God, and consequently His providence, are merely the order of nature—that is, when Scripture describes an event as accomplished by God or God's will, we must understand merely that it was in accordance with the law and order of nature, not, as most people believe, that nature had for a season ceased to act, or that her order was temporarily interrupted. But Scripture does not directly teach matters unconnected with its doctrine, wherefore it has no care to explain things by their natural causes, nor to expound matters merely speculative. Wherefore our conclusion must be gathered by inference from those Scriptural narratives which happen to be written more at length and circumstantially than usual. Of these I will cite a few.

In the first book of Samuel, ix. 15, 16, it is related that God revealed to Samuel that He would send Saul to him, yet God did not send Saul to Samuel as people are wont to send one man to another. His "sending" was merely the ordinary course of nature. Saul was looking for the asses he had lost, and was meditating a return home without them, when, at the suggestion of his servant, he went to the prophet Samuel, to learn from him where he might find them. From no part of the narrative does it appear that Saul had any command from God to visit Samuel beyond this natural motive.

.    .    .    .    .    .    .    .

In Psalm civ. 4, wind and fire are called the angels and ministers of God, and various other passages of the same sort are found in Scripture, clearly showing that the decree, commandment, fiat, and word of God are merely expressions for the action and order of nature.

Thus it is plain that all the events narrated in Scripture came to pass naturally, and are referred directly to God because Scripture, as we have shown, does not aim at explaining things by their natural causes, but only at narrating what appeals to the popular imagination, and doing so in the manner best calculated to excite wonder, and consequently to impress the minds of the masses with devotion. If, therefore, events are found in the Bible which we cannot refer to their causes, nay, which seem entirely to contradict the order of nature, we must not come to a stand, but assuredly believe that whatever did really happen happened naturally. This view is confirmed by the fact that in the case of every miracle there were many attendant circumstances, though these were not always related, especially where the narrative was of a poetic character.

The circumstances of the miracles clearly show, I maintain, that natural causes were needed. For instance, in order to infect the Egyptians with blains, it was necessary that Moses should scatter ashes in the air (Exod. ix. 10); the locusts also came upon the land of Egypt by a command of God in accordance with nature, namely, by an east wind blowing for a whole day and night; and they departed by a very strong west wind (Exod. x. 14, 19). By a similar Divine mandate the sea opened a way for the Jews (Exod. xiv. 21), namely, by an east wind which blew very strongly all night.

So, too, when Elisha would revive the boy who was believed to be dead, he was obliged to bend over him several times until the flesh of the child waxed warm, and at last he opened his eyes (2 Kings iv. 34, 35).

Again, in John's Gospel (chap. ix.) certain acts are mentioned as performed by Christ preparatory to healing the blind man, and there are numerous other instances showing that something further than the absolute fiat of God is required for working a miracle.

Wherefore we may believe that, although the circumstances attending miracles are not related always or in full detail, yet a miracle was never performed without them.

This is confirmed by Exodus xiv. 27, where it is simply stated that "Moses stretched forth his hand, and the waters of the sea returned to their strength in the morning," no mention being made of a wind; but in the song of Moses (Exod. xv. 10) we read, "Thou didst blow with Thy wind (*i.e.* with a very strong wind), and the sea covered them." Thus the attendant circumstance is omitted in the history, and the miracle is thereby enhanced.

But perhaps someone will insist that we find many things in Scripture which seem in nowise explicable by natural causes, as for instance, that the sins of men and their prayers can be the cause of rain and of the earth's fertility, or that faith can heal the blind, and so on. But I think I have already made sufficient answer: I have shown that Scripture does not explain things by their secondary causes, but only narrates them in the order and the style which has most power to move men, and especially uneducated men, to devotion; and therefore it speaks inaccurately of God and of events, seeing that its object is not to convince the reason, but to attract and lay hold of the imagination. If the Bible were to describe the destruction of an empire in the style of political historians, the masses would remain unstirred, whereas the contrary is the case when it adopts the method of poetic description, and refers all things immediately to God. When, therefore, the Bible says that the earth is barren because of men's sins, or that the blind were healed by faith, we ought to take no more notice than when it says that God is angry at men's sins, that He is sad, that He repents of the good He has promised and done; or that on seeing a sign he remembers something He had promised, and other similar expressions, which are either thrown out poetically or related according to the opinion and prejudices of the writer.

We may, then, be absolutely certain that every event which is truly described in Scripture necessarily happened, like everything else, according to natural laws; and if anything is there set down which can be proved in set terms to contravene the order of nature, or not to be deducible therefrom, we must believe it to have been foisted into the sacred writings by irreligious hands; for whatsoever is contrary to nature is also contrary to reason, and whatsoever is contrary to reason is absurd, and, *ipso facto*, to be rejected.

.    .    .    .    .    .    .    .

*Note*

1. I do not mean here by "nature," merely matter and its modifications, but infinite other things besides matter.


## John Locke, "A Discourse of Miracles" (1706)

To discourse of miracles without defining what one means by the word miracle, is to make a show, but in effect to talk of nothing.

A miracle then I take to be a sensible operation, which, being above the comprehension of the spectator, and in his opinion contrary to the established course of nature, is taken by him to be divine.

He that is present at the fact, is a spectator: he that believes the history of the fact, puts himself in the place of a spectator.

This definition, it is probable, will not escape these two exceptions.

1. That hereby what is a miracle is made very uncertain; for it depending on the opinion of the spectator, that will be a miracle to one which will not be so to another.

In answer to which, it is enough to say, that this objection is of no force, but in the mouth of one who can produce a definition of a miracle not liable to the same exception, which I think not easy to do; for it being agreed, that a miracle must be that which surpasses the force of nature in the established, steady laws of causes and effects, nothing can be taken to be a miracle but what is judged to exceed those laws. Now every one being able to judge of those laws only by his own acquaintance with nature, and notions of its force (which are different in different men), it is unavoidable that that should be a miracle to one, which is not so to another.

2. Another objection to this definition will be, that the notion of a miracle, thus enlarged, may come sometimes to take in operations that

have nothing extraordinary or supernatural in them, and thereby invalidate the use of miracles for the attesting of divine revelation.

To which I answer, not at all, if the testimony which divine revelation receives from miracles be rightly considered.

To know that any revelation is from God, it is necessary to know that the messenger that delivers it is sent from God, and that cannot be known but by some credentials given him by God himself. Let us see then whether miracles, in my sense, be not such credentials, and will not infallibly direct us right in the search of divine revelation.

It is to be considered, that divine revelation receives testimony from no other miracles, but such as are wrought to witness his mission from God who delivers the revelation. All other miracles that are done in the world, how many or great soever, revelation is not concerned in. Cases wherein there has been, or can be need of miracles for the confirmation of revelation, are fewer than perhaps is imagined. The heathen world, amidst an infinite and uncertain jumble of deities, fables, and worships, had no room for a divine attestation of any one against the rest. Those owners of many gods were at liberty in their worship; and no one of their divinities pretending to be the one only true God, no one of them could be supposed in the pagan scheme to make use of miracles to establish his worship alone, or to abolish that of the other; much less was there any use of miracles to confirm any articles of faith, since no one of them had any such to propose as necessary to be believed by their votaries. And therefore I do not remember any miracles recorded in the Greek or Roman writers, as done to confirm any one's mission and doctrine. Conformable hereunto we find St. Paul, I Cor. i. 22, takes notice that the Jews (it is true) required miracles, but as for the Greeks they looked after something else; they knew no need or use there was of miracles to recommend any religion to them. And indeed it is an astonishing mark how far the god of this world had blinded men's minds, if we consider that the Gentile world received and stuck to a religion, which, not being derived from reason, had no sure foundation in revelation. They knew not its original, nor the authors of it, nor seemed concerned to know from whence it came, or by whose authority delivered; and so had no mention or use of miracles for its confirmation. For though there were here and there some pretences to revelation, yet there were not so much as pretences to miracles that attested it.

If we will direct our thoughts by what has been, we must conclude that miracles, as the credentials of a messenger delivering a divine religion, have no place but upon a supposition of one only true God; and that it is so in the nature of the thing, and cannot be otherwise, I think will be made appear in the sequel of this discourse. Of such who have come in the name of the one only true God, professing to bring a law from him, we have in history a clear account but of three, viz. Moses, Jesus, and Mahomet. For what the Persees say of their Zoroaster, or the Indians of their Brama (not to mention all the wild stories of the religions farther East) is so obscure, or so manifestly fabulous, that no account can be made of it. Now of the three before-mentioned, Mahomet having none to produce, pretends to no miracles for the vouching his mission; so that the only revelations that come attested by miracles, being those of Moses and Christ, and they confirming each other; the business of miracles, as it stands really in matter of fact, has no manner of difficulty in it; and I think the most scrupulous or sceptical cannot from miracles raise the least doubt against the divine revelation of the Gospel.

But since the speculative and learned will be putting of cases which never were, and it may be presumed never will be; since scholars and disputants will be raising of questions where there are none, and enter upon debates whereof there is no need; I crave leave to say, that he who comes with a message from God to be delivered to the world, cannot be refused belief if he vouches his mission by a miracle, because his credentials have a right to it. For every rational thinking man must conclude, as Nicodemus did, "we know that thou art a teacher come from God, for no man can do these signs which thou doest, except God be with him."

For example, Jesus of Nazareth professes himself sent from God: he with a word calms a tempest at sea. This one looks on as a miracle, and consequently cannot but receive his doctrine. Another thinks this might be the effect of chance, or skill in the weather, and no miracle, and so stands out; but afterwards seeing him walk on the sea, owns that for a miracle, and believes: which yet upon another has not that force, who suspects it may possibly be done by the assistance of a spirit. But yet the same person, seeing afterwards our Saviour cure an inveterate palsy by a word, admits that for a miracle, and becomes a convert. Another overlooking it in this instance, afterwards finds a miracle in his giving sight to one born blind, or in raising the dead, or his raising himself from the dead, and so receiving his doctrine as a revelation coming from God. By all which it is plain, that where the miracle is admitted, the doctrine cannot be rejected; it comes with the assurance of a divine attestation to him that allows the miracle, and he cannot question its truth.

The next thing then is, what shall be a sufficient inducement to take any extraordinary operation to be a miracle, i.e. wrought by God himself for the attestation of a revelation from him?

And to this I answer, the carrying with it the marks of a greater power than appears in opposition to it. For,

1. First, this removes the main difficulty where it presses hardest, and clears the matter from doubt, when extraordinary and supernatural operations are brought to support opposite missions, about which methinks more dust has been raised by men of leisure than so plain a matter needed. For since God's power is paramount to all, and no opposition can be made against him with an equal force to his; and since his honour and goodness can never be supposed to suffer his messenger and his truth to be borne down by the appearance of a greater power on the side of an impostor, and in favour of a lie; wherever there is an opposition, and two pretending to be sent from heaven clash, the signs, which carry with

them the evident marks of a greater power, will always be a certain and unquestionable evidence, that the truth and divine mission are on that side on which they appear. For though the discovery, how the lying wonders are or can be produced, be beyond the capacity of the ignorant, and often beyond the conception of the most knowing spectator, who is therefore forced to allow them in his apprehension to be above the force of natural causes and effects; yet he cannot but know they are not seals set by God to his truth for the attesting of it, since they are opposed by miracles that carry the evident marks of a greater and superior power, and therefore they cannot at all shake the authority of one so supported. God can never be thought to suffer that a lie, set up in opposition to a truth coming from him, should be backed with a greater power than he will show for the confirmation and propagation of a doctrine which he has revealed, to the end it might be believed. The producing of serpents, blood, and frogs, by the Egyptian sorcerers and by Moses's, could not to the spectators but appear equally miraculous: which of the pretenders then had their mission from God, and the truth on their side, could not have been determined, if the matter had rested there. But when Moses's serpents eat up theirs, when he produced lice, which they could not, the decision was easy. It was plain Jannes and Jambres acted by an inferior power, and their operations, how marvellous and extraordinary soever, could not in the least bring in question Moses's mission; that stood the firmer for this opposition, and remained the more unquestionable after this, than if no such signs had been brought against it.

So likewise the number, variety, and greatness of the miracles wrought for the confirmation of the doctrine delivered by Jesus Christ, carry with them such strong marks of an extraordinary divine power, that the truth of his mission will stand firm and unquestionable, till any one rising up in opposition to him shall do greater miracles than he and his apostles did. For any thing less will not be of weight to turn the scales in the opinion of any one, whether of an inferior or more exalted understanding. This is one of those palpable truths and trials, of which all mankind are judges; and there needs no assistance of learning, no deep thought, to come to a certainty in it. Such care has God taken that no pretended revelation should stand in competition with what is truly divine, that we need but open our eyes to see and be sure which came from him. The marks of his over-ruling power accompany it; and therefore to this day we find, that wherever the Gospel comes, it prevails to the beating down the strong holds of Satan, and the dislodging the prince of the power of darkness, driving him away with all his lying wonders; which is a standing miracle, carrying with it the testimony of superiority.

What is the uttermost power of natural agents or created beings, men of the greatest reach cannot discover; but that it is not equal to God's omnipotency, is obvious to every one's understanding; so that the superior power is an easy as well as sure guide to divine revelation, attested by miracles, where they are brought as credentials to an embassy from God.

And thus upon the same grounds of superiority of power, uncontes.. revelation will stand too.

For the explaining of which, it may be necessary to premise,

1. That no mission can be looked on to be divine, that delivers any thing derogating from the honour of the one, only, true, invisible God, or inconsistent with natural religion and the rules of morality: because God having discovered to men the unity and majesty of his eternal god-head, and the truths of natural religion and morality, by the light of reason, he cannot be supposed to back the contrary by revelation; for that would be to destroy the evidence and the use of reason, without which men cannot be able to distinguish divine revelation from diabolical imposture.

2. That it cannot be expected that God should send any one into the world on purpose to inform men of things indifferent, and of small moment, or that are knowable by the use of their natural faculties. This would be to lessen the dignity of his majesty in favour of our sloth, and in prejudice to our reason.

3. The only case, then, wherein a mission of any one from heaven can be reconciled to the high and awful thoughts men ought to have of the Deity, must be the revelation of some supernatural truths relating to the glory of God, and some great concern of men. Super-natural operations attesting such a revelation may with reason be taken to be miracles, as carrying the marks of a superior and over-ruling power, as long as no revelation accompanied with marks of a greater power appears against it. Such supernatural signs may justly stand good, and be received for divine, i.e. wrought by a power superior to all, till a mission attested by operations of a greater force shall disprove them: because it cannot be supposed God should suffer his prerogative to be so far usurped by any inferior being, as to permit any creature, depending on him, to set his seals, the marks of his divine authority, to a mission coming from him. For these supernatural signs being the only means God is conceived to have to satisfy men, as rational creatures of the certainty of anything he would reveal, as coming from himself, can never consent that it should be wrested out of his hands, to serve the ends and establish the authority of an inferior agent that rivals him. His power being known to have no equal, always will, and always may be, safely depended on, to show its superiority in vindicating his authority, and maintaining every truth that he hath revealed. So that the marks of a superior power accompanying it, always have been, and always will be, a visible and sure guide to divine revelation; by which men may conduct themselves in their examining of revealed religions, and be satisfied which they ought to receive as coming from God; though they have by no means ability precisely to determine what is or is not above the force of any created being; or what operations can be performed by none but a divine power, and require the immediate hand of the Almighty. And therefore we see it is by that our Saviour measures the great unbelief of the Jews, John xv. 24, saying, "If I had

not done among them the works which no other man did, they had not had sin; but now have they both seen and hated both me and my Father;" declaring, that they could not but see the power and presence of God in those many miracles he did, which were greater than ever any other man had done. When God sent Moses to the children of Israel with a message, that now, according to his promise, he would redeem them by his hand out of Egypt, and furnished him with signs and credentials of his mission; it is very remarkable what God himself says of those signs, Exod. iv. 8, "And it shall come to pass, if they will not believe thee, nor hearken to the voice of the first sign" (which was turning his rod into a serpent), that "they will believe the voice of the latter sign" (which was the making his hand leprous by putting it in his bosom). God farther adds, ver. 9, "And it shall come to pass, if they will not believe also these two signs, neither hearken unto thy voice, that thou shalt take of the water of the river, and pour upon the dry land: and the water which thou takest out of the river shall become blood upon the dry land." Which of those operations was or was not above the force of all created beings, will, I suppose, be hard for any man, too hard for a poor brick-maker, to determine; and therefore the credit and certain reception of the mission was annexed to neither of them, but the prevailing of their attestation was heightened by the increase of their number; two supernatural operations showing more power than one, and three more than two. God allowed that it was natural, that the marks of greater power should have a greater impression on the minds and belief of the spectators. Accordingly the Jews, by this estimate, judged of the miracles of our Saviour, John vii. 31, where we have this account, "And many of the people believed in him, and said, When Christ cometh, will he do more miracles than these which this man hath done?" This, perhaps, as it is the plainest, so it is also the surest way to preserve the testimony of miracles in its due force to all sorts and degrees of people. For miracles being the basis on which divine mission is always established, and consequently that foundation on which the believers of any divine revelation must ultimately bottom their faith, this use of them would be lost, if not to all mankind, yet at least to the simple and illiterate (which is the far greatest part) if miracles be defined to be none but such divine operations as are in themselves beyond the power of all created beings, or at least operations contrary to the fixed and established laws of nature. For as to the latter of those, what are the fixed and established laws of nature, philosophers alone, if at least they, can pretend to determine. And if they are to be operations performable only by divine power, I doubt whether any man, learned or unlearned, can in most cases be able to say of any particular operation, that can fall under his senses, that it is certainly a miracle. Before he can come to that certainty, he must know that no created being has a power to perform it. We know good and bad angels have abilities and excellencies exceedingly beyond all our poor performances or narrow comprehensions. But to define what is the utmost extent of power that any of them has, is a bold undertaking of a man in the dark, that pronounces without seeing, and sets bounds in his narrow cell to things at an infinite distance from his model and comprehension.

Such definitions, therefore, of miracles, however specious in discourse and theory, fail us when we come to use, and an application of them in particular cases.[1]

*Note*

1. These thoughts concerning miracles were occasioned by my reading Mr. Fleetwood's Essay on Miracles, and the letter writ to him on that subject. The one of them defining a miracle to be an extraordinary operation performable by God alone: and the other writing of miracles without any definition of a miracle at all.

## Samuel Clarke, "A Discourse Concerning the Unalterable Obligations of Natural Religion, and the Truth and Certainty of the Christian Revelations" (1705)

. . . . . . . . .

The Christian Revelation is positively and directly proved, to be actually and immediately sent to us from God, by the many infallible *Signs and Miracles*, which the Author of it worked publicly as the Evidence of his Divine Commission.

Besides the great Excellency and Reasonableness of the *Doctrine* considered in it self, of which I have already treated; 'Tis here of no small moment to observe, that the *Author* of it (separate from all external Proof of his Divine Commission) appeared in all his Behavior, Words and Actions, to be neither an *Impostor* nor an *Enthusiast*. His Life was Innocent and Spotless, spent entirely in serving the Ends of Holiness and Charity, in doing good to the Souls and Bodies of Men, in exhorting them to Repentance, and inviting them to serve and glorify God. When his bitterest Enemies accused him, in order to take away his Life; they could not charge him with any appearance of Vice or Immorality. And so far was he from being guilty of what they *did* accuse him of, namely of Vainglory and attempting to move Sedition; that once, when the admiring People would by force have taken him and made him their King, he chose even to work a Miracle to avoid that, which was the only thing that could be imagined to have been the Design of an *Impostor*. In like manner, whoever seriously considers the Answers he gave to all Questions whether moral or captious, his occasional Discourses to his Disciples, and more especially the Wisdom and Excellency of his Sermon upon the Mount, which is as it were the System and Summary of his Doctrine, manifestly surpassing all the moral Instructions of the most celebrated Philosophers that ever lived; cannot without the extremest Malice and Obstinacy in the World, charge him with *Enthusiasm*.

These Considerations cannot but add great Weight and Authority to his Doctrine, and make his own Testimony concerning himself exceedingly credible. But the *positive and direct* proof of his Divine Commission, are the *Miracles* which he worked for that purpose: His healing the Sick: His giving Sight to the Blind: His casting out Devils: His raising the Dead: The Wonders that attended his Crucifixion: His own Resurrection from the Dead: His Appearance afterwards to his Disciples: And his Ascension visibly into Heaven.

These, and the rest of his stupendous Miracles, were, *to the Disciples that saw them*, sensible Demonstrations of our Lord's Divine Commission. And *to those who have lived since that Age*, they are as certain Demonstrations of the same Truth, as the Testimony of those first Disciples, who were Eye-witnesses of them, is certain and true.

To the *Disciples that saw them*, these Miracles were sensible and complete Demonstrations of our Lord's Divine Commission; because they were so *great*, and so *many*, and so *public*, and so *evident*, that it was absolutely impossible they should be the Effect of any *Art of Man*, of any *Chance* or *Fallacy*: And the Doctrine they were brought to confirm, was of so good and holy a Tendency, that it was impossible he should be inabled to work them by the Power and Assistance of *Evil Spirits*: So that, consequently they must of necessity have been performed, either *immediately* or *mediately*, by *God* himself.

But here, because there have been many Questions raised, and some Perplexity introduced, by the Disputes and different Opinions of learned Men, concerning the *Power of Working Miracles*, and concerning the *Extent of the Evidence* which Miracles give to the Truth of any Doctrine; And because it hath been much controverted, whether true Miracles can be worked by any less Power, than the immediate Power of God; and whether to complete the Evidence of a Miracle, the Nature of the Doctrine pretended to be proved thereby, is requisite to be taken into the Consideration, or no: It may not perhaps be improper, upon this Occasion, to endeavor to set this whole Matter in its true Light, as briefly and clearly as I can.

1st, then: In respect of the *Power of God*, and in respect to the *Nature of the things themselves* absolutely speaking, all things that are possible at all, that is, which imply not a direct contradiction, are *equally and alike easy* to be done. The Power of God, extends equally to great things, as to small; and to many, as to few: And the one makes no more Difficulty at all, or Resistance to his Will, than the other.

'Tis not therefore a right Distinction, to define or distinguish *a Miracle* by any *absolute Difficulty* in the Nature of the thing itself to be done; As if the things we call *natural*, were absolutely and in their own Nature easier to be effected, than those that we look upon as *miraculous*. On the contrary, 'tis evident and undeniable, that 'tis at least as great an Act of Power, to cause *the Sun* or *a Planet to move at all;* as to cause it to *stand still at any Time.* Yet this latter, we call a Miracle; the former, not. And, *to restore the Dead to Life,* which is an Instance of an extraordinary Miracle; is in itself plainly altogether as easy, as to dispose matter at first into such order, as to *form a humane Body* in that which we commonly call a natural way. So that, absolutely speaking, in *This strict and Philosophical Sense;* either *nothing* is miraculous, namely, if we have respect to the Power of God; or, if we regard our own Power and Understanding, then almost *every thing,* as well what we call natural, as what we call supernatural, *is* in *this Sense* really miraculous; and 'tis only *usualness* or *unusualness* that makes the distinction.

2. What *degrees of Power* God may reasonably be supposed to have communicated to *Created Beings,* to *subordinate Intelligences,* to *good or evil Angels;* is by no means possible for us to determine. Some Things absolutely impossible for *Men* to effect, 'tis evident may easily be within the natural Powers of *Angels;* and some Things beyond the Power of *inferior Angels,* may as easily be supposed to be within the Natural Power of others that are *superior* to Them; and so on. So that (unless we knew the Limit of *communicable* and *incommunicable* Power) we can hardly affirm *with any Certainty,* that any particular Effect, how great or miraculous soever it may seem to us, is beyond the Power of all Created Beings in the Universe to have produced.

'Tis not therefore a right Distinction, to define *a Miracle* (as some very learned and very pious Men have done,) to be such an Effect, as could not have been produced by any less Power than the *Divine Omnipotence.* There is no Instance of any Miracle in Scripture, which to an ordinary Spectator would *necessarily* imply the immediate operation of *original, absolute,* and *underived* Power: And consequently such a Spectator could never be *certain,* that the miraculous Effect was beyond the Power of all created Beings in the Universe to produce. There is one Supposition indeed, upon which the Opinion of *all Miracles being necessarily the immediate Effects of the Divine Omnipotence,* may be defended; And that is, if God, together with the natural Powers wherewith he hath indued all subordinate Intelligent Beings, has likewise given a Law or Restraint, whereby they be hindered from ever interposing in this lower World, to produce any of those Effects which we call miraculous or supernatural: But then, how certain soever it is, that all Created Beings are under some particular Laws and Restraints; yet it can never be proved, that they are under such Restraints universally, perpetually, and without exception: And without this, a Spectator that sees a Miracle, can never be certain that it was not done by some Created Intelligence. Reducing the natural Power of Created Beings to as low a degree as any one can desire to suppose, will help nothing in this matter; For, supposing (which is very unreasonable to suppose) that the natural Powers of the highest Angels, were no greater than the natural Powers of Men; yet since thereby an Angel would be inabled to do all That invisibly, which a Man can do visibly; he would even in this Supposition be naturally able to do numberless things, which we should esteem the greatest of Miracles.

3. All things that are *Done* in the World, are done either immediately by God himself, or by *created Intelligent Beings: Matter* being evidently not at all capable of any *Laws* or *Powers* whatsoever, any more than it is capable of Intelligence; excepting only this One *Negative Power*, that every part of it will, of itself, always and necessarily continue in that State, whether of *Rest* or *Motion*, wherein it at present is. So that all those things which we commonly say are the Effects of the *Natural Powers of Matter*, and *Laws of Motion; of Gravitation, Attraction*, or the like; are indeed (if we will speak strictly and properly) the Effects of *God's* acting upon Matter continually and every moment, either immediately by himself, or mediately by some created intelligent Beings: (Which Observation, by the way, furnishes us, as has been before noted, with an excellent natural Demonstration of *Providence*.) Consequently there is no such thing, as what Men commonly call the *Course of Nature*, or the *Power of Nature*. The Course of Nature, truly and properly speaking, is nothing else but the *Will of God* producing certain Effects in a continued, regular, constant and uniform Manner: Which Course or Manner of Acting, being in every Moment perfectly *Arbitrary*, is as easy to be *altered* at any time, as to be *preserved*. And if, (as seems most probable,) this continual Acting upon Matter, be performed by the subserviency of created Intelligences appointed to that purpose by the Supreme Creator; then 'tis as easy for any of Them, and as much within their natural Power, (by the Permission of God,) to *alter* the Course of Nature at any time, or in any respect, as to *preserve* or *continue* it.

'Tis not therefore a right Distinction; to define a *Miracle* to be That which is *against the Course of Nature:* meaning, by the *Course of Nature*, the *Power of Nature*, or the *Natural Powers of Created Agents*. For, in this Sense, 'tis no more against the Course of Nature, for an Angel to *keep a Man from sinking in the Water*, than for a Man to *hold a Stone from falling in the Air*, by overpowering the Law of Gravitation; And yet the one is a Miracle, the other not so. In like manner, 'tis no more above the natural Power of a created Intelligence, to *stop the Motion of the Sun* or of a Planet, than to *continue to carry it on in its usual Course*: And yet the former is a Miracle, the latter not so. But if by the *Course of Nature*, be meant only (as it truly signifies) *the constant and uniform manner* of God's acting either immediately or mediately in preserving and continuing the Order of the World; then, in That Sense, indeed a Miracle may be rightly defined to be an Effect produced contrary to the usual Course or Order of Nature, by the unusual Interposition of some Intelligent Being Superior to Men; As I shall have occasion presently to observe more particularly.

And from this Observation, we may easily discover the Vanity and Unreasonableness of that obstinate Prejudice, which Modern Deists have universally taken up, against the Belief of Miracles in general. They see, that things generally go on in a constant and regular Method; that the

Frame and Order of the World, is preserved by things being disposed and managed in an Uniform manner: that certain Causes produce certain Effects in a continued Succession, according to certain fixed Laws or Rules; And from hence they conclude, very weakly and unphilosophically, that there are in *Matter* certain necessary *Laws* or *Powers*, the Result of which is That which they call the *Course of Nature*; which they think is impossible to be changed or altered, and consequently that there can be no such thing as *Miracles*. Whereas on the contrary, if they would consider things duly; they could not but see, that dull and lifeless Matter is utterly uncapable of obeying any *Laws*, or of being indued with any *Powers*; and that therefore That Order and Disposition of Things, which they vulgarly call the *Course of Nature*, cannot possibly be any thing else, but the *Arbitrary Will and Pleasure of God* exerting itself and acting upon Matter continually, either immediately by itself, or mediately by some subordinate Intelligent Agents, according to certain Rules of uniformity and proportion, fixed indeed and constant, but which yet are made such merely by Arbitrary Constitution, not by any sort of Necessity in the things themselves; as has been abundantly proved in my *former Discourse;* And consequently it cannot be denied, but that 'tis altogether as easy to *alter the Course of Nature*, as to *preserve* it; that is, that Miracles, excepting only that they are more unusual, are in *themselves*, and *in the Nature and Reason of the thing*, as credible in all respects, and as easy to be believed, as any of those we call natural Effects.

4. Those Effects which are produced in the World *regularly and constantly*, which we call the *Works of Nature;* prove to us in general, the Being, the Power, and the other Attributes of God. Those Effects, which, upon any *rare and extraordinary Occasion*, are produced in such manner, that 'tis manifest they could neither have been done by any *Power or Art of Man*, nor by what we call *Chance*, that is, by any Composition or result of those Laws which are God's *constant and uniform* Actings upon Matter; These undeniably prove to us the immediate and *occasional* Interposition either of God himself, or at least of some intelligent Agent Superior to Men, at That particular Time, and on That particular Account. For instance: The regular and continual Effects of the *Power of Gravitation*, and of the *Laws of Motion;* of the *Mechanic*, and of the *Animal Powers;* All these prove to us in general, the Being, the Power, the Presence, and the constant Operation, either immediate or mediate, of God in the World. But if, upon any particular Occasion, we should see a *Stone suspended in the Air*, or a *Man walking upon the Water*, without any visible support; a *chronical Disease cured by a word speaking*, or a *dead and corrupted Body restored to life in a moment;* We could not then doubt, but there was an *extraordinary* Interposition either of God himself, in order to signify his Pleasure upon that particular Occasion; or at least of some Intelligent Agent far superior to Man, in order to bring about some particular Design.

And now from these few clear and undeniable Propositions, it evidently follows:

1st. That the true *Definition* of a *Miracle*, in the *Theological* Sense of the Word, is this; that it is work effected in a manner *unusual*, or different from the common and regular Method of Providence, by the interposition either of God himself, or of some Intelligent Agent superior to Man, for the Proof or Evidence of some particular Doctrine, or in attestation to the Authority of some particular Person. And if a Miracle so worked, be not opposed by some plainly superior Power; nor be brought to attest a Doctrine either *contradictory* in itself, or *vicious* in its consequences; (a Doctrine of which kind, no Miracles in the World can be sufficient to prove;) then the Doctrine so attested must necessarily be looked upon as Divine, and the Worker of the Miracle entertained as having infallibly a Commission from God.

2. From hence it appears, that the complete *Demonstration* of our Savior's being a Teacher sent from God, was, to the Disciples who *saw his Miracles*, plainly This: That the *Doctrine* he taught, being in itself possible, and in its consequences Tending to promote the Honor of God and true Righteousness among Men; and the *Miracles* he worked, being such, that there neither was nor could be any pretence of more or greater Miracles to be set up in opposition to them; it was as infallibly certain that he had truly a Divine Commission, as it was certain that God would not himself impose upon Men: necessary and invincible Error.

## *Thomas Sherlock*, The Tryal of the Witnesses of the Resurrection of Jesus *(11th ed., 1729)*

WE were, not long since, some Gentlemen of the Inns of Court together, each to other so well known, that no Man's Presence was a Confinement to any other, from speaking his Mind on any Subject that happen'd to arise in Conversation. The Meeting was without Design, and the Discourse, as in like Cases, various. Among other things we fell upon the Subject of *Woolston's* Tryal and Conviction, which had happen'd some few Days before: That led to a Debate how the Law stands in such Cases, what Punishment it inflicts; and, in general, whether the Law ought at all to interpose in Controversies of this kind. We were not agreed in those Points. One, who maintain'd the favourable side to *Woolston*, discover'd a great Liking and Approbation of his Discourses against the Miracles of Christ, and seem'd to think his Arguments unanswerable. To which another replyed, I wonder that one of your Abilities, and bred to the Profession of the Law, which teaches us to consider the Nature of Evidence, and its proper Weight, can be of that Opinion; I am sure you would be unwilling to determine a Property of Five Shillings upon such Evidence, as you now think material enough to overthrow the Miracles of Christ.

It may easily be imagin'd that this open'd a Door to much Dispute, and determin'd the Conversation for the Remainder of the Evening to this Subject. The Dispute ran thro' almost all the Particulars mention'd in *Woolston's* Pieces; but the Thread of it was broken by several Digressions, and the Pursuit of things which were brought accidentally in the Discourse. At length one of the Company said pleasantly, Gentlemen, you don't argue like Lawyers; If I were Judge in this Cause, I would hold you better to the Point. The Company took the Hint, and cry'd, they should be glad to have the Cause re-heard, and him to be the Judge. The Gentlemen who had engaged with Mettle and Spirit in a Dispute which arose accidentally, seem'd very unwilling to be drawn into a formal Controversy: and especially the Gentleman who argu'd against *Woolston*, thought the Matter grew too serious for him, and excus'd himself from undertaking a Controversy in Religion, of all others the most momentous: But he was told, that the Argument should be confin'd merely to the Nature of the Evidence, and that might be consider'd without entering into any such Controversy as he would avoid; and to bring the Matter within Bounds, and under one View, the Evidence of Christ's Resurrection, and the Exceptions taken to it, should be the only Subject of the Conference. With much Persuasion he suffered himself to be persuaded, and promised to give the Company, and their new-made Judge, a Meeting that Day Fortnight. The Judge and the rest of the Company were for bringing on the Cause a Week sooner; but the Counsel for *Woolston* took the Matter up, and said, Consider, Sir, the Gentleman is not to argue out of *Littleton*, *Plowden*, or *Coke*, Authors to him well known; but he must have his Authorities from *Matthew*, *Mark*, *Luke*, and *John*; and a Fortnight is time little enough of all conscience to gain a Familiarity with a new Acquaintance; and, turning to the Gentleman, he said, I'll call upon you before the Fortnight is out, to see how reverend an Appearance you make behind *Hammond* on the new Testament, a Concordance on one Hand, and a Folio Bible with References on the other. You shall be welcome, Sir, reply'd the Gentleman, and perhaps you may find some Company more to your own Taste; he is but a poor Counsel who studies on one side of the Question only; and therefore I will have your Friend *Woolston*, T———l, C———s, to entertain you when you do me the Favour of the Visit. Upon this we parted in good Humour, and all pleased with the Appointment made, except the two Gentlemen who were to provide the Entertainment.

## The Second Day

THE Company met at the Time appointed: But it happen'd in this, as in like Cases it often does, that some Friends to some of the Company, who were not of the Party the First Day, had got notice of the Meeting; and the Gentlemen who were to debate the Question, found they had a more numerous Audience than they expected or desired. He especially who was to maintain the Evidence of the Resurrection, began to excuse the Necessity he was under of disappointing their Expectation, alledging that he was not prepared; and he had persisted in excusing himself, but that the Strangers who perceived what the Case was, offered to withdraw, which the Gentleman would by no Means consent to: They insisting to go, he said, he would much rather submit himself to their Candor, unprepared as he was, than be guilty of so much Rudeness, as to force them to leave the Company. Upon which one of the Company, smiling said, It happens luckily that our Number is encreased; when we were last together, we appointed a Judge, but we quite forgot a Jury, and now, I think, we are good Men and true, sufficient to make one. This Thought was pursued in several Allusions to legal Proceedings, which created some Mirth, and had this good Effect, that it dispersed the solemn Air which the mutual Compliments upon the Difficulty before-mentioned had introduced, and restored the Ease, and Good-humour natural to the Conversation of Gentlemen.

The Judge perceiving the Disposition of the Company, thought it a proper Time to begin, and called out, Gentlemen of the Jury take your Places; and immediately seated himself at the upper End of the Table: The Company sat round him, and the Judge called upon the Counsel for *Woolston* to begin.

.    .    .    .    .    .    .    .    .

Mr. *A*. I shall trouble you, Sir, but with one Observation more, which is this; that altho' in common Life we act in a thousand Instances upon the Faith and Credit of human Testimony, yet the Reason for so doing is not the same in the Case before us; in common Affairs, where nothing is asserted but what is probable and possible, and according to the usual Course of Nature, a reasonable degree of Evidence ought to determine every Man; for the very Probability or Possibility of the Thing is a Support to the Evidence, and in such Cases we have no doubt but a Man's Senses qualify him to be a Witness; but when the Thing testify'd is contrary to the Order of Nature, and, at first sight at least, impossible, what Evidence can be sufficient to overturn the constant Evidence of Nature, which she gives us in the constant and regular Method of her Operations? If a Man tells me he has been in *France*, I ought to give a Reason for not believing him; but if he tells me he comes from the Grave, what Reason can he give why I should believe him? In the Case before us, since the Body rais'd from the Grave differ'd from common natural Bodies, as we have before seen, how can I be assur'd that the Apostles Senses qualified them to judge at all of this Body, whether it was the same or not the same which was bury'd? They handled the Body, which yet could pass through Doors and Walls; they saw it, and sometimes knew it, at other times knew it not; in a word, it seems to be a Case exempt from human Evidence. Men have limited Senses, and a limited Reason; when they act within their

Limits we may give Credit to them, but when they talk of things remov'd beyond the reach of their Senses and Reason, we must quit our own if we believe theirs.

Mr. *B.* . . . The Gentleman allows it to be reasonable in many cases to act upon the Testimony and Credit of others, but he thinks this should be confin'd to such Cases where the thing testify'd is *probable, possible,* and *according to the usual Course of Nature.* The Gentleman does not, I suppose, pretend to know the Extent of all natural Possibilities, much less will he suppose them to be generally known; and therefore his Meaning must be, that the Testimony of Witnesses is to be receiv'd only in Cases which appear to us to be possible; in any other Sense we can have no Dispute; for mere Impossibilities, which can never exist, can never be prov'd; taking the Observation therefore in this Sense, the Proposition is this; that the Testimony of others ought not to be admitted but in such Matters as appear probable, at least possible to our Conceptions: For Instance; a Man who lives in a warm Climate, and never saw Ice, ought upon no Evidence to believe that Rivers freeze and grow hard in cold Countries; for it is improbable, contrary to the usual Course of Nature, and impossible according to his Notion of Things; and yet we all know that this is a plain, manifest Case, discernible by the Senses of Men, of which therefore they are qualify'd to be good Witnesses. An hundred such Instances might be nam'd, but it is needless; for surely nothing is more apparently absurd, than to make one Man's Ability in discerning, and his Veracity in reporting plain Facts, depend upon the Skill or Ignorance of the Hearer. And what has the Gentleman said upon this Occasion against the Resurrection, more than any Man who never saw Ice might say against an hundred honest Witnesses, who assert that Water turns to Ice in cold Climates?

It is very true that Men do not so easily believe, upon Testimony of others, things which to them seem improbable or impossible, but the reason is not because the thing itself admits of no Evidence, but because the Hearer's pre-conceiv'd Opinion outweighs the Credit of the Reporter, and makes his Veracity to be call'd in question; for Instance, it is natural for a Stone to roll down-hill, it is unnatural for it to roll up-hill; but a Stone moving up-hill is as much the Object of Sense as a Stone moving down-hill; and all Men in their Senses are as capable of seeing, and judging, and reporting the Fact in one Case as in the other. Should a Man then tell you that he saw a Stone go up-hill of its own accord, you might question his Veracity, but you could not say the thing admitted no Evidence because it was contrary to the Law and usual Course of Nature; for the Law of Nature form'd to yourself from your own Experience and Reasoning, is quite independent of the Matter of Fact which the Man testifies; and whenever you see Facts yourself which contradict your Notions of the Law of Nature, you admit the Facts because you believe yourself; when you do not admit like Facts upon the Evidence of others, it is because you do not believe them, and not because the Facts in their own nature exclude all Evidence.

Suppose a Man should tell you that he was come from the Dead, you would be apt to suspect his Evidence; but what would you suspect? that he was not alive, when you heard him, saw him, felt him, and convers'd with him? You could not suspect this without giving up all your Senses, and acting in this Case as you act in no other; here then you would question whether the Man had ever been dead; but would you say that it is incapable of being made plain by human Testimony that this or that Man dy'd a Year ago? It can't be said. Evidence in this Case is admitted in all Courts perpetually.

Consider it the other way. Suppose you saw a Man publickly executed, his Body afterwards wounded by the Executioner, and carry'd and laid in the Grave; that after this you should be told, that the Man was come to Life again; what would you suspect in this Case? not that the Man had never been dead, for that you saw your self; but you would suspect whether he was now alive: But would you say this Case excluded all human Testimony, and that Men could not possibly discern whether one with whom they convers'd familiarily was alive or no? Upon what ground could you say this? A Man rising from the Grave is an Object of Sense, and can give the same Evidence of his being alive as any other Man in the World can give. So that a Resurrection consider'd only as a Fact to be prov'd by Evidence, is a plain Case; it requires no greater Ability in the Witnesses, then that they be able to distinguish between a Man dead and a Man alive; a Point, in which I believe every Man living thinks himself a Judge.

I do allow that this Case, and others of like nature, require more Evidence to give them Credit than ordinary Cases do; you may therefore require more Evidence in these than in other Cases; but it is absurd to say that such Cases admit no Evidence, when the things in question are manifestly Objects of Sense.

I allow further, that the Gentleman has rightly stated the Difficulty upon the Foot of common Prejudice, and that it arises from hence that such Cases appear to be contrary to the Course of Nature; but I desire him to consider what this Course of Nature is; every Man, from the lowest Countryman to the highest Philosopher, frames to himself from his Experience and Observation a Notion of a Course of Nature, and is ready to say of every thing reported to him that contradicts his Experience, that it is contrary to Nature; but will the Gentleman say that every thing is impossible, or even improbable, that contradicts the Notion which Men frame to themselves of the Course of Nature? I think he will not say it; and if he will, he must say that Water can never freeze, for it is absolutely inconsistent with the Notion which Men have of the Course of Nature who live in the warm Climates; and hence it appears, that when Men talk of the Course of Nature, they really talk of their own Prejudice and Imaginations, and that Sense and Reason are not so much concern'd in the Case as the Gentleman imagines. For I ask, Is it from the Evidence of Sense or the Evidence of Reason that People of warm Climates think it contrary to Nature that Water should grow solid and become Ice? As for Sense, they see indeed that Water with them is always liquid, but none of their Senses tell them that it can never grow solid; as for Reason, it can never so inform them, for right Reason can never contradict the Truth of Things. Our Senses then inform us rightly what the usual Course of Things is; but when we conclude that Things cannot be otherwise, we outrun the Information of our Senses, and the Conclusion stands upon Prejudice, and not upon Reason; and yet such Conclusions form what is generally call'd the Course of Nature; and when Men upon proper Evidence and Informations admit things contrary to this presuppos'd Course of Nature, they do not, as the Gentleman expresses it, *quit their own Sense and Reason,* but in truth they quit their own Mistakes and Prejudices.

In the Case before us, the Case of the Resurrection, the great Difficulty arises from the like Prejudice. We all know by Experience that all Men die, and rise no more; therefore we conclude, that for a dead Man to rise to Life again, is contrary to the Course of Nature; and certainly it is contrary to the uniform and settled Course of things; but if we argue from hence, that it is contrary and repugnant to the real Laws of Nature, and absolutely impossible on that account, we argue without any Foundation to support us, either from our Senses or our Reason. We cannot learn from our Eyes, or Feeling, or any other Sense, that it is impossible for a dead Body to live again; if we learn it at all, it must be from our Reason; and yet what one Maxim of Reason is contradicted by the Supposition of a Resurrection? For my own part, when I consider how I live; that all the animal Motions necessary to my Life are independent of my Will; that my Heart beats without my Consent, and without my Direction; that Digestion and Nutrition are preform'd by Methods to which I am not conscious; that my Blood moves in a perpetual round, which is contrary to all known Laws of Motion, I cannot but think that the Preservation of my Life, in every Moment of it, is as great an Act of Power as is necessary to raise a dead Man to Life; and whoever so far reflects upon his own Being as to acknowledge that he owes it to a superior Power, must needs think that the same Power which gave Life to senseless Matter at first, and set all the Springs and Movements a going at the beginning, can restore Life to a dead Body; for surely it is not a greater thing to give Life to a Body once dead than to a Body that never was alive.

·   ·   ·   ·   ·   ·   ·   ·

*Judge.*   Very well. Gentlemen of the Jury, you have heard the Proofs and Arguments on both Sides, and it is now your Part to give a Verdict.

*Here the Gentlemen whisper'd together, and the Foreman stood up.*

*Foreman.*   My Lord, the Cause has been long, and consists of several Articles, therefore the Jury hope you will give them your Directions.

*Judge.*   No, no; you are very able to judge without my Help.

Mr. A.  My Lord, Pray consider, you appointed this Meeting, and chose your Office; Mr. B. and I have gone thro' our Parts, and have some Right to insist on your doing your Part.

Mr. B.  I must join, Sir, in that Request.

Judge.  I have often heard that all Honour has a Burden attending it, but I did not suspect it in this Office, which I conferr'd upon my self; but since it must be so, I will recollect and lay before you, as well as I can, the Substance of the Debate.

Gentlemen of the Jury, the Question before you is, Whether the Witnesses of the Resurrection of Christ are guilty of giving false Evidence or no?

.   .   .   .   .   .   .   .

The Council for *Woolston*, among other Difficulties, started one, which if well grounded, excludes all Evidence out of this Case. The Resurrection being a thing out of the Course of Nature, he thinks the Testimony of Nature, held forth to us in her constant Method of working, a stronger Evidence against the Possibility of a Resurrection, than any human Evidence can be for the Reality of one.

In answer to this, it is said on the other Side,

*First*, That a Resurrection is a thing to be judg'd of by Mens Senses; and this cannot be doubted. We all know when a Man is dead; and should he come to life again, we might judge whether he was alive or no by the very same Means by which we judge those about us to be living Men.

*Secondly*, That the Notion of a Resurrection contradicts no one Principle of right Reason, interferes with no Law of Nature; and that whoever admits that God gave Man Life at first, cannot possibly doubt of his Power to restore it when lost.

*Thirdly*, That appealing to the settled Course of Nature, is referring the Matter in dispute not to Rulers or Maxims of Reason and true Philosophy, but to the Prejudices and Mistakes of Men, which are various and infinite, and differ sometimes according to the Climate Men live in; because Men form a Notion of Nature from what they see; and therefore in cold Countries all Men judge it to be according to the Course of Nature for Water to freeze, in warm Countries they judge it to be unnatural; consequently, that it is not enough to prove any thing to be contrary to the Laws of Nature, to say that it is usually or constantly to our Observation otherwise; and therefore tho' Men in the Ordinary Course die, and do not rise again (which is certainly a Prejudice against the Belief of a Resurrection) yet is it not an Argument against the Possibility of a Resurrection.

.   .   .   .   .   .   .   .

Gentlemen of the Jury, I have laid before you the Substance of what has been said on both Sides, you are now to consider of it, and to give your Verdict.

*The Jury consulted together, and the Foreman rose up.*

*Foreman.*  My Lord, we are ready to give our Verdict.

*Judge.*  Are you all agreed?

*Jury.*  Yes.

*Judge.* Who shall speak for you?

*Jury.* Our Foreman.

*Judge.* What say you? Are the Apostles guilty of giving false Evidence in the Case of the Resurrection of Jesus, or not guilty?

*Foreman.* Not guilty.

*Judge.* Very well. And now, Gentlemen, I resign my Commission, and am your humble Servant.

## *Peter Annet,* The Resurrection of Jesus Considered: In Answer to the Tryal of the Witnesses *(1744)*

Having examined the evidence of the witnesses, so called, I now proceed to the rest of the tryal. To the question [in Sherlock], *Why did not Christ appear publicly to all the people, especially to the Magistrates? Why were some witnesses cull'd and chosen out, and others excluded?* Mr. B. answers, *It may be sufficient to say, where there are witnesses enow, no judge, no jury, complains for want of more; and therefore, if the witnesses we have are sufficient, 'tis no objection that we have not others and more.* But can there be sufficient witnesses, when their evidence is not sufficient to prove the fact? Then he compares it to a will which requires but three witnesses, cull'd out that they may be good ones; and adds, *How comes it to pass then that the very thing which shuts out all suspicion, in other cases, should, in this case, be of all others the most suspicious thing itself?* It is because this case, of all others is, the most uncommon. If it were of no more consequence than any ordinary affair, why do they make such a stir about it? Is the proof of a relation's will, and the proof of the will of God, a parallel case? Or a legacy in this world, and eternal life, of the same value? Should not the proof be as clear as the importance of the case requires? Is it not very absurd, that the meanest witnesses should be pick'd and cull'd out for the best, in the greatest affairs? That matters of the highest concern, and of the most extraordinary nature, should be, or said to be, sufficiently attested by the most doubtful evidence! That those who are principally interested in a will, the very executors and legatees, should be allowed to be the best and only witnesses of the said will: This wou'd not be pleaded for, or granted in any court in Christendom, nor pass any tryal, but in this.

The following improbabilities and absurdities, shew, what reason there is of complaint, That Jesus should be said publically to predict his own resurrection, and not fulfil it in public. That he should promise it to be the sign of his mission to that evil generation, yet never shew them the sign. That he should inform the people that he would rise again the third day, yet disappoint all their expectations in seeing him. That he should put the proof of his mission on the reality of his rising again; yet never discover that fact to them, by rising before them, nor by appearing to them afterwards. Had it been publically known to all *Jerusalem* that Jesus would rise again the third day, all *Jerusalem*, that believed it, would have expected to see him. If they were disappointed in their expectations, what was it but deceiving them in that very point, in which of all others, he should have satisfied them. Not to appear to them, if he promis'd it, and put the truth of his mission on it, was denying the truth of his mission, and falsifying his word. They said (Matt. xxvii, 42), *Let him come down from the cross, and we will believe in him:* And would they not have believed in him, if he had come up from the dead? Is it probable, that an extraordinary action, done for an extraordinary end, and highly necessary to be known to mankind, should be so secretly done, that no man saw it! That so great an action should be done so improper a way! That Jesus should require men to believe his Disciples, rather than their own senses, in an affair where reason can be of no assistance! That such a surprising method should be taken to save all men in such a manner, that scarce any man, that examines it, can believe it! That a miracle should be wrought in secret to convince men, and never manifest itself to the satisfaction of mankind; nor leave any footsteps, or any marks on earth of its having ever been, yet absolutely necessary to be believed! That he appeared in such a manner to his Disciples, which scarce convinced themselves; yet sent them to convince the world! That he was with them forty days, yet appeared but four times, or but now and then; and that he should not abide constant as before, nor be seen by others!

The witnesses give us no account where he spent the rest of his time, and to what end. Whether the spirit of God *drove* (Mark i. 12, 13) or *led* him into the wilderness to the devil again, for 'tis said (Luke iv. 13), he only *departed from him for a season;* where, and with whom, he staid forty days before to no purpose.[1] Choice company for the Son of God! Since Jesus might do and say all that is related of him, after his resurrection, in less than forty hours; and of all the forty nights, he never, that we hear of, lodg'd one night with any of his Disciples. These things are as surprising as his resurrection. That Jesus rose again from the dead, staid forty days afterwards, no body knows where, and purposely avoided the most right and rational method of its being certainly known to the world, viz. By avoiding to appear to the world! That after the Watch had spread lyes about, he did not shew himself to the Rulers, nor the people, to convince them of the contrary! That he, who was the messenger of truth, should countenance lyes by his silence and absence! They could not have put him to death again, if they would, for he could appear and disappear at pleasure. No doubt but the sight of Jesus would have struck them with sufficient awe and terror, from attempting it. Why did he not, after his resurrection, undeceive his Disciples in their notions of temporal victory and grandeur, when they ask'd him about it? Or take possession of the kingdom of *Israel*, fulfill the scriptures of the Prophets, and prove himself the Messiah? Why not appear in public for the public good, maintain the public cause of his nation and people? And why did he, at the very last, leave his Disciples, in expectation of it, and baulk all their expectations: Promise to come again presently (Matt. x. 23), and is not come yet? These disappointments give too much reason to cry out, *Why is his chariot so long in coming? Why tarry the wheels of his chariot?* Is he not risen? Did he not ascend? Has he not triumph'd over death and the grave, and led captivity captive?

.    .    .    .    .    .    .    .

Mr. *B.* remarks, That *since all men have an equal right to demand a special and particular evidence, why may not the same be demanded for every country and every age?* I know not why every country and age should have it, since they have an equal right to demand it. A special and particular action requires a special and particular proof, to every country and age, that are especially and particularly concerned in the case. If it needs a miraculous one, because it admits of no natural proof, miraculous proof should be given: For the proof of an action, which must be credited, ought to be such as is sufficient and fit to prove the action.

If miracles are once necessary to prove a fact, they are always necessary; because the same proof, or an adequate one, is always necessary to prove the same operation. The distance of time and place makes not less, but rather more necessary. A history of an extraordinary uncommon kind should have more than common proof. That is, The proofs given should be equal to the things to be proved. And the more momentous the affair is, or is esteem'd, so much the more plain, and certain, should be the evidence.

.    .    .    .    .    .    .    .

Now having gone thro' the whole affair, with as much clearness and brevity as I am able; I proceed to consider what was before pass'd over of Mr. *B*'s arguments in favor of the natural possibility of miracles in general.

To prove the possibility of things improbable to reason, the Gentleman argues That what nature produces in one country, may be incredible to people in another; as cold congealing waters to ice may be to a man that lives in a hot climate, who never saw such a thing. Be it so. In this case here's all the evidence of sense to prove the thing where it is; and of this there are places and witnesses enow. He that cannot believe, may go and have sensible conviction, And, *if an hundred such instances might be named, 'tis needless.* For tho' *nothing is more apparently absurd, than to make one man's ability in discerning, and his veracity in reporting plain facts, depend upon the skill of ignorance of the hearer;* yet if something be reported to me, or imposed on me for truth, which appears the less to be so, the more I examine it: Must I deny my discerning faculties, and my own veracity in examining; and depend upon the art or authority of the reporter or impostor? If (as 'tis called) the *plain fact* reported be a plain absurdity to my sense and understanding, and contradictory to the constant course of nature, should I renounce the evidence of what senses are alone capable of trying it, and of men's common and constant experience of the known laws thereof; to depend on the reporters or imposers judgment and veracity; one or both of which may be to me as questionable as the report. If the plain fact pretended have no other evidence but the bare report, and such as is inconsistent with itself, as well as with the reason of man, and the nature of things; let all impartial men judge, whether it is my *pre-conceived opinion*, or the want of good evidence, *that outweighs the credit of reporters, and makes their veracity to be called into question*. What no man's senses ever discerned, was never the object of any man's sense. If [reference to Sherlock] a stone appeared to roll up a hill of its own accord to my sight, I should think I had reason to doubt the veracity of my eye-sight, or of the object. Therefore I cannot admit the like fact on the evidence of others: Because pretended facts, which are contrary to nature, can have no natural evidence, tho' they may be called positive; that is, they are positively asserted, and must be positively believed; for evidence there is none. What conceptions any man frames to himself of the course of nature, from his own *experience and observation*, are not *prejudices and imaginations*; but what *sense and reason* are concern'd about. This is the very foundation of that right reason, which *can never contradict the truth of things*.

Any romantic story said to be seen, and heard, may be called a *plain manifest case, discernible by the senses of men; of which they are therefore qualified to be good Witnesses*, Things asserted, which are contrary to experience, and reason of all mankind; *and to what they know of the law and usual course of nature*, are, to the common sense and understanding of men, utterly impossible; because such assertions contradict all men's notions of those laws, that are known by common experience. Therefore they cannot admit the facts asserted on *any* evidence; because *they in their own nature exclude all evidence*; as all impossibilities must consequently do. Every miraculous fact then should be most exactly scrutiniz'd in every part, to attain a full assurance of the possibility of it. If in any one point it escapes examination, therein the fallacy may consist; which not being discern'd it may pass for a real miracle, tho' a notorious fraud. *Nothing is therefore more apparently absurd*, than to make some men's positive assertions, without being ever able to know their veracity, or the truth of the fact, to be the standard of other men's faith.

*If our senses inform us rightly what the usual course of things is*, and we conclude that it may be otherwise, without proper and infallible proof; we outrun the information of our senses, and the conclusion stands upon presumption, not upon sense and reason. Yet such conclusions do men form, who recede from that general course, and entertain mistakes and prejudices. As we know by experience that all men die, and rise no more, therefore we conclude, for a dead man to rise to life again, is contrary to the uniform and settled course of nature. Yet if we argue, that it is not contrary nor repugnant to the real laws thereof, as the Gentleman insinuates, we make the uniform and settled course, and the real laws of nature, two different things. Thus, we argue without any foundation, either from sense or reason; all which inform us, that it is impossible for a dead body to live again: To believe it possible contradicts this maxim, *That nature is steady in her operations*: For one miracle or action, done contrary to her laws, contradicts all her steady uniform springs and movements; and all that mankind call truth and reason. Therefore, I cannot but believe, till the course of nature is changed, that it is infinitely a greater thing to give life to a body once dead, than to give life and being, in a natural way, to ten thousand bodies that never had it; for the latter is done daily, the former never. I see no reason to allow that possible to be done, which admits no possible proof: For then a way is opened to allow any impossibility. It is very easy for any one to believe what is commonly done; but what is never done, or never can be proved, may be called faith, but has no foundation. Because I cannot account for whatever is demanded, must I believe whatever is proposed? He that is persuaded to believe anything contrary to the known laws of nature, because there are things he does not know, is seduced to renounce his understanding; and, because he knows not all possible things, is per-suaded to believe all things are possible. Positive and presumptive evi-dence is of no weight against the reason and nature of things. Such evidence should be rejected, rather than the nature of things should be subverted to support such evidence.

It may be objected, That God can do things contrary to nature. But what proof is there that God ever did, or will, if tradition be set aside, and men may suspend their belief, till rationally convinced, and the rod of damnation removed from them for doubting, which drives faith into the timorous, as a mallet does a wedge into a block; and in like manner divides, rends, and weakens the understanding. Where is the proof of it even in any one miracle, which tradition informs us of. If the evidence given be insufficient, what method of conviction remains? Were we to go to the place where reports says it was done, there are no signs of it left. If we enquire of those among whom it was said to be done, they know nothing of the matter, nor can we be sure they ever did. The Apostles are said to have proved the resurrection by miracles, but not one believer can prove it by any now, if the salvation of all mankind depended on it; tho' the power of working miracles was promised to all believers, yet none have it. If the true way of proving the faith is lost, there can be no proof, that the true faith itself is not lost.

Truth requires no man's assent without conviction. Therefore [refer-ence to Sherlock] *the testimony of others ought not to be admitted, but in such matters as appear probable, or at least possible to our conceptions;* or we may admit any thing. Such things as may be probable or possible in nature, but not to our conceptions, require better proof, in proportion as they appear improbable or impossible to our apprehensions. It cannot then be criminal in any man to with-hold his assent to a proposition, or story related, till he is fully convinced of the truth of it; but it may be safe for a man to yield his assent to what he is not fully convinced of; for this precludes further examination, and establishes error, with all its consequences.

It is knavery for one man knowingly to mislead another, folly to deceive ourselves, and weakness to suffer ourselves to be deceived. If we err, we may lead others into error. If we would not beguile ourselves, we should not encourage others to do it, but be strictly upon our guard against deceit; for sincerity, which is also called fidelity and honest, is the life and soul of true religion; deception and hypocrisy the bane of it. Wicked and designing men, who have trumped up a power superior to nature and reason, to destroy both, have depreciated the true born daughter of God, *faithfulness*, and anointed the bastard *faith* in her room. Those, who found religion on extraordinary pretensions, say, that nature, which is the offspring of God, is degenerate and deficient; but it is their extraordinary art that makes it appear so. Miraculous causes must have miraculous effects; but it cannot be proved that the latter have never appeared, therefore the former want proof.

Natural powers are fit to answer all the ends of virtue and religion; therefore supernatural powers are needless. A man of honesty and understanding needs no supernatural endowments, to instruct mankind in unspotted sanctity of heart and manners, such as may render them acceptable to God, and useful to one another; and consequently make then happy as they can be. No extraordinary or uncommon inspiration is necessary to teach the most excellent morals that were ever taught, with the reasonable belief of one God, and providence; witness Confucius, the great Philosopher of *China*, who was inferior to none, yet neither a God, nor a Prophet. He was the reviver of a religion of which nature was the author, which is as old as their race, and their country; which their wise men still esteem and enjoy; and which God never abolish'd; tho' he has permitted fools, that dislike it, to chuse another. I never read, that it was either given, or confirm'd by miracles; but truth has no need of them; and that which has, hath reason to be suspected; for they may be pretended to, to gloss over error, and establish iniquity, but cannot make that true and good, which is in its own nature otherwise.

A power to work miracles is a power superior to the universal laws, by which the systems of things are govern'd. This is the power of imagination only; and contrary to the attributes of God; to that which is most clear of all others, his unchangeableness. The same causes must always produce the same effects. But miracles are urged to prove a change in the will of God; this is, impossible things are pretended, to prove an impossibility, or the truth of a falsehood. As this cannot be proved, no such proofs were ever given; and 'tis impossible they should be. As the will of God cannot change, neither can the execution of his power; which is directed by his will. If no such change can be, no such change can be manifested. If God can alter his will, or if the displaying his eternal wisdom is not equally as constant and uniform as that wisdom is, he is then changeable, and may cease to be wise and good.

The power of God is under the direction of his wisdom and goodness, and limited thereby. A power to do whatever is consistent with these attributes, denotes absolute perfection. The whole production then of this wisdom, goodness, and power, must be a perfect work, therefore cannot be better. There is no room here for any superior or other power to interfere. God therefore made, and governs the world in the best manner, or it would be an imperfect work, and not shew forth the perfections, but the defect of the operator; and, if best already, it cannot be made better. If God is a perfect being, his works are perfect, and cannot be mended; because he could not limit his wisdom, goodness, or power, in producing it, without being guilty of folly, evil, or weakness. And, if God has in creation displayed his attributes, then all things, at least, collectively taken, and rightly understood, witness the perfection of his nature. And if so, God need not, or cannot exhibit any superior power, and proof of his perfection, than what is commonly known, and constantly manifest. If the power of God is always directed by perfect wisdom, no greater can be displayed, for perfection cannot be mended. The works of a wise operator shew forth his skill in the best manner possible; so that the performance may not bring a reflection on the artist, by its want of extraordinary repairs afterwards. If God be then perfectly wise, his work is a perfect work, and wants no miraculous mending power, nor can admit of it; it may marr, but cannot mend that which is best already. As the work is, such is the workman. As the seed is, so will be the produce. From hence it appears, that, as there is no need of such power, so the impossibility of it is evident.

But if miracles were ever necessary, whether the divine and human nature, or the nature of things be changeable or unchangeable, they must always be necessary. For, if God ever wrought miracles, as the proof of the revelation of his will, he will always pursue the same method, if he is an unchangeable being. If the nature of things are unchangeable, the method of attaining the knowledge of God's will must always be the same: And, if human nature be ever the same, it will ever require the same method of conviction, or of attaining the knowledge of the will of God.

If God's will be changeable, then there is a necessity for his constant working miracles, to discover such a change of his will to man; for so extraordinary a will can never be known to us, without an extraordinary revelation or discovery of it, that we may be certain we are not deceived.

.    .    .    .    .    .    .    .

We are told, that God has wrought wonders for the satisfaction of one generation, and not for another; tho' they are equally necessary and useful to all people; but the justice, mercy, goodness, and wisdom of God, is degraded hereby; because, by this, God is represented to us as partial being. Therefore, the belief of past miracles is destructive to the moral character of the Deity. The wonders, which are said to be wrought in one age, can never convince a sober thinker in the next, unless there be such lasting monuments of them, and they are so clearly and fully evidenced, that they appear to be true against all contradiction; nor is it fit that they should; for to believe miracles were performed in a certain manner, time, and place, of which no shadow of proof remains more than the bare report, is putting faith in the reporters, not in the operator: Thus I may be always amused by fabulous tales, as often as simple or bad men please to relate them; unless I can be sure that no man will lye to serve a turn, nor can be impos'd upon to believe a false story.

But if God acts towards mankind, as the moral fitness of things requires, there is no occasion for miracles; for if reasonable exhortations to virtue, and dehortations from vice; if prudent persuasion, and just laws, will not make people virtuous, nothing can. But miracles rather force the passions by violent, than guide them by gentle means, and drive men on without sense, than drive sense into them. The surprise seizes the imagination, the person no longer hesitates concerning truth, or deliberates of virtue; but is carried away in the full gale of his passions, by the rapid torrent of an astonishing power, that bears down all before it.

The more men are amused with miraculous tales, they will be diverted from employing their reason. But, when truth is valued, the rational faculties will be exercised, enthusiasm sinks of course, and superstition its offspring. The more respect is paid to any thing substituted in the room of truth, and moral righteousness; the less are these regarded. The resurrection of these is death to the false righteousness of faith and formality. When men know they are to have nothing but what they work for, when they are assured they are not born to an estate in the kingdom of heaven of another's purchasing, they will not idly live on the faith of it, but go to work, and endeavour their utmost to *work out their own salvation* with care and diligence.

To conclude, I am therefore not without hopes, that, whether this treatise be answered or not, it will prove a real service to religion, and make men's practices better; when they shall find they have nothing else to depend on for happiness here and hereafter, but their own personal righteousness, with their love of wisdom, and Truth. For, if it be answered, Deists will be silenced, and infidelity shall stop her mouth. But if those learned Gentlemen, who are the directors of others, will not think fit to do it, but chuse to give up speculative principles, and an historical faith, rather than contend about them, and to insist only on that practice which will recommend men in every religion to the favor of God, the good-will of men, and the peace of their own consciences, and own, that the whole Christian religion, which is worth contending for, are all relative and social virtues, then the contention between *Christian* and *Deist* will drop. Censoriousness, and reviling, and slander, and persecution, and uncharitableness, for the sake of religion, shall cease among us. Then *faithfulness shall be the girdle of our loins*. The blossoms of wisdom, and fruits of righteousness, will be the glory of our isle, *and the Lord alone shall be exalted in that day*. We shall give glory to that Unchangeable God, whose power forms, and whose wisdom governs all; who has no partner in the one, nor director in the other; whose goodness and mercy is not purchased with the blood of a victim. . . .

If these things CAN be refuted, let them, for the Truth's sake. Whenever violence is used for argument, 'tis for want of better against INVINCIBLE TRUTH. But *the wrath of man worketh not the righteousness of God; as St. James saith, But if ye have bitter envyings and strife in your hearts, glory not, and* LIE *not against the truth. This wisdom decendeth not from above, but is earthly, sensual, and devilish. For where envying and strife is, there is confusion, and every evil work. But the wisdom that is from above is first and pure, then peaceable, gentle, and easy to be intreated, full of mercy and good fruits, without* PARTIALITY *and without hypocrisy.*

*Note*

1. This story, if elsewhere, would seem blasphemous and fabulous.

## *David Hume*, Enquiry Concerning Human Understanding *(1777)*, *Section 10, "Of Miracles"*

### Part 1

There is, in Dr. Tillotson's writings, an argument against the *real presence*, which is as concise, and elegant, and strong as any argument can possibly be supposed against a doctrine, so little worthy of a serious refutation. It is acknowledged on all hands, says that learned prelate, that the authority, either of the scripture or of tradition, is founded merely in the testimony of the apostles, who were eye-witnesses to those miracles of our Saviour, by which he proved his divine mission. Our evidence, then, for the truth of the *Christian* religion is less than the evidence for the truth of our senses; because, even in the first authors of our religion, it was no greater; and it is evident it must diminish in passing from them to their disciples; nor can any one rest such confidence in their testimony, as in the immediate object of his senses. But a weaker evidence can never destroy a stronger; and therefore were the doctrine of the real presence ever so clearly revealed in scripture, it were directly contrary to the rules of just reasoning to give our assent to it. It contradicts sense, though both the scripture and tradition, on which it is supposed to be built, carry not such evidence with them as sense; when they are considered merely as external evidences, and are not brought home to every one's breast, by the immediate operation of the Holy Spirit.

Nothing is so convenient as a decisive argument of this kind, which must at least *silence* the most arrogant bigotry and superstition, and free us from their impertinent solicitations. I flatter myself, that I have discovered an argument of a like nature, which, if just, will, with the wise and learned, be an everlasting check to all kinds of superstitious delusion, and consequently, will be useful as long as the world endures. For so long, I presume, will the accounts of miracles and prodigies be found in all history, sacred and profane.[1]

Though experience be our only guide in reasoning concerning matters of fact; it must be acknowledged, that this guide is not altogether infallible, but in some cases is apt to lead us into errors. One, who in our climate, should expect better weather in any week of JUNE than in one of DECEMBER, would reason justly, and conformably to experience; but it is certain, that he may happen, in the event, to find himself mistaken. However, we may observe, that, in such a case, he would have no cause to complain of experience; because it commonly informs us beforehand of the uncertainty, by that contrariety of events, which we may learn from a diligent observation. All effects follow not with like certainty from their supposed causes. Some events are found, in all countries and all ages, to have been constantly conjoined together: Others are found to have been more variable, and sometimes to disappoint our expectations; so that, in our reasonings concerning matter of fact, there are all imaginable degrees of assurance, from the highest certainty to the lowest species of moral evidence.

A wise man, therefore, proportions his belief to the evidence. In such conclusions as are founded on an infallible experience, he expects the event with the last degree of assurance, and regards his past experience as a full *proof* of the future existence of that event. In other cases, he proceeds with more caution: He weighs the opposite experiments. He considers which side is supported by the greater number of experiments: To that side he inclines, with doubt and hesitation; and when at last he fixes his judgment, the evidence exceeds not what we properly call *probability*. All probability, then, supposes an opposition of experiments and observations, where the one side is found to overbalance the other, and to produce a degree of evidence, proportioned to the superiority. A hundred instances or experiments on one side, and fifty on another, afford a doubtful expectation of any event; though a hundred uniform experiments, with only one that is contradictory, reasonably beget a pretty strong degree of assurance. In all cases, we must balance the opposite experiments, where they are opposite, and deduct the smaller number from the greater, in order to know the exact force of the superior evidence.

To apply these principles to a particular instance; we may observe, that there is no species of reasoning more common, more useful, and even necessary to human life, than that which is derived from the testimony of men, and the reports of eye-witnesses and spectators. This species of reasoning, perhaps, one may deny to be founded on the relation of cause and effect. I shall not dispute about a word. It will be sufficient to observe, that our assurance in any argument of this kind is derived from no other principle than our observation of the veracity of human testimony, and of the usual conformity of facts to the reports of witnesses. It being a general maxim, that no objects have any discoverable connexion together, and that all the inferences, which we can draw from one to another, are founded merely on our experience of their constant and regular conjunction; it is evident, that we ought not to make an exception to this maxim in favour of human testimony, whose connexion with any event seems, in itself, as little necessary as any other.[2] Were not the memory tenacious to a certain degree; had not men commonly an inclination to truth and a principle of probity; were they not sensible to shame, when detected in a falsehood: Were not these, I say, discovered by *experience* to be qualities, inherent in human nature, we should never repose the least confidence in human testimony. A man delirious, or noted for falsehood and villany, has no manner of authority with us.

And as the evidence, derived from witnesses and human testimony, is founded on past experience, so it varies with the experience, and is regarded either as a *proof* or a *probability*, according as the conjunction between any particular kind of report and any kind of object has been found to be constant or variable. There are a number of circumstances to be taken into consideration in all judgments of this kind; and the ultimate standard, by which we determine all disputes, that may arise concerning them, is always derived from experience and observation. Where this experience is not entirely uniform on any side, it is attended with an unavoidable contrariety in our judgments, and with the same opposition and mutual destruction of argument as in every other kind of evidence. We frequently hesitate concerning reports of others. We balance the opposite circumstances, which cause any doubt or uncertainty; and when we discover a superiority on any side, we incline to it; but still with a diminution of assurance, in proportion to the force of its antagonist.

This contrariety of evidence, in the present case, may be derived from several different causes; from the opposition of contrary testimony; from the character or number of the witnesses; from the manner of their delivering their testimony; or from the union of all these circumstances. We entertain a suspicion concerning any matter of fact, when the witnesses contradict each other; when they are but few, or of a doubtful character; when they have an interest in what they affirm; when they deliver their testimony with hesitation, or on the contrary, with too violent asseverations. There are many other particulars of the same kind, which may diminish or destroy the force of any argument, derived from human testimony.

Suppose, for instance, that the fact, which the testimony endeavours to establish, partakes of the extraordinary and the marvellous; in that case, the evidence, resulting from the testimony, admits of a diminution, greater or less, in proportion as the fact is more or less unusual. The reason, why we place any credit in witnesses and historians, is not derived from any *connexion*, which we perceive *a priori*, between testimony and reality, but because we are accustomed to find a conformity between them. But when the fact attested is such a one as has seldom fallen under our observation, here is a contest of two opposite experiences; of which the one destroys the other, as far as its force goes, and the superior can only operate on the mind by the force, which remains. The very same principle of experience, which gives us a certain degree of assurance in the testimony of witnesses, gives us also, in this case, another degree of assurance against the fact, which they endeavour to establish; from which contradiction there necessarily arises a counterpoise, and mutual destruction of belief and authority.

³*I should not believe such a story were it told to me by* CATO; was a proverbial saying in ROME, even during the lifetime of that philosophical patriot.⁴ The incredibility of a fact, it was allowed, might invalidate so great an authority.

⁵The INDIAN prince, who refused to believe the first relations concerning the effects of frost, reasoned justly; and it naturally required very strong testimony to engage his assent to facts, that arose from a state of nature, with which he was unacquainted, and which bore so little analogy to those events, of which he had had constant and uniform experience. Though they were not contrary to his experience, they were not conformable to it.⁶

But in order to encrease the probability against the testimony of witnesses, let us suppose, that the fact, which they affirm, instead of being only marvellous, is really miraculous; and suppose also, that the testimony, considered apart and in itself, amounts to an entire proof; in that case, there is proof against proof, of which the strongest must prevail, but still with a diminution of its force, in proportion to that of its antagonist.

A miracle is a violation of the laws of nature; and as a firm and unalterable experience has established these laws, the proof against a miracle, from the very nature of the fact, is as entire as any argument from experience can possibly be imagined. Why is it more than probable that all men must die; that lead cannot, of itself, remain suspended in the air; that fire consumes wood, and is extinguished by water; unless it be, that these events are found agreeable to the laws of nature, and there is required a violation of these laws, or in other words, a miracle to prevent them? Nothing is esteemed a miracle, if it ever happen in the common course of nature. It is no miracle that a man, seemingly in good health, should die on a sudden: because such a kind of death, though more unusual than any other, has yet been frequently observed to happen. But it is a miracle, that a dead man should come to life; because that has never been observed, in any age or country. There must, therefore, be a uniform experience against every miraculous event, otherwise the event would not merit that appellation. And as an uniform experience amounts to a proof, there is here a direct and full *proof*, from the nature of the fact, against the existence of any miracle; nor can such a proof be destroyed, or the miracle rendered credible, but by an opposite proof, which is superior.[7]

The plain consequence is (and it is a general maxim worthy of our attention), 'That no testimony is sufficient to establish a miracle, unless the testimony be of such a kind, that its falsehood would be more miraculous, than the fact, which it endeavours to establish: And even in that case there is a mutual destruction of arguments, and the superior only gives us an assurance suitable to that degree of force, which remains, after deducting the inferior.' When any one tells me, that he saw a dead man restored to life, I immediately consider with myself, whether it be more probable, that this person should either deceive or be deceived, or that the fact, which he relates, should really have happened. I weigh the one miracle against the other; and according to the superiority, which I discover, I pronounce my decision, and always reject the greater miracle. If the falsehood of his testimony would be more miraculous, than the event which he relates; then, and not till then, can he pretend to command my belief or opinion.

## Part 2

In the foregoing reasoning we have supposed, that the testimony, upon which a miracle is founded, may possibly amount to an entire proof, and that the falsehood of that testimony would be a real prodigy: But it is easy to shew, that we have been a great deal too liberal in our concession, and that there never was a miraculous event[8] established on so full an evidence.

For *first*, there is not to be found in all history, any miracle attested by a sufficient number of men, of such unquestioned good-sense, education, and learning, as to secure us against all delusion in themselves; of such undoubted integrity, as to place them beyond all suspicion of any design to deceive others; of such credit and reputation in the eyes of mankind, as to have a great deal to lose in case of their being detected in any falsehood; and at the same time, attesting facts, performed in such a public manner, and in so celebrated a part of the world, as to render the detection unavoidable: All which circumstances are requisite to give us a full assurance in the testimony of men.

*Secondly.* We may observe in human nature a principle, which, if strictly examined, will be found to diminish extremely the assurance, which we might, from human testimony, have, in any kind of prodigy. The maxim, by which we commonly conduct ourselves in our reasonings, is, that the objects, of which we have no experience, resemble those, of which we have; that what we have found to be most usual is always most probable; and that where there is an opposition of arguments, we ought to give the preference to such as are founded on the greatest number of past observations. But though, in proceeding by this rule, we readily reject any fact which is unusual and incredible in an ordinary degree; yet in advancing farther, the mind observes not always the same rule; but when anything is affirmed utterly absurd and miraculous, it rather the more readily admits of such a fact, upon account of that very circumstance, which ought to destroy all its authority. The passion of *surprise* and *wonder*, arising from miracles, being an agreeable emotion, gives a sensible tendency towards the belief of those events, from which it is derived. And this goes so far, that even those who cannot enjoy this pleasure immediately, nor can believe those miraculous events, of which they are informed, yet love to partake of the satisfaction at second-hand or by rebound, and place a pride and delight in exciting the admiration of others.

With what greediness are the miraculous accounts of travellers received, their descriptions of sea and land monsters, their relations of wonderful adventures, strange men, and uncouth manners? But if the spirit of religion join itself to the love of wonder, there is an end of common sense; and human testimony, in these circumstances, loses all pretensions to authority. A religionist may be an enthusiast, and imagine he sees what has no reality: He may know his narrative to be false, and yet persevere in it, with the best intentions in the world, for the sake of promoting so holy a cause: Or even where this delusion has not place, vanity, excited by so strong a temptation, operates on him more powerfully than on the rest of mankind in any other circumstances; and self-interest with equal force. His auditors may not have, and commonly have not, sufficient judgment to canvass his evidence: What judgment they have, they renounce by principle, in these sublime and mysterious subjects: Or if they were ever so willing to employ it, passion and a heated imagination disturb the regularity of its operations. Their credulity encreases his impudence: And his impudence overpowers their credulity.

Eloquence, when at its highest pitch, leaves little room for reason or reflection; but addressing itself entirely to the fancy or the affections, captivates the willing hearers, and subdues their understanding. Happily, this pitch it seldom attains. But what a TULLY or a DEMOSTHENES could scarcely effect over a ROMAN or ATHENIAN audience, every *Capuchin*, every itinerant or stationary teacher can perform over the generality of mankind, and in a higher degree, by touching such gross and vulgar passions.

[9]The many instances of forged miracles, and prophecies, and supernatural events, which, in all ages, have either been detected by contrary evidence, or which detect themselves by their absurdity, prove sufficiently the strong propensity of mankind to the extraordinary and the marvellous, and ought reasonably to beget a suspicion against all relations of this kind. This is our natural way of thinking, even with regard to the most common and most credible events. For instance: There is no kind of report, which rises so easily, and spreads so quickly, especially in country places and provincial towns, as those concerning marriages; insomuch that two young persons of equal condition never see each other twice, but the whole neighbourhood immediately join them together. The

pleasure of telling a piece of news so interesting, of propagating it, and of being the first reporters of it, spreads the intelligence. And this is so well known, that no man of sense gives attention to these reports, till he find them confirmed by some greater evidence. Do not the same passions, and others still stronger, incline the generality of mankind to believe and report, with the greatest vehemence and assurance, all religious miracles?

*Thirdly.* It forms a strong presumption against all supernatural and miraculous relations, that they are observed chiefly to abound among ignorant and barbarous nations; or if a civilized people has ever given admission to any of them, that people will be found to have received them from ignorant and barbarous ancestors, who transmitted them with that inviolable sanction and authority, which always attend received opinions. When we peruse the first histories of all nations, we are apt to imagine ourselves transported into some new world; where the whole frame of nature is disjointed and every element performs its operations in a different manner, from what it does at present. Battles, revolutions, pestilence, famine, and death, are never the effect of those natural causes, which we experience. Prodigies, omens, oracles, judgments, quite obscure the few natural events, that are intermingled with them. But as the former grow thinner every page, in proportion as we advance nearer the enlightened ages, we soon learn, that there is nothing mysterious or supernatural in the case, but that all proceeds from the usual propensity of mankind towards the marvellous, and that, though this inclination may at intervals receive a check from sense and learning, it can never be thoroughly extirpated from human nature.

*It is strange,* a judicious reader is apt to say, upon the perusal of these wonderful historians, *that such prodigious events never happen in our days.* But it is nothing strange, I hope, that men should lie in all ages. You must surely have seen instances enow of that frailty. You have yourself heard many such marvellous relations started, which, being treated with scorn by all the wise and judicious, have at last been abandoned even by the vulgar. Be assured, that those renowned lies, which have spread and flourished to such a monstrous height, arose from like beginnings; but being sown in a more proper soil, shot up at last into prodigies almost equal to those which they relate.

It was a wise policy in that [10]false prophet, ALEXANDER, who, though now forgotten, was once so famous, to lay the first scene of his impostures in PAPHLAGONIA, where, as LUCIAN tells us, the people were extremely ignorant and stupid, and ready to swallow even the grossest delusion. People at a distance, who are weak enough to think the matter at all worth enquiry, have no opportunity of receiving better information. The stories come magnified to them by a hundred circumstances. Fools are industrious in propagating the imposture; while the wise and learned are contented, in general, to deride its absurdity, without informing themselves of the particular facts, by which it may be distinctly refuted. And thus the impostor above-mentioned was enabled to proceed, from his ignorant PAPHLAGONIANS, to the enlisting of votaries, even among the

GRECIAN philosophers, and men of the most eminent rank and distinction in ROME: Nay, could engage the attention of the sage emperor MARCUS AURELIUS; so far as to make him trust the success of a military expedition to his delusive prophecies.

The advantages are so great, of starting an imposture among an ignorant people, that, even though the delusion should be too gross to impose on the generality of them (*which, though seldom, is sometimes the case*) it has a much better chance for succeeding in remote countries, than if the first scene has been laid in a city renowned for arts and knowledge. The most ignorant and barbarous of these barbarians carry the report abroad. None of their countrymen have a large correspondence, or sufficient credit and authority to contradict and beat down the delusion. Men's inclination to the marvellous has full opportunity to display itself. And thus a story, which is universally exploded in the place where it was first started, shall pass for certain at a thousand miles distance. But had ALEXANDER fixed his residence at ATHENS, the philosophers of that renowned mart of learning had immediately spread, throughout the whole ROMAN empire, their sense of the matter; which, being supported by so great authority, and displayed by all the force of reason and eloquence, had entirely opened the eyes of mankind. It is true; LUCIAN, passing by chance through PAPHLAGONIA, had an opportunity of performing this good office. But, though much to be wished, it does not always happen, that every ALEXANDER meets with a LUCIAN, ready to expose and detect his impostures.[11]

I may add as a *fourth* reason, which diminishes the authority of prodigies, that there is no testimony for any, even those which have not been expressly detected, that is not opposed by an infinite number of witnesses; so that not only the miracle destroys the credit of testimony, but the testimony destroys itself. To make this the better understood, let us consider, that, in matters of religion, whatever is different is contrary; and that it is impossible the religions of ancient ROME, of TURKEY, of SIAM, and of CHINA should, all of them, be established on any solid foundation. Every miracle, therefore, pretended to have been wrought in any of these religions (and all of them abound in miracles), as its direct scope is to establish the particular system to which it is attributed; so has it the same force, though more indirectly, to overthrow every other system. In destroying a rival system, it likewise destroys the credit of those miracles, on which that system was established; so that all the prodigies of different religions are to be regarded as contrary facts, and the evidences of these prodigies, whether weak or strong, as opposite to each other. According to this method of reasoning, when we believe any miracle of MAHOMET or his successors, we have for our warrant the testimony of a few barbarous ARABIANS: And on the other hand, we are to regard the authority of TITUS LIVIUS, PLUTARCH, TACITUS, and, in short, of all the authors and witnesses, GRECIAN, CHINESE, and ROMAN CATHOLIC, who have related any miracle in their particular religion; I say, we are to regard their testimony in the same light as if they had mentioned that MAHOMETAN miracle, and had in express terms contradicted it, with the same certainty as they have for the miracle they relate. This argument may appear over subtile and refined; but is not in reality different from the reasoning of a judge, who supposes, that the credit of two witnesses, maintaining a crime against any one, is destroyed by the testimony of two others, who affirm him to have been two hundred leagues distant, at the same instant when the crime is said to have been committed.

One of the best attested miracles in all profane history, is that which TACITUS reports of VESPASIAN, who cured a blind man in ALEXANDRIA, by means of his spittle, and a lame man by the mere touch of his foot; in obedience to a vision of the god SERAPIS, who had enjoined them to have recourse to the Emperor, for these miraculous cures. The story may be seen in that fine historian;[12] where every circumstance seems to add weight to the testimony, and might be displayed at large with all the force of argument and eloquence, if any one were now concerned to enforce the evidence of that exploded and idolatrous superstition. The gravity, solidity, age, and probity of so great an emperor, who, through the whole course of his life, conversed in a familiar manner with his friends and courtiers, and never affected those extraordinary airs of divinity assumed by ALEXANDER and DEMETRIUS. The historian, a cotemporary writer, noted for candour and veracity, and withal, the greatest and most penetrating genius, perhaps, of all antiquity; and so free from any tendency to credulity, that he even lies under the contrary imputation, of atheism and profaneness: The persons, from whose authority he related the miracle, of established character for judgment and veracity, as we may well presume; eye-witnesses of the fact, and confirming their testimony, after the FLAVIAN family was despoiled of the empire, and could no longer give any reward, as the price of a lie. *Utrumque, qui interfuere, nunc quoque memorant, post quam nullum mendacio pretium.* To which if we add the public nature of the facts, as related, it will appear, that no evidence can well be supposed stronger for so gross and so palpable a falsehood.

There is also a memorable story related by Cardinal DE RETZ, which may well deserve our consideration. When that intriguing politician fled into SPAIN, to avoid the persecution of his enemies, he passed through SARAGOSSA, the capital of ARRAGON, where he was shewn, in the ca-thedral, a man, who had served [13]seven years as a door-keeper, and was well known to every body in town, that had ever paid his devotions at that church. He had been seen, for so long a time, wanting a leg; but recovered that limb by the rubbing of holy oil upon the stump;[14] and the cardinal assures us that he saw him with two legs. This miracle was vouched by all the canons of the church; and the whole company in town were appealed to for a confirmation of the fact; whom the cardinal found, by their zealous devotion, to be thorough believers of the miracle. Here the relater was also contemporary to the supposed prodigy, of an incredulous and libertine character, as well as of great genius; the miracle of so *singular* a nature as could scarcely admit of a counterfeit, and the witnesses very numerous, and all of them, in a manner, spectators of the fact, to which they gave their testimony. And what adds mightily to the force of the evidence, and may double our surprize on this occasion, is, that the cardinal himself, who relates the story, seems not to give any credit to it, and consequently cannot be suspected of any concurrence in the holy fraud. He considered justly, that it was not requisite, in order to reject a fact of this nature, to be able accurately to disprove the testimony, and to trace its falsehood, through all the circumstances of knavery and credulity which produced it. He knew, that, as this was commonly altogether impossible at any small distance of time and place; so was it extremely difficult, even where one was immediately present, by reason of the bigotry, ignorance, cunning, and roguery of a great part of mankind. He therefore concluded, like a just reasoner, that such an evidence carried falsehood upon the very face of it, and that a miracle supported by any human testimony, was more properly a subject of derision than of argument.

There surely never was a greater number of miracles ascribed to one person, than those, which were lately said to have been wrought in FRANCE upon the tomb of Abbé PARIS, the famous JANSENIST, with whose sanctity the people were so long deluded. The curing of the sick, giving hearing to the deaf, and sight to the blind, were every where talked of as the usual effects of that holy sepulchre. But what is more extraordinary; many of the miracles were immediately proved upon the spot, before judges of unquestioned integrity, attested by witnesses of credit and distinction, in a learned age, and on the most eminent theatre that is now in the world. Nor is this all: A relation of them was published and dispersed every where; nor were the *Jesuits*, though a learned body, supported by the civil magistrate, and determined enemies to those opinions, in whose favour the miracles were said to have been wrought, ever able distinctly to refute or detect them.[15] Where shall we find such a number of circumstances, agreeing to the corroboration of one fact? And what have we to oppose to such a cloud of witnesses, but the absolute impossibility or miraculous nature of the events, which they relate? And this surely, in the eyes of all reasonable people, will alone be regarded as a sufficient refutation.

Is the consequence just, because some human testimony has the utmost force and authority in some cases, when it relates the battle of PHILIPPI or PHARSALIA for instance; that therefore all kinds of testimony must, in all cases, have equal force and authority? Suppose that the CAESAREAN and POMPEIAN factions had, each of them, claimed the victory in these battles, and that the historians of each party had uniformly ascribed the advantage to their own side; how could mankind, at this distance, have been able to determine between them? The contrariety is equally strong between the miracles related by HERODOTUS or PLUTARCH, and those delivered by MARIANA, BEDE, or any monkish historian.

The wise lend a very academic faith to every report which favours the passion of the reporter; whether it magnifies his country, his family, or himself, or in any other way strikes in with his natural inclinations and propensities. But what greater temptation than to appear a missionary, a prophet, an ambassador from heaven? Who would not encounter many dangers and difficulties, in order to attain so sublime a character? Or if, by the help of vanity and a heated imagination, a man has first made a convert of himself, and entered seriously into the delusion; who ever scruples to make use of pious frauds, in support of so holy and meritorious a cause?

The smallest spark may here kindle into the greatest flame; because the materials are always prepared for it. The *avidum genus auricularum*[16] the gazing populace, receive greedily, without examination, whatever sooths superstition, and promotes wonder.

How many stories of this nature, have, in all ages, been detected and exploded in their infancy? How many more have been celebrated for a time, and have afterwards sunk into neglect and oblivion? Where such reports, therefore, fly about, the solution of the phenomenon is obvious; and we judge in conformity to regular experience and observation, when we account for it by the known and natural principles of credulity and delusion. And shall we, rather than have a recourse to so natural a solution, allow of a miraculous violation of the most established laws of nature?

I need not mention the difficulty of detecting a falsehood in any private or even public history, at the place, where it is said to happen; much more when the scene is removed to ever so small a distance. Even a court of judicature, with all the authority, accuracy, and judgment, which they can employ, find themselves often at a loss to distinguish between truth and falsehood in the most recent actions. But the matter never comes to any issue, if trusted to the common method of altercation and debate and flying rumours; especially when men's passions have taken part on either side.

In the infancy of new religions, the wise and learned commonly esteem the matter too inconsiderable to deserve their attention or regard. And when afterwards they would willingly detect the cheat, in order to undeceive the deluded multitude, the season is now past, and the records and witnesses, which might clear up the matter, have perished beyond recovery.

No means of detection remain, but those which must be drawn from the very testimony itself of the reporters: And these, though always sufficient with the judicious and knowing, are commonly too fine to fall under the comprehension of the vulgar.

Upon the whole, then, it appears, that no testimony for any kind of miracle [17]has ever amounted to a probability, much less to a proof; and that, even supposing it amounted to a proof, it would be opposed by another proof, derived from the very nature of the fact, which it would endeavour to establish. It is experience only, which gives authority to human testimony; and it is the same experience, which assures us of the laws of nature. When, therefore, these two kinds of experience are contrary, we have nothing to do but substract the one from the other, and embrace an opinion, either on one side or the other, with that assurance which arises from the remainder. But according to the principle here explained, this substraction, with regard to all popular religions, amounts to an entire annihilation; and therefore we may establish it as a maxim, that no human testimony can have such force as to prove a miracle, and make it a just foundation for any such system of religion.

[18]I beg the limitations here made may be remarked, when I say, that a miracle can never be proved, so as to be the foundation of a system of religion. For I own, that otherwise, there may possibly be miracles, or violations of the usual course of nature, of such a kind as to admit of proof from human testimony; though, perhaps, it will be impossible to find any such in all the records of history. Thus, suppose, all authors, in all languages, agree, that, from the first of JANUARY 1600, there was total darkness over the whole earth for eight days: Suppose that the tradition of this extraordinary event is still strong and lively among the people: That all travellers, who return from foreign countries, bring accounts of the same tradition, without the least variation or contradiction: It is evident that our present philosophers, instead of doubting the fact, ought to receive it as certain, and ought to search for the causes whence it might be derived.[19] The decay, corruption, and dissolution of nature, is an event rendered probable by so many analogies, that any phaenomenon, which seems to have a tendency towards catastrophe, comes within the reach of human testimony, if that testimony be very extensive and uniform.

But suppose, that all the historians who treat of ENGLAND, should agree, that, on the first of JANUARY 1600, Queen ELIZABETH dies; that both before and after her death she was seen by her physicians and the whole court, as is usual with persons of her rank; that her successor was acknowledged and proclaimed by the parliament; and that, after being interred a month, she again appeared, resumed the throne, and governed ENGLAND for three years: I must confess that I should be surprised at the occurrence of so many odd circumstances, but should not have the least inclination to believe so miraculous an event. I should not doubt of her pretended death, and of those other public circumstances that followed it: I should only assert it to have been pretended, and that it neither was, nor possibly could be real. You would in vain object to me the difficulty, and almost impossibility of deceiving the world in an affair of such consequence; the wisdom[20] and solid judgment of that renowned queen; with the little or advantage which she could reap from so poor an artifice: All this might astonish me; but I would still reply, that such the knavery and folly of men are such common phaenomena, that I should rather believe the most extraordinary events to arise from their concurrence, than admit of so signal a violation of the laws of nature.

But should this miracle be ascribed to any new system of religion; men, in all ages, have been so much imposed on by ridiculous stories of that kind, that this very circumstance would be a full proof of a cheat, and sufficient, with all men of sense, not only to make them reject the fact, but reject it without farther examination. Though the Being to whom the miracle is ascribed, be, in this case, Almighty, it does not, upon that account, become a whit more probable; since it is impossible for us to know the attributes or actions of such a Being, otherwise than from the experience which we have of his productions, in the usual course of nature. This still reduces us to past observation, and obliges us to compare the instances of the violation of truth in the testimony of men, with those of the violation of the laws of nature by miracles, in order to judge which of them is most likely and probable. As the violations of truth are more common in the testimony concerning religious miracles, than in that concerning any other matter of fact; this must diminish very much the authority of the former testimony, and make us form a general resolution, never to lend any attention to it, with whatever specious pretence it may be covered.

[21]Lord BACON seems to have embraced the same principles of reasoning. 'We ought,' says he, 'to make a collection or particular history of all monsters and prodigious births or productions, and in a word of every thing new, rare, and extraordinary in nature. But this must be done with the most severe scrutiny, lest we depart from truth. Above all, every relation must be considered as suspicious, which depends in any degree upon religion, as the prodigies of LIVY: And no less so, every thing that is to be found in the writers of natural magic or alchimy, or such authors, who seem, all of them, to have an unconquerable appetite for falsehood and fable.'[22]

I am the better pleased with the method of reasoning here delivered, as I think it may serve to confound those dangerous friends or disguised enemies to the *Christian Religion*, who have undertaken to defend it by the principles of human reason. Our most holy religion is founded on *Faith*, not on reason, and it is a sure method of exposing it to put it to such a trial as it is, by no means, fitted to endure. To make this more evident, let us examine those miracles, related in scripture; and not to lose ourselves in too wide a field, let us confine ourselves to such as we find in the *Pentateuch*, which we shall examine, according to the principles of those pretended Christians, not as the word or testimony of God himself, but as the production of a mere human writer and historian. Here then we are first to consider a book, presented to us by a barbarous and ignorant people, written in an age when they were still more barbarous, and in all probability long after the facts which it relates, corroborated by no concurring testimony, and resembling those fabulous accounts, which every nation gives of its origin. Upon reading this book, we find it full of prodigies and miracles. It gives an account of a state of the world and of human nature entirely different from the present: Of our fall from that state: Of the age of man, extended to near a thousand years: Of the destruction of the world by a deluge: Of the arbitrary choice of one people, as the favourites of heaven; and that people the countrymen of the author: Of their deliverance from bondage by prodigies the most astonishing imaginable: I desire any one to lay his hand upon his heart, and after a serious consideration declare, whether he thinks that the falsehood of such a book, supported by such a testimony, would be more extraordinary and miraculous than all the miracles it relates; which is, however, necessary to make it be received, according to the measures of probability above established.

What we have said of miracles may be applied, without any variation, to prophecies; and indeed, all prophecies are real miracles, and as such only, can be admitted as proofs of any revelation. If it did not exceed the capacity of human nature to foretel future events, it would be absurd to employ any prophecy as an argument for a divine mission or authority from heaven. So that upon the whole, we may conclude, that the *Christian Religion* not only was at first attended with miracles, but even at this day cannot be believed by any reasonable person without one. Mere reason is insufficient to convince us of its veracity: And whoever is moved by *Faith* to assent to it, is conscious of a continued miracle in his own person, which subverts all the principles of his understanding, and gives him a determination to believe what is most contrary to custom and experience.

### Notes

Edition E. *Philosophical Essays Concerning Human Understanding.* London: A Millar, 1748.
Edition F. Ditto. 2nd ed. London: Printed for M. Cooper, MDCCLI.
Edition K. *Essays and Treatises on Several Subjects.* London: A Millar, MDCCLIII–IV.
Edition M. *Essays and Treatises on Several Subjects.* London: A Millar, MDCCLVIII.
Edition N. Ditto. MDCCLX.
Edition O. Ditto. MDCCLXIV.
Edition P. Ditto. Printed for A. Millar, A. Kincaid, J. Bell, and A. Donaldson in Edinburgh. MDCCLXVIII.
Edition Q. Ditto. Printed for T. Cadell, MDCCLXX.

1. [In all prophane history: Editions E and F.]
2. [Editions E to K substitute: Did not Men's Imagination naturally follow their Memory.]
3. [This paragraph was added in Edition K.]
4. PLUTARCH, in vita Catonis Min. 19.
5. [This paragraph was added in Edition F.]
6. NO INDIAN, it is evident, could have experience that water did not freeze in cold climates. This is placing nature in a situation quite unknown to him; and it is impossible for him to tell *a priori* what will result from it. It is making a new experiment, the consequence of which is always uncertain. One may sometime conjecture from analogy what will follow; but still this is but conjecture. And it must be confessed, that, in the present case of freezing, the event follows contrary to the rules of analogy, and is such as a rational INDIAN would not look for. The operations of cold upon water are not gradual, according to the degrees of cold; but

whenever it come to the freezing point, the water passes in a moment, from the utmost liquidity to perfect hardness. Such an event, therefore, may be denominated *extraordinary*, and requires a pretty strong testimony, to render it credible to people in a warm climate: But still it is not *miraculous*, nor contrary to uniform experience of the course of nature in cases where all the circumstances are the same. The inhabitants of SUMATRA have always seen water fluid in their own climate, and the freezing of their rivers ought to be deemed a prodigy: But they never saw water in MOSCOVY during the winter; and therefore they cannot reasonably be positive what would there be the consequence. [This note first appears in the last page of Edition F, with the preface: The distance of the Author from the Press is the Cause, why the following Passage arriv'd not in time to be inserted in its proper Place.]

7. Sometimes an event may not, *in itself, seem* to be contrary to the laws of nature, and yet, if it were real, it might, by reason of some Circumstances, be denominated a miracle; because, in *fact*, it is contrary to these laws. Thus if a person, claiming a divine authority, should command a sick person to be well, a healthful man to fall down dead, the clouds to pour rain, the winds to blow, in short, should order many natural events, which immediately follow upon his command; these might justly be esteemed miracles, because they are really, in this case, contrary to the laws of nature. For if any suspicion remain, that the event and command concurred by accident, there is no miracle and no transgression of the laws of nature. If this suspicion be removed, there is evidently a miracle, and a transgression of these laws; because nothing can be more contrary to nature than that the voice or command of a man should have such an influence. A miracle may be accurately defined, *a transgression of a law of nature by a particular volition of the Deity, or by the interposition of some invisible agent.* A miracle may either be discoverable by men or not. This alters not its nature and essence. The raising of a house or ship into the air is a visible miracle. The raising of a feather, when the wind wants ever so little a force requisite for that purpose, is as real a miracle, though not so sensible with regard to us.

8. [In any History: Editions E and F.]

9. [This paragraph was printed as a note in Editions E to P.]

10. [Cunning impostor: Editions E to P.]

11. [Editions E to P append the following note: It may here, perhaps, be objected, that I proceed rashly, and form my notions of ALEXANDER merely from the account given of him by LUCIAN, a professed enemy. It were, indeed, to be wished, that some of the accounts published by his followers and accomplices had remained. The opposition and contrast between the character and conduct of the same man, as drawn by friend or enemy, is as strong, even in common life, much more in these religious matters, as that betwixt any two men in the world, betwixt ALEXANDER and St. PAUL, for instance. See a letter to GILBERT WEST, Esq; on the conversion and apostleship pf St. PAUL.]

12. Hist. Lib. v. cap. 8. SUETONIUS gives nearly the same account *in vita* VESP. 7. [The reference to Suetonius was added in the Eratta to Edition F.].

13. [20: Editions E to N.]

14. [Editions E and F substitute: And when the Cardinal examin'd it, he found it to be a true natural Leg, like the other.]

15. This book was writ by Mons. MONTERON, counsellor or judge of the par-
hammet of PARIS, a man of a figure and character, who was also a
martyr to the cause, and is now said to be somewhere in a dungeon on
account of his book.

There is another book in three volumes (called *Recueil des Miracles de
l'Abbé* PARIS) giving an account of many of these miracles, and accompanied with prefatory discourses, which are very well written. There runs,
however, through the whole of these a ridiculous comparison between
the miracles of our Saviour and those of the Abbé; wherein it is asserted,
that the evidence for the latter is equal to that for the former: As if the
testimony of men could ever be put in the balance with that of God
himself, who conducted the pen of the inspired writers. If these writers,
indeed, were to be considered merely as human testimony, the FRENCH
author is very moderate in his comparison: since he might, with some
appearance of reason, pretend, that the JANSENIST miracles much surpass
the other ill evidence and authority. The following circumstances are
drawn from authentic papers, inserted in the above-mentioned book.

Many of the miracles of Abbé PARIS were proved immediately by witnesses before the officiality or bishop's court at PARIS, under the eye of
cardinal NOAILLES, whose character for integrity and capacity was never
contested even by his enemies.

His [M. de Ventimille,-ED] successor in the archbishopric was an enemy
to the JANSENISTS, and for that reason promoted to the see by the court.
Yet 22 rectors or *curés* of PARIS with infinite earnestness, press him to
examine those miracles, which they assert to be known to the whole
world, and undisputably certain: But he wisely forbore.

The MOLINIST party had tried to discredit these miracles in one instance, that of Mademoiselle le FRANC. But, besides that their proceedings
were in many respects the most irregular in the world, particularly in
citing only a few of the JANSENIST witnesses, whom they tampered with:
Besides this, I say, they soon found themselves overwhelmed by a cloud
of new witnesses, one hundred and twenty in number, most of them
persons of credit and substance in PARIS, who gave oath for the miracle.
This was accompanied with a solemn and earnest appeal to the parliament. But the parliament were forbidden by authority to meddle in the
affair. It was at last observed, that where men are heated by zeal and
enthusiasm, there is no degree of human testimony so strong as may not
be procured for the greatest absurdity: And those who will be so silly as
to examine the affair by that medium, and seek particular flaw in the
testimony, are almost sure to be confounded. It must be a miserable imposture, indeed, that does not prevail in that contest.

All who have been in FRANCE about that time have heard of the reputation of Mons. HERAUT, the *lieutenant de Police*, whose vigilance, penetration, activity, and extensive intelligence have been much talked of.
This magistrate, who by the nature of his office is almost absolute, was
invested with full powers, on purpose to suppress or discredit these miracles; and he frequently seized immediately, and examined the witnesses
and subjects of them: But never could reach any thing satisfactory
against them.

In the case of Mademoiselle THIBAUT he sent the famous DE SYLVA to
examine her; whose evidence is very curious. The physician declares, that

it was impossible she could have been so ill as was proved by witnesses; because it was impossible she could, in so short a time, have recovered so perfectly as he found her. He reasoned, like a man of sense, from natural causes; but the opposite party told him that the whole was a miracle, and that his evidence was the very best proof of it.

The MOLINISTS were in a sad dilemma. They durst not assert the absolute insufficiency of human evidence, to prove a miracle. They were obliged to say, that these miracles were wrought by witchcraft and the devil. But they were told, that this was the resource of the JEWS of old.

No JANSENIST was ever embarrassed to account for the cessation of the miracles, when the church-yard was shut up by the king's edict. It was the touch of the tomb, which produced these extraordinary effects, and when no one could approach the tomb, no effects could be expected. God, indeed, could have thrown down the walls in a moment; but he is master of his own graces and works, and it belongs not to us to account for them. He did not throw down the walls of every city like those of JERICHO, on the sounding of the rams' horns, nor break up the prison of every apostle, like that of St. PAUL.

No less a man, than the Duc de CHATILLION, a duke and peer of FRANCE, of the highest rank and family, gives evidence of a miraculous cure, performed upon a servant of his, who had lived several years in his house with a visible and palpable infirmity.

I shall conclude with observing, that no clergy are more celebrated for strictness of life and manners than the secular clergy of FRANCE, particularly the rectors or cures of PARIS, who bear testimony to these impostures.

The learning, genius, and probity of the gentlemen, and the austerity of the nuns of PORT-ROYAL, have been much celebrated all over EUROPE. Yet they all give evidence for a miracle, wrought on the niece of the famous PASCAL, whose sanctity of life, as well as extraordinary capacity, is well known. [Edition F adds: Tho' *he* also was a Believer, in that and in many other Miracles, which he had less opportunity of being inform'd of. See his Life. Here Edition F. stops.] The famous RACINE gives an account of this miracle in his famous history of PORT-ROYAL, and fortifies it with all the proofs, which a multitude of nuns, priests, physicians, and men of the world, all of them of undoubted credit, could bestow upon it. Several men of letters, particularly the bishop of TOURNAY, thought this miracle so certain, as to employ it in the refutation of atheists and free-thinkers. The queen-regent of FRANCE, who was extremely prejudiced against the PORT-ROYAL, sent her own physician to examine the miracle, who returned an absolute convert. In short, the supernatural cure was so uncontestable, that it saved, for a time, that famous monastery from the ruin with which it was threatened by the JESUITS. Had it been a cheat, it had certainly been detected by such sagacious and powerful antagonists, and must have hastened the ruin of the contrivers. Our divines, who can build up a formidable castle from such despicable materials, what a prodigious fabric could they have reared from these and many other circumstances, which I have not mentioned! How often would the great names of PASCAL, RACINE, ARNAUD, NICOLE, have resounded in our ears? But if they be wise, they had better adopt the miracle, as being more worth, a thousand times, than all the rest of their collection. Besides, it may serve very much to their purpose. For that miracle was really performed by the touch of an authentic holy prickle of the holy thorn, which composed the holy crown, which, &c. [This note was added in Edition F.]

16. LUCRET. iv. 594. [This reference was added in Edition F, and the mistranslation was inserted in the text in Edition M.]

17. [Can ever possibly amount to: Editions E and F.]

18. [This and the three following paragraphs are given as a note in Editions E to P.]

19. [This sentence was added in Edition K.]

20. [And integrity: Editions E to P.]

21. [This paragraph, which is not found in Editions E and F, is also put in the note in Editions K to P. It is quoted in Latin in Editions K to Q.]

22. Nov. Org. lib. ii. aph. 29.

## *Richard Price*, Four Dissertations *(2d ed. 1768)*, Dissertation IV, *"On the Importance of Christianity and the Nature of Historical Evidence, and Miracles"*

## Section I

*Introductory Observations, relating to the importance of Christianity, Its Evidences, and the Objections which have been made to it.*

One of the objections that deserves most to be attended to, is that taken from the nature of the principal facts recorded in the scriptures. These are *miraculous*, and, as such, (it has been said) "have a *particular incredibility* in them, which does not belong to *common* events. When we look into the Bible, we find ourselves transported, as it were, into a new world, where the course of nature is altered, and every thing is different from what we have been used to observe. Could we, in any other case, receive a book filled with visions and prodigies, and containing so much of the *marvellous?* Ought not such a book to startle our minds? Or can there be any evidence sufficient to establish its authority?"—Some have gone so far in this way of objecting, as to assert in general, that all relations of facts which contradict experience, or imply a deviation from the usual course of nature, are their own confutation, and should be at once rejected as incapable of proof, and impossible to be true.—One cannot be better employed than in inquiring how far such sentiments are right, and what regard is really due to *testimony*, when its reports do not agree with *experience*. I shall endeavour to state this matter as accurately as possible, by entering into a critical examination of the grounds of belief in this case, and of the nature and force of historical evidence.

In what follows, I shall confine myself to the examination of the *principles* on which the objection I have mentioned is founded. When these are proved to be fallacious, the way will be open to an easier admission of the *direct evidences* of christianity, and they will operate with greater force.—It is well known, that this objection has lately been urged in all its strength by Mr. *Hume,* a writer whose genius and abilities are so distinguished, as to be above any of *my* commendations. Several excellent answers have been published[1]; and it is not without some pain, after what has been so well and so effectually said by others, that I determine to take up this subject. I imagine, however, that it admits of further discussion, and that there remain still some observations to be made, which have not been enough attended to.—Before I proceed, it will be proper to give a more distinct and full account of the objection to be considered.

## Section II

### The Nature and Grounds of the Regard due to Experience and to the Evidence of Testimony, stated and compared.

"Experience, we have been told, is the ground of the credit we give to *human testimony.* We have found, in past instances, that men have informed us right, and therefore, are disposed to believe them in future instances. But this experience is by no means constant; for we often find that men prevaricate and deceive.—On the other hand: What assures us of those laws of nature, in the violation of which the notion of a miracle consists, is, in like manner, experience. But, this is an experience that has never been interrupted. We have never been deceived in our expectations, that the dead will not come to life, or that the command of a man will not immediately cure a disease. There arises, therefore, from hence, a proof against accounts of miracles which is the strongest of the kind possible, and to believe such accounts on the authority of human testimony, is to prefer a weaker proof to a stronger; to leave a guide that *never* has deceived us, in order to follow one that has *often* deceived us; or to receive, upon the credit of an experience that is *weak* and *variable,* what is contrary to *invariable* experience."

In other words: "A miracle is an event, from the nature of it, inconsistent with all the experience we ever had, and in the highest degree incredible and extraordinary. In the falsehood of testimony, on the contrary, there is no such inconsistency, nor any such incredibility, scarcely any thing being more common. No regard, therefore, can be due to the latter, when it is applied as a proof of the former.—According to this reasoning, we are always to compare the improbability of a fact, with the improbability of the falsehood of the testimony which asserts it, and to determine our assent to that side on which the least improbability lies. Or, in the case of miracles, we are to consider which is most likely, that such events should happen, or that men should either deceive or be deceived. And, as there is nothing more unlikely than the former, or much more common than the latter, particularly, where religion is concerned; it will be right to form a *general resolution, never to lend any attention to accounts of miracles, with whatever specious pretexts they may be covered.*[2]

"It is," says Mr. Hume, "*a maxim worthy of our attention, that no testimony is sufficient to establish a miracle, unless the testimony be of such a kind, that its falsehood would be more miraculous than the fact which it endeavours to establish. And even in that case, there is a mutual destruction of arguments, and the superior only gives us an assurance suitable to that degree of force, which remains after deducting the inferior. When any one tells me that he saw a dead man restored to life, I immediately consider with myself, whether it be more probable that the person should either deceive or be deceived, or that the fact he relates should really have happened. I weigh the one miracle against the other, and according to the superiority which I discover, I pronounce my decision, and always reject the greater miracle. If the falsehood of his testimony would be more miraculous than the event which he relates, then, and not till then, can he pretend to command my belief or opinion.*"[3]—For such reasons as these, Mr. Hume asserts, "*That the evidence of testimony, when applied to a miracle, carries falsehood upon the very face of it, and is more properly a subject of derision than of argument;*[4] and that whoever believes the truth of the christian religion, *is conscious of a continued miracle in his own person, which subverts all the principles of his understanding, and gives him a determination to believe what is most contrary to custom and experience.*"[5]

This is the objection in its complete force. It has, we see, a plausible appearance, and is urged with much confidence. But I cannot hesitate in asserting that it is founded on false principles; and, I think, this must appear to be true, to any one who will bestow attention on the following observations.

The principles on which this objection is built are chiefly, "That the credit we give to testimony, is derived *solely* from experience;" "That a miracle is a fact *contrary* to experience;" "That the previous improbability of a fact is a proof against it, diminishing, in proportion to the degree of it, the proof from testimony for it;" and "That no testimony should ever gain credit to an event, unless it is more extraordinary that it should be false, than that the event should have happened." I will, as briefly as possible, examine each of these assertions in the order in which they have been now mentioned.

With this view it is necessary first to consider the nature and the foundation of that assurance which experience gives us of the laws of nature. This assurance is nothing but the conviction we have, that future events will be agreeable to what we have hitherto found to be the course of nature, or the *expectation* arising in us, upon having observed that an event has happened in former experiments, that it will happen again in *future* experiments. This expectation has been represented as one of the greatest mysteries, and the result of an ingenious and elaborate disquisition about it is, that it cannot be founded on any reason, and consists only in an association of ideas derived from habit, or a disposition in our imaginations to pass from the idea of one object to the idea of another which we have found to be its usual attendant.[6] But surely, never before were such difficulties raised on a point so plain.—If I was to draw a slip of paper out of a wheel, where I knew there were more white than black papers, I should intuitively see, that there was a probability of drawing a white paper, and therefore should *expect* this; and he who should make a mystery of such an expectation, or apprehend any difficulty in accounting for it, would not deserve to be seriously argued with.—In like manner; if, out of a wheel, the particular contents of which I am ignorant of, I should draw a white paper a hundred times together, I should see that it was probable, that it had in it more white papers than black, and therefore should expect to draw a white paper the next trial. There is no more difficulty in this case than in the former; and it is equally absurd in both cases to ascribe the *expectation,* not to *knowledge,* but to *instinct.*—The case of our assurance of the laws of nature, as far as we are ignorant of the causes that operate in nature, is exactly the same with this. An experiment which has often succeeded, we expect to succeed again, because we perceive intuitively, that such a constancy of event must proceed from something in the constitution of natural causes, disposing them to produce it; nor will it be possible to deny this, till it can be proved, that it is not a first principle of reason, that of every thing that comes to pass there must be some account or cause; or, that a constant re-currency of the same event is not a fact which requires any cause.—In a word: We trust experience, and expect that the future should resemble the past in the course of nature, for the very same reason that, supporting ourselves otherwise in the dark, we should conclude that a dye which has turned an ace oftenest in *past* trials is mostly marked with aces, and consequently should expect, that it will go on to turn the same number oftenest in *future* trials.—The ground of the expectation produced by experience being this, it is obvious that it will always be weaker or stronger, in proportion to the greater or less constancy and uniformity of our experience. Thus from the happening of an event in every trial a million of times, we should conclude more confidently, that it will happen again the next trial, than if it had happened less frequently, or if in some of these instances it had failed. The plain reason is, that in the former case it would appear that the causes producing the event are probably of a more fixed-nature, and less liable to be counteracted by opposite causes.—It must, however, be remembered, that the greatest uniformity and frequency of experience will not afford a proper *proof,* that an event will happen in a future trial, or even render it so much as probable, that it will *always* happen in all future trials.—In order to explain this, let us suppose a solid which, for ought we know, may be constituted in any one of an infinity of different ways, and that we can judge of it only from experiments made in throwing it. The oftener we suppose ourselves to have seen it turn the same face, the more we should reckon upon its turning the same face, when thrown next. But though we knew, that it had turned the same face in every trial a million of times, there would be no *certainty*, that it would turn this face again in any particular future trial, nor even the least *probability*, that it would *never* turn any other face. What would appear would be only, that it was *likely*, that it had about a million and a half more of these sides than of all others;[7] or, that its nature was such as disposed it to turn this side oftener, in this proportion, than any other; not that it had no other sides, or that it would never turn any others. In reality, there would be the greatest probability against this.—These observations are applicable in the exactest manner, to what passes in the course of nature, as far as *experience* is our guide. Upon observing, that any natural event has happened often or invariably, we have only reason to expect that it will happen again, with an assurance proportioned to the frequency of our observations. But, we have no *absolute proof* that it will happen again in any particular future trial; nor the least reason to believe that it will always happen.[8] For ought we know, there may be occasions on which it will fail, and secret causes in the frame of things which *sometimes* may counteract those by which it is produced.

But to say no more at present of this. Let us, in the next place, consider what is the ground of the regard we pay to *human testimony*.—We may, I think, see plainly, that it is not experience only; meaning, all along, that kind of experience to which we owe our expectation of natural events, the causes of which are unknown to us. Were this the case, the regard we ought to pay to testimony, would be in proportion to the number of instances, in which we have found, that it has given us right information, compared with those in which it has deceived us; and it might be calculated in the same manner with the regard due to any conclusions derived from induction. But this is by no means the truth. One action, or one conversation with a man, may convince us of his integrity and induce us to believe his testimony, though we had never, in a single instance, experienced his veracity. His manner of telling his story, its being corroborated by other testimony, and various particulars in the nature and circumstances of it, may satisfy us that it must be true. We feel in ourselves that a regard to truth is one principle in human nature; and we know, that there must be such a principle in every reasonable being, and that there is a necessary repugnancy between the perception of moral distinctions and deliberate falsehood. To this, chiefly, is owing the credit we give to human testimony. And from hence, in particular, must be derived our belief of veracity in the Deity.—It might be shown here in many ways, that there is a great difference between the conviction produced by testimony, and the conviction produced by experience. But I will content myself with just taking notice, that the one is capable of being carried much higher than the other. When any events, in the course of nature, have often happened, we are sure properly, of nothing but the past fact. Nor, I think, is there in general, antecedently to their happening, any comparison between the assurance we have that they will happen, and that which we have of many facts the knowledge of which we derive from testimony. For example; we are not so certain that the tide will go on to ebb and flow, and the sun to rise and set in the manner they have hitherto done, a year longer, as we are that there has been such a man as *Alexander*, or such an empire as the *Roman*.[9]

From these observations it follows, that to use *testimony* to prove a *miracle* implies no absurdity. 'Tis not using a *feebler* experience to overthrow another of the same kind, which is *stronger:* But, using an argument to establish an event, which yields a direct and positive proof and is capable of producing the strongest conviction to overthrow another founded on different principles, and which, at best, can prove no more than that, previously to the event, there would have appeared to us a presumption against its happening.

What I now mean will be greatly confirmed by observing, that a miracle cannot, with strict propriety, be styled an event *contrary* to experience. This is the second of the assertions in Mr. *Hume*'s argument, which I have before mentioned, and to which there is, I think, reason to object. A miracle is more properly an event *different* from experience than *contrary* to it. Were I to see a tempest calmed instantaneously by the word of a man, all my past experience would remain the same; and were I to affirm that I saw what was contrary to it, I could only mean, that I saw what I never before had any experience of. In like manner; was I to be assured by eye witnesses that, on a particular occasion, some event, different from the usual course of things, had happened, testimony, in this case, would afford direct and peremptory evidence for the fact. But what information would experience give?—It would only tell me what happened on other occasions, and in other instances. Its evidence, therefore, would be entirely negative.[10] It would afford no proper proof that the event did not happen, for it can be no part of any one's experience, that the course of nature will continue always the same.—It cannot then be proper to assert (as Mr. *Hume*[11] does) that, in every case of a miracle supported by testimony, there is a contest of two opposite experiences, the strongest of which ought always to determine our judgments.

But this leads me to take notice of the fundamental error in this argument: an error which, I fancy, every person must be sensible of when it is mentioned, and for the sake of pointing out which chiefly this dissertation is written.—The error I mean is contained in the assertion, that "if, previously to an event, there was a greater probability *against* its happening, than there is *for* the truth of the testimony endeavoring to establish it, the former destroys the latter, and renders the event unlikely to have happened in proportion to its superiority." That this is a fundamental point in Mr. *Hume*'s objection must be apparent to those who have considered it. By the contest between two opposite experiences in miraculous facts supported by testimony, the greatest of which always destroys the other as far as its force goes; he cannot consistently mean any thing but this. One of the opposite experiences must be that which acquaints us with the course of nature, and by which, as before explained, it is rendered probable, in proportion to the number of instances in which an event has happened, that it will happen in future trials. The other must be that from whence the credit we give to testimony is derived, which, according to Mr. *Hume*, being our observation of the usual conformity of facts to the reports of witnesses, makes it probable that any event reported by witnesses has happened, in proportion to what we have experienced of this conformity. Now, as in the case of miraculous facts these probabilities oppose one another, and the greatest, according to Mr. Hume, must be the first, because the experience which produces it is constant and invariable; it follows, that there must be always a great overbalance of evidence against their reality. He seems to lay it down as a general maxim, that if it is more improbable that any fact should have really happened, than that men should either deceive or be deceived, it should be rejected by us.—But, it must be needless to take any pains to show, that the turning point in Mr. Hume's argument is that which I have mentioned; or, in other words, the principle, that no testimony should engage our belief, except the improbability in the falsehood of it is greater than that in the event which it attests.[12]

In order to make it appear that this is an error, what I desire may be considered is, the degree of improbability which there is against almost all the most common facts, independently of the evidence of testimony for them. In many cases of particular histories which are immediately believed upon the slightest testimony, there would have appeared to us, previously to this testimony, an improbability of almost infinity to one against their reality, as any one must perceive, who will think how sure he is of the falsehood of all facts that have *no* evidence to support them, or which he has only *imagined* to himself. It is then very common for the slightest testimony to overcome an almost infinite improbability.

To make this more evident: Let us suppose, that testimony informed us rightly ten times to one in which it deceived us; and that there was nothing to direct our judgments concerning the regard due to witnesses, besides the degree of conformity which we have experienced in past events to their reports. In this case, there would be the probability of ten to one for the reality of every fact supported by testimony. Suppose then that it informs me of the success of a person in an affair, against the success of which there was the probability of a hundred to one, or of any other event previously improbable in this proportion. I ask, What, on this supposition, would be, on the whole, the probability that the event really happened? Would the right way of computing be, to compare the probability of the truth of the testimony with the probability that the event would not happen, and to reject the event with a confidence proportioned to the superiority of the latter above the former? This Mr. *Hume* directs; but certainly contrary to all reason.—The truth is, that the testimony would give the probability of ten to one to the event, unabated by the supposed probability against it. And one reason of this is, that the very experience which teaches us to give credit to testimony, is an experience by which we have found, that it has informed us rightly concerning facts, in which there would have appeared to us, previously, a great improbability.

But to be yet more explicit; Let us suppose the event reported by testimony to be, that a particular side of a die was thrown twice in two trials, and that the testimony is of such a nature that it has as often informed us wrong as right. In this case, there would plainly be an equal chance for the reality of the event, though, previously, there was the probability of thirty-five to one against it: And every one would see, that it would be absurd to say, that there being so considerable a probability against the event, and no probability at all for the truth of the testimony; or, that having had much more frequent experience that two trials have not turned up the same face of a die, than of the conformity of facts to the supposed testimony, therefore, no regard is due to the testimony.— An evidence that is *often* connected with truth, though not *oftener* than with falsehood, is real evidence, and deserves regard. To reject such evidence would be to fall *often* into error, whatever improbabilities may attend the events to which it is applied; and to assert the contrary, would be to assert a manifest contradiction.

The end of a news-paper confines it, in a great measure, to the relation of such facts as are uncommon. Suppose that it reports truth only twice in three times, and that there are *nine* such uncommon facts reported by it as, that a certain person is alive in his hundredth year, that another was struck dead by lightning, or that a woman has been delivered of three children at a birth; Would it be right to reject *all* these facts, because more extraordinary than the report of falsehood by the news-paper? To say this, would be to say, that what, by supposition, reports truth *six* times in *nine*, does not report truth *once* in nine times.

But let us take a higher case of this kind. The improbability of drawing a lottery in any particular assigned manner, independently of the evidence of testimony, or of our own senses, acquainting us that it *has* been drawn in that manner, is such as exceeds all conception.[13] And yet the most common testimony is sufficient to put us out of doubt about it. Suppose here a person was to reject the evidence offered him on the pretence, that the improbability of the falsehood of it is almost infinitely less than that of the event;[14] or, suppose, that universally a person was to reject all accounts which he reads or hears of facts which are more uncommon, than it is that he should read or hear what is false: What would be thought of such a person? How soon would he be made to see and acknowledge his mistake?

In the case I have mentioned of a news-paper supposed to report truth twice in three times, the odds of *two to one*, would overcome the odds of *thousands to one*. This is no more than saying, that an evidence which, in cases where there were great odds against an event, has been found true twice in three times, *is* true in such cases twice in three times, and communicates the probability of 2 to 1 to the event to which it is applied. Every one will see that this is an assertion so plainly true as to be trifling; and yet the principal part of what I am here asserting may be reduced to it.—The previous improbability of most common facts, that is, the improbability we should see to be in them were they unconnected with all evidence for them, is, I have observed, very great. We have, generally, found testimony right, when applied to such facts. It is therefore reasonable to give credit to it when so applied, tho' not so likely to be true as it was that the facts should not happen: And saying this, is only saying, that an evidence *generally* right ought to be received as being so, notwithstanding improbabilities by which we have found it not be to affected; I will add, and by which too we know that it is its *nature* not to be affected.

What has been last said requires explanation; and it will be proper to dwell a little upon it, in order more fully to show the nature of historical evidence, and the reason and truth of all I have said concerning it.— What I desire may be here attended to is chiefly the following assertion, "that improbabilities *as such* do not lessen the capacity of testimony to report truth."—The only causes of falsehood in testimony are the intention to deceive, and the danger of being deceived. Setting aside the former, let us, for the sake of greater precision, confine our views at present to the latter, or suppose a case where there are no motives to deceive, and where therefore the only source of mis-information from testimony is the danger of being deceived. Let us likewise suppose that this danger is such as makes testimony liable to be wrong once in ten times. Now, I say, that such testimony would communicate its own probability to *every* event reported by it of which sense is *equally* a judge, whether the odds against that event, or the previous improbability in it is more or less.—For instance. A person, who in the dark should take a black-ball out of a heap of 67 white-balls, and 33 black would do what there were the odds of two to one against his doing. He, therefore, who should report this, would report an event which was improbable as two to one; and a person who should affirm that there was no improbability to be removed by the report, would affirm a palpable falsehood. Now, to this fact, the testimony I have supposed, would give the probability of *nine* to one, notwithstanding its previous improbability. Such a testimony would do the same if its report was, that a black-ball had been in the same manner taken out of a heap containing 90 white-balls and ten black, or 99 white and one black. That is, it would afford equal evidence whether the improbability of the event was 2 to 1, 10 to 1, or 99 to 1.—The like will appear, if we suppose the reports of such a testimony applied to the particular faces thrown with a set of dies. It would make no difference, whether its reports were applied to the faces thrown with a set of dies of 6 sides or a thousand sides, or to any *different* faces thrown with them, or any *coincidence* of faces. Supposing any considerable number of such reports, the nature of the thing implies, that an equal proportion of them would be found to be true in either case; because, by supposition, however different the improbabilities are, the only cause of mis-information, namely the danger of a deception of the senses, does not operate more in one case than in the other.—In other words. The improbabilities I mean, being no hindrance to the perceptions of sense, make no opposition to the testimony of a witness who reports honestly from sense; and, therefore, saying that such a testimony, tho' the probability of its own truth is but 9 to 1, will overcome equally an improbability of 2 to 1, 10 to 1, or 99 to 1, is no more than saying, that it is equally an over-match for any one of a number of things, by which it is not opposed.—In short. TESTIMONY is truly no more than SENSE at second-hand; and improbabilities, in the circumstances now supposed, can have no more effect on the evidence of the one, than on the evidence of the other.

It is obvious that similar observations might be made on the other cause which I have mentioned of falsehood in testimony. If in any case it cannot be supposed that a witness is deceived, his report will give an event that precise degree of probability which there is of his not intending to deceive, be the event what it will.

A due attention to these observations will, I think, show the reason of the little effect which, in numberless instances, very great previous improbabilities have, when set against the weakest direct testimony. No one can be at a loss to account for this where he has the evidence of *sense*. It appears that there is no greater difficulty in accounting for it, where we have the evidence of *testimony*.

It should be remembered, that nothing I have said implies, that improbabilities ought never to have any influence on our opinion of testimony. Improbabilities, I have observed, *as such*, do not affect the *capacity* of testimony to report truth. They have no *direct* and necessary operation upon it, and should not be considered as a *counter-evidence* invalidating, in proportion to their degree, its reports.—But tho' this is true, it by no means follows, that they may not in many circumstances affect the *credit* of testimony, or cause us to question its veracity. They have sometimes this effect on even the[15] reports on sense, and, therefore, may also on the reports of testimony. This will happen, first, when they are of such a nature as to carry the appearance of *impossibilities*. Every such appearance is indeed properly a counter-evidence; and testimony, when applied in such circumstances, cannot gain credit any further than there is a greater probability of its truth, than there is of the impossibility of the fact. Thus; if I was to hear a report, that a person was in *one* place at a time when I apprehended him to be in *another*, I could not give my assent till it appeared, that I had less reason for thinking myself right in this apprehension, than for believing the report. The same is true in all cases where seeming impossibilities or inconsistencies are reported. But, between *impossibilities* and *improbabilities*, however apt we may be to confound them, there is an infinite difference; and no conclusion can be drawn from the one to the other. There are few of the most *incredible* facts that can, with any reason, be called *impossible*. With respect to *miracles*, particularly, there are no arguments which have a tendency to prove this concerning them; or were it even true, that there are such arguments, their utmost effect, agreeably to the observation just made, would be, not to *destroy* the evidence of christianity, but to *counter-balance* it; and there might be still reason to believe christianity, unless it appeared that their force was such as to *outweigh* the force of the evidence for it. Testimony sometimes has convinced men of facts which they judged to be impossible; that is, it has convinced them that they were wrong in this opinion. Kindling spirits by a touch from ice would appear to a common person, impossible. The evidence of sense, however, would immediately convince him of the contrary; and from the preceding reasoning, I think, it appears, that there is nothing which sense is capable of proving that testimony may not also prove.

But, *Secondly*, The chief reason of the effect of improbabilities on our regard to testimony is, their tendency to influence the principles of deceit in the human mind. They have *of themselves*, I have said, no effect on the perceptions of sense, and therefore none on any faithful reports from sense. They may, however, *when perceived*, lead us to question the faithfulness of a report, and give just ground to suspect a design to misrepresent or exaggerate. A *given probability* of testimony communicates itself always entire to an event; but an event may be of such a nature as to lead us to doubt, whether there is that probability or not.—My meaning here will be explained by the following considerations.

Whenever any particular improbabilities appear, or a fact has any thing of the air of the marvellous, the passions are necessarily engaged, and we know that a temptation to deceive takes place in order to draw attention and excite wonder. On the contrary; when a fact is such as not at all to *interest*, or to give any room for imagining that men can intend deceit, we immediately believe it, without minding any previous improbabilities. It is for this reason, that we easily believe any story of a common nature, however complicated, tho' improbable, when the support of testimony is taken from it, almost as infinity to one. But when a story is told us, which is attended with any circumstances not common, or in any way calculated to produce surprize, we place ourselves on our guard, and very reasonably give our assent with caution, because we see that in this case there is room for fearing the operation of the principles of deceit.—Thus; were we to receive an account that number 1500 was the *first* drawn in a lottery, we should immediately believe it; but were we to hear that number 1 was the *first* drawn, we should hesitate and doubt, tho' the improbability of the event gives no more reason for hesitation in the one case than the other; it being certainly no more unlikely, that number 1 should be *first* drawn, than number 1500.

Were we sure in instances of this kind, that the story which surprizes, and the story which does not surprize, came to us from persons who had no more thought of deceiving in one case than in the other, we should in both cases give our assent with equal readiness; and it would be unreasonable to do otherwise. For instance; were a person to tell us that, in passing through Guildhall at the time of drawing a lottery, he happened to hear his age, the day of the month, and the date of the year drawn together, we should scarcely believe him, tho' we know that he was not more unlikely to hear these numbers drawn, than any other particular numbers. But if the same person was only to tell us the numbers themselves, and the co-incidence which strikes us was entirely our own discovery, we should have just the same reason for believing his account, as if there had been no such co-incidence. In like manner; if before the beginning of drawing a lottery, we suppose a wager laid in a company, that a particular number shall be first drawn, and if afterwards one who only knows of the wager, without being any way interested in it, should come and report to the company that he had heard that very number first drawn, he would not easily gain credit. But if a stranger, ignorant of the wager, was to come accidentally, and to make the same report, he would be believed. The reason is obvious. It would appear that probably the last of these reporters had nothing but the reality of the fact to lead him to report this number rather than any other; whereas the contrary would appear to be true of the other.

These observations may be applied to every case in which historical evidence is concerned. A *given* force of testimony never wants ability to produce belief proportioned to its degree; but the situation of reporters and the circumstances of facts may be such as may render us doubtful whether that *given force* is *really* applied. As far as it appears that there is no ground for any doubts of this kind, we are equally forced to believe in all cases. Were we even to receive an account that a lottery had been drawn in the very order of the numbers, in a manner which gave us as little reason to suspect the danger of mistake and deceit, as there is when we are informed that it has been drawn in any other order, we should be obliged to give our assent.

All that has been here asserted may be justly applied to the case of miracles reported by testimony.—Uncommon facts, *as such*, are not less subject to the cognizance of *sense* than the most ordinary. It is as competent a judge, for instance, of a man eight feet high, as of a man five or six feet high, and of the restoration of a withered limb, or the instantaneous cure of a disease, by speaking a word, as of the amputation of a limb, or the gradual cure of a disease by the use of medicines: And were a set of such facts to be related to us by eye and ear-witnesses, who appeared no more to mean deceit than persons in general do when they relate any thing of a common nature, we should be under a necessity of believing them.—In particular; were there no more reason to question the sincerity of the Apostles when they tell us, that they saw Jesus perform his wonderful works, that they conversed with him familiarly for many days after his resurrection; that he ascended to heaven before their eyes, and that afterwards, in consequence of being endued *with power from on high* agreeably to his promise, they went about thro' all the world preaching the doctrine of *eternal life through him*, and converting men from idolatry and vice, God himself bearing witness with them *by divers miracles, and wonders, and gifts of the Holy Ghost*:[16] Were there, I say, no more reason to question the honesty of the Apostles when they deliver this part of their history, than when they give an account of the affairs of the Jews and Romans, of the ignominious suffering and crucifixion of Christ under Pilate, of Peter's denial, Judas's treachery, and other events of a similar nature, we should be obliged alike to receive both. This, indeed, seems to me to be nearly the truth.[17] The *extraordinary* facts they relate are so blended with the *common*, and told with so much of the appearance of a like artless simplicity in both cases, as has, I think, a strong tendency to impress an attentive and impartial mind.

## Section III

### Of the Credibility of Miracles, and the Force of Testimony when employed to prove them.

It has, I hope, been sufficiently proved in the last section, that the influence of improbabilities on historical evidence is by no means such as Mr. Hume asserts, and that there cannot be any such incredibility in miracles as renders them incapable of being proved by testimony. We have seen that testimony is continually overcoming greater improbabilities than those of its own falsehood, and that, like the evidence of *sense*, the capacity of doing this is implied in its very nature.—The objection therefore, grounded on the supposed absurdity of trusting a feebler experience in opposition to a stronger, or of believing testimony, when it reports facts more improbable and extraordinary than falsehood and deception, is fallacious.

I must add what deserves particular notice, that what has been said shows us that Mr. Hume's argument would prove nothing even tho' one of the principles before opposed were granted, namely, that we derive our regard to testimony from experience in the same manner with our assurance of the laws and course of nature.

It is not necessary to the purpose of this Dissertation that I should proceed any further. The improbability, however, attending miracles being a point that strongly affects the minds of many persons, I cannot help entering a little further into the consideration of it, in order to shew more fully how much it has been magnified, and with what propriety and effect testimony may be employed to gain credit to the supernatural facts of christianity.—This shall be my business in the greatest part of what remains of this Dissertation.

There are many events, not miraculous, which yet have a previous incredibility in them similar to that of miracles, and by no means inferior to it. The events I mean, are all such *phenomena* in nature as are quite new and strange to us. No one can doubt whether these are capable of full proof by testimony.—I could, for instance, engage by my own single testimony to convince any reasonable person, that I have known one of the human species, neither deformed nor an idiot, and only thirty inches high, who arrived at his most mature state at seven years of age, and weighed then eighteen pounds; but from that time gradually declined, and died at seventeen weighing only twelve pounds, and with almost every mark of old age upon him.—Now, according to Mr. Hume's argument, no testimony can prove such a fact; for it might be said, that nothing being more *common* than the falsehood of testimony, nor more *uncommon* than such a fact, it must be contrary to all reason to believe it on the evidence of testimony.

It deserves particular notice here, that in judging from experience concerning the probability of events, we should always take care to satisfy ourselves, that there is nothing wanting to render the cases, from which we argue, perfectly alike. Our knowledge that an event has always or generally happened in certain circumstances, gives no reason for believing that the same event will happen, when these circumstances are altered: And, in Truth, we are so ignorant of the constitution of the world and of the springs of events, that it is seldom possible for us to know what different *phenomena* may take place, on any the least change in the situation of nature, or the circumstances of objects. It was inattention to this that occasioned the mistake of that king of *Siam*, mentioned by Mr. *Locke*, who rejected, as utterly incredible, the account which was given him of the effects of cold upon water in Europe. His unbelief was plainly the effect of ignorance. And this indeed is almost as often the case with unbelief, as with its contrary. Give to a common man an account of the most remarkable experiments in natural philosophy: Tell him that you can *freeze* him to death by blowing warm air upon him before a good *fire;* or that you often divert yourself with bottling up lightning and discharging it through the bodies of your acquaintance; and he will perhaps look upon you as crazy, or, at least, he will think himself sure that you mean to deceive him. Could we suppose him to have adopted Mr. Hume's method of reasoning, he might say, "That what you acquaint him with is contrary to uniform experience; that he cannot believe you without quitting a guide that has never deceived him, to follow one which is continually deceiving him; and that, therefore, such facts, when reported by testimony, are more properly subjects of *derision* than *argument.*"—But, how obvious would be the weakness of his reasoning?—A person in such circumstances, who thought justly, would consider how complicated and extensive the frame of nature is, and how little a way his observations have reached. This would show him that he can be no competent judge of the powers of nature, and lead him to expect to find in it things strange and wonderful, and consequently to enquire what regard is due to the testimony which informs him of such facts, rather than hastily to reject them.—One cannot help being greatly disgusted with the inclination which shews itself in many persons, to treat with contempt whatever they hear, be it ever so well attested, if it happens that they are not able to account for it, or that it does not coincide with their experience, just as if they knew all that can take place in nature, or, as if their experience was the standard of truth and the measure of possibility. This is to give themselves up to the influence of a principle which has a tendency to unfit them for society, and, in effect, barring their minds against light and improvement. If we would be truly wise, we ought, at the same time that we are upon our guard against deception, to avoid carefully a vain scepticism, preserving openness with respect to *any* evidence that can be offered to us on every subject, from a sense of our own ignorance and narrow views.—But to come more directly to the subject under consideration.

There is, I have said, no greater incredibility in a miracle, than in such facts as those I have mentioned. It has been already shewn, p. 393, &c. that the most uniform experience affords no reason for concluding, that the course of nature will *never* be interrupted, or that any natural event which has hitherto happened, will *always* happen. It has appeared, on the contrary, that there must be always reason *against* this conclusion. There may, I have said, be secret causes which will sometimes counteract those by which the course of nature is carried on. We are under no more necessity of thinking that it must be the same in all *ages* than in all *climates*. During the continuance of a world, there may be periods and emergencies in which its affairs may take a new turn, and very extraordinary events happen.—In particular, there are, for ought we know, superior beings who may sometimes interpose in our affairs, and over-rule the usual operations of natural causes.[18] We are so far from having any reason to deny this, that if any end worthy of such an interposition appears, nothing is more credible.—There was, undoubtedly, a time when this earth was reduced into its present habitable state and form. This must have been a time of miracles, or of the exertion of supernatural power. Why must this power have then so entirely withdrawn itself, as never to appear afterwards? The vanishing of old stars, and the appearance of new ones, is probably owing to the destruction of old worlds, and the creation of new worlds. It is reasonable to believe that events of this kind are continually happening in the immense universe; and it is certain, that they must be brought about under the direction of some superior power. There is, therefore, the constant exertion of such power in the universe. Why must it be thought that, in the lapse of six thousand years, there have been no occasions on which it has been exerted on our globe?

What I am now saying is true on the supposition that a miracle, according to the common opinion, implies a *violation* or *suspension* of the laws of nature. But, in reality, this is by no means necessarily included in the idea of a miracle. A sensible and *extraordinary effect* produced by *superior power*, no more implies that a law of nature is *violated*, than any *common effect* produced by *human power*. This has been explained in the dissertation on Providence, and it has a considerable tendency to render the admission of a miracle more easy.

These observations demonstrate, that there is nothing of the improbability in miracles which some have imagined. I may even venture to say, that they have in them a much less degree of improbability, than there was, antecedently to observations and experiments, in such *phenomena* as *comets*, or such powers as those of *magnetism* and *electricity*. My reason for this assertion is, that it is far more likely that the course of nature should some time or other fail, than that any particular powers or effects should exist in nature, which we could before-hand guess.

A due attention to these arguments will necessarily dispose a candid enquirer to give a patient hearing to any testimony which assures him, that there actually have been miracles. It appears that to decline this, under the pretence that nothing different from the common course of things can be proved by testimony, is extremely unreasonable.—The miracles of the New Testament, in particular, have many circumstances attending them which recommend them strongly to our good opinion, and which lay us under indispensable obligations to give the evidence for them a fair and patient examination.—Such is the state of mankind, that there is nothing more credible, than that our affairs have not always been suffered to go on entirely of themselves. A revelation to instruct and reform a sinful and degenerate world is so far from implying any absurdity, that it is an effect of divine goodness which might very reasonably be hoped for. There appears to have been great need of it; and it seems to be certain, that there must have been a revelation at the beginning of the world. If we reject the miracles mentioned in the New Testament, it will not be possible to give any tolerable account of the establishment of such a religion as the christian among mankind, by a few persons of no education or learning, in opposition to all the prejudices and powers of the world. The excellence of the end for which they were wrought; the myriads of mankind which they brought over to piety and goodness, and the amazing turn they gave to the state of religion by destroying, in a few years, a system of idolatry which had been the work of ages, and establishing on its ruins the knowledge and worship of the one true God; these, and various other undeniable facts which might be enumerated, give them a high credibility. We see here an occasion worthy of the use of such means, and a probability that, if ever since the creation there has been any interposition of superior power, this was the time.

*Notes*

1. By Dr. *Adams* in his *Essay on Miracles, in answer to Mr. Hume's Essay;* and by the author of the *Criterion, or, Miracles examined, &c.*—And also by Dr. Campbell, *principal of the Marishal college at Aberdeen,* in a Treatise, entitled, *A Dissertation on Miracles, containing an Examination of the Principles advanced by David Hume, Esq; in an Essay on Miracles.*—The last of these answers was published several years after the others. I mention this because, from Dr. Campbell's never referring to any other answers, as well as from his manner of expressing himself sometimes, an inattentive reader might be led to conclude that at the time he wrote the subject was quite open to him. His book, however, has uncommon merit, and the public is much indebted to him for it.
2. See the *Essay on Miracles,* in *Mr. Hume's Philosophical Essays concerning human Understanding,* p. 205, 2nd edition, in the Note.

3. Ib. P. 182—P. 206. *I desire any one to lay his hand on his heart, and after serious consideration declare, whether he thinks that the falsehood of such a book,* (the Pentateuch) *supported by such testimony, would be more extraordinary and miraculous than all the miracles it relates; which is however necessary, to make it be received, according to the measures of probability above established.*

4. Page 195.

5. Page 207.

6. See Mr. Hume's Philosophical Essays, Essay 4th and 5th.

7. If any one wants a further explication of what is here said, let him consider, that as there is only a *high probability*, not a *certainty*, that the supposed solid, after turning the same side a million of times without once failing, would turn again this side in the next trial, the probability must be less, that it would turn this side in *two* future trials, and still less, that it would do it in *three* future trials; and thus, the probability will decrease continually as the number of the supposed trials is increased, till, at last, it will become an equal chance, and from thence pass into an improbability.—This may be a little differently represented thus. Let a solid be supposed that has 1,600,000 sides of the same sort, to one of any other sort. There is a probability, that in a million of trials, such a solid would turn constantly the same side. Such a supposition, therefore, would completely account for this event, supposing it to happen; *and nothing further could, with reason, be concluded from it.* But, there is an *infinity* of other suppositions that will also account for it, of which the particular supposition that it has no sides of any other sort, and that, therefore, it will never turn any other, is *only one*. Against the truth, therefore, of this particular supposition, there must be, in the circumstances of ignorance above supposed, the greatest probability.

8. In an essay published in vol. 53d of the *Philosophical Transactions*, what is said here and in the last note, is proved by mathematical demonstration, and a method shown of determining the exact probability of all conclusions founded on induction.—This is plainly a curious and important problem, and it has so near a relation to the subject of this dissertation, that it will be proper just to mention the results of the solution of it in a few particular cases.

Suppose, all we know of an event to be, that it has happened ten times without failing, and that it is inquired, what reason we shall have for thinking ourselves right, if we judge, that the probability of its happening in a single trial, lies somewhere between sixteen to one and two to one.—The answer is, that the chance for being right, would be .5013, or very nearly an equal chance.—Take next, the particular case mentioned above, and suppose, that a solid or dye of whose number of sides and constitution we know nothing, except from experiments made in throwing it, has turned constantly the same face in a million of trials.—In these circumstances, it would be *improbable*, that it had *less* than 1,400,000 more of these sides or faces than of all others; and it would be also *improbable*, that it had *above* 1,600,000 more. The chance for the latter is .4647, and for the former .4895. There would, therefore, be no reason for thinking, that it would never turn any other side. On the contrary, it would be likely that this would happen in 1,600,000 trials.—In like manner, with respect to any event in nature, suppose the flowing of the tide, if it has flowed at the end of a certain interval a million of times, there would be the probability expressed by .5105, that the odds for its flowing again at the usual period was *greater* than 1,400,000 to 1, and the probability expressed by .5352, that the odds was *less* than 1,600,000 to one.

Such are the conclusions which *uniform* experience warrants.—What follows is a *specimen* of the expectations, which it is reasonable to entertain in the case of *interrupted* or *variable* experience.—If we know no more of an event than that it has happened ten times in eleven trials, and failed once, and we should conclude from hence, that the probability of its happening in a single trial lies between the odds of nine to one and eleven to one, there would be twelve to one *against* being right.—If it has happened a hundred times, and failed ten times, there would also be the odds of near three to one *against* being right in such a conclusion.—If it has happened a thousand times and failed a hundred, there would be an odds *for* being right of a little more than two to one. And, supposing the same *ratio* preserved of the number of happenings to the number of failures, and the same guess made, this odds will go on increasing for ever, as the number of trials is increased.—He who would see this explained and proved at large may consult the essay in the Philosophical Transactions, to which I have referred; and also the supplement to it in the 54th volume.—The specimen now given is enough to show how very inaccurately we are apt to speak and judge on this subject, previously to calculation. See Mr. Hume's Essay on Miracles, p. 175, 176, &c. and Dr Campbell's, Essay, Sect. 2nd, p. 35.—It also demonstrates, that the order of events in nature is derived from permanent causes established by an intelligent Being in the constitution of nature, and not from any of the powers of chance. And it further proves, that so far is it from being true, that the understanding is not the faculty which teaches us to rely on experience, that it is capable of determining, *in all cases*, what conclusions ought to be drawn from it, and what *precise degree* of confidence should be placed in it.

9. It might have been added here, as another observation of considerable importance, that the greatest part of what is commonly called experience is merely the report of testimony. "Our own experience (says an excellent writer) reaches around, and goes back but a little way; but the experience of others, on which we chiefly depend, is derived to us wholly from testimony." Dr. *Adams's Essay on Miracles*, page 5th.—In proportion, therefore, as we weaken the evidence of testimony, we weaken also that of experience; and in comparing them we ought in reason to oppose to the former, only what remains of the latter after that part of it which is derived from the former, that is, after much the greatest part of it is deducted.

10. See Dr. *Adams's Essay*, p. 9–24. 2d Edit. p. 10–31. 3d Edit.

11. *Essay on Miracles*, Page 179.

12. Let it be remembered, that the improbability of event here mentioned, must mean the improbability which we should have seen there was of its happening independently of any evidence for it, or, previously to the evidence of testimony informing us that it *has* happened. No other improbability can be meant, because the whole dispute is about the im-

probability that remains after the evidence of testimony given for the event.

13. This improbability is as the number of different ways which there are of drawing the lottery; or, as the number of permutations which a number of things, equal to that of the tickets in the lottery, admits of. In a lottery, therefore, of 50,000 tickets, this improbability is expressed by the proportion of $1 \times 2 \times 3 \times 4 \times 5 \times 6$, &c. continued to 50,000 to one. Or, it is the same with that of drawing such a lottery exactly in the order of the numbers, first 1, then 2, and so on to the last. Most persons will scarcely be able to persuade themselves, that this is not an absolute impossibility; and yet in truth, it is equally possible, and was beforehand equally probable with that very way in which, after drawing the lottery, we believe it has been drawn: And what is similar to this is true of almost every thing that can be offered to our assent, independently of any evidence for it; and particularly, of numberless facts which are the objects of testimony, and which are continually believed, without the least hesitation, upon its authority.

14. The false principle, which is the foundation of this method of reasoning, has been too easily received. Several considerable writers, as well as Mr. Hume, seem to have been deceived by it. Had not this been, in some degree, true of even Dr. Campbell, he would perhaps have expressed himself differently in some parts of the first and sixth sections of the first part of his very judicious dissertation before mentioned.—In the case he supposes, of the loss of a passage boat which had crossed a river two thousand times safely; it is plain, that an evidence of much less weight than the probability, that an experiment which had succeeded two thousand times will succeed the next time, would be sufficient to convince us of the reality of the event. Any report that has been oftener found to be true than false would engage belief, though the conviction we should have had, supposing no such report, that the event did not happen, would have been much stronger than any that the report itself is capable of producing. The reason of this has been assigned above.

15. Were we to *see* any thing very strange and incredible, it would be natural at first to doubt whether our eyes did not deceive us. But if it appeared to us repeatedly, and for a length of time, and others saw the same, we should soon be as well convinced of its reality, as of any other object of sense.—The like is true in the case of *testimony*. If any thing reported to us is so strange that we cannot trust any single witness so far as to believe it, the agreement of a number of independent witnesses may produce such an increase of evidence, as shall leave no more possibility of doubting about it than if we had been ourselves witnesses of it.

16. Heb. ii. 4.—Rom. xv. 18, 19.

17. "The Gospels and the Acts afford us the same historical evidence of the miracles of Christ and the Apostles, as of the common matters related in them. This indeed could not have been affirmed by any reasonable man, if the authors of these books like many other historians had appeared to aim at an entertaining manner of writing, tho' they had in their works interspersed miracles at proper distances and on proper occasions. These might have animated a dull relation, amused the reader and engaged his attention.—But the facts, both miraculous and natural

in scripture, are related in plain unadorned narratives; and both of them appear in all respects to stand upon the same foot of historical evidence." Butler's Analogy, Part II, Chap. 7.

18. Sure it is, that Mr. Hume, at least, cannot dispute the credibility of this, who has said of the system of pagan *mythology*, that it seems *more than probable* that, somewhere or other in the universe, it is really carried into execution. *Natural History of Religion*, Sect. 11th.


## *George Campbell*, A Dissertation on Miracles *(1762)*

### Part I. Miracles Are Capable of Proof from Testimony, and Religious Miracles Are Not Less Capable of This Evidence Than Others.

#### *Section I. Mr. Hume's favourite argument is founded on a false hypothesis.*

It is not the aim of this author to evince, that miracles, if admitted to be true, would not be a sufficient evidence of a divine mission: his design is solely to prove, that miracles which have not been the objects of our own senses, at least such as are said to have been performed in attestation of any religious system, cannot reasonably be admitted by us, or believed on the testimony of others. "A miracle," says he, "supported by any human testimony, is more properly a subject of derision than of argument." Again, in the conclusion of his Essay, "Upon the whole it appears, that no testimony for *any kind* of miracle can ever possibly amount to a probability, much less to a proof." Here he concludes against all miracles: "*Any kind* of miracle" are his express words. He seems, however, immediately sensible, that, in asserting this, he has gone too far; and therefore, in the end of the same paragraph, retracts part of what he had advanced in the beginning: "We may establish it as a maxim, that no human testimony can have such force as to prove a miracle, and make it a just foundation for any system of religion." In the note on this passage he has these words: "I beg the limitation here made may be remarked, when I say, that a miracle can never be proved, so as to be the foundation of a system of religion: For I own that otherwise there may possibly be miracles, or violations of the usual course of nature, of such a kind as to admit of proof from human testimony."

So much for that cardinal point which the Essayist labors so strenuously to evince; and which, if true, will not only be subversive of revelation, as received by us on the testimony of the apostles, and prophets, and martyrs, but will directly lead to this general conclusion, "That it is impossible for God Almighty to give a revelation, attended with such evidence that it can be reasonably believed in after-ages, or even in the same age, by any person who hath not been an eye-witness of the miracles by which it is supported."

Now by what wonderful process of reasoning is this strange conclusion made out? Several topics have been employed for the purpose by this subtle disputant. Among these there is one principal argument, which he is at great pains to set off to the best advantage. Here indeed he claims a particular concern, having discovered it himself. His title to the honor of the discovery, it is not my business to controvert; I confine myself entirely to the consideration of its importance. To this end I shall now lay before the reader the unanswerable argument, as he flatters himself it will be found; taking the freedom, for brevity's sake, to compendize the reasoning, and to omit whatever is said merely for illustration. To do otherwise, would lay me under the necessity of transcribing the greater part of the Essay.

"Experience," says he, "is our only guide in reasoning concerning matters of fact. Experience is in some things variable, in some things uniform. A variable experience gives rise only to probability; an uniform experience amounts to a proof. Probability always supposes an opposition of experiments and observations, where the one side is found to overbalance the other, and to produce a degree of evidence proportioned to the superiority. In such cases we must balance the opposite experiments, and deduct the lesser number from the greater, in order to know the exact force of the superior evidence. Our belief or assurance of any fact, from the report of eye-witnesses, is derived from no other principle than experience; that is, our observation of the veracity of human testimony, and of the usual conformity of facts to the reports of witnesses. Now if the fact attested partakes of the marvellous, if it is such as has seldom fallen under our observation, here is a contest of two opposite experiences, of which the one destroys the other, as far as its force goes, and the superior can only operate on the mind by the force which remains. The very same principle of experience, which gives a certain degree of assurance in the testimony of witnesses, gives us also, in this case, another degree of assurance against the fact which they endeavor to establish; from which contradiction there necessarily arises a counterpoise, and mutual destruction of belief and authority. Further, if the fact affirmed by the witnesses, instead of being only marvelous, is really miraculous; if, besides, the testimony considered apart and in itself amounts to an entire proof; in that case there is proof against proof, of which the strongest must prevail, but still with a diminution of its force, in proportion to that of its antagonist. A miracle is a violation of the laws of nature; and as a firm and unalterable experience has established these laws, the proof against a miracle, from the very nature of the fact, is as entire, as any argument from experience can possibly be imagined. And if so, it is an undeniable consequence, that it cannot be surmounted by any proof whatever from testimony. A miracle therefore, however attested, can never be rendered credible, even in the lowest degree."—This, in my apprehension, is the sum of the argument on which my ingenious opponent rests the strength of his cause.

.     .     .     .     .     .     .     .

But how, says Mr. Hume, is testimony then to be refuted? Principally in one or other of these two ways:—*first*, and most directly, By contradictory testimony; that is, when an equal or greater number of witnesses, equally or more credible, attest the contrary: *secondly*, By such evidence, either of the incapacity or of the bad character of the witnesses, as is sufficient to discredit them. What, rejoins my antagonist, cannot then testimony be confuted by the extraordinary nature of the fact attested? Has this consideration no weight at all?—That this consideration has no weight at all, it was never my intention to maintain; that by itself it can very rarely, if ever, amount to a refutation against ample and unexceptionable testimony, I hope to make extremely plain. Who has ever denied, that the uncommonness of an event related is a presumption against its reality; and that chiefly on account of the tendency, which, experience teaches us, and this author has observed, some people have to sacrifice truth to the love of wonder? The question only is, How far does this presumption extend? In the extent which Mr. Hume has assigned it, he has greatly exceeded the limits of nature, and consequently of all just reasoning.

In his opinion, "When the fact attested is such as has seldom fallen under our observation, there is a contest of two opposite experiences, of which the one destroys the other, as far as its force goes, and the superior can only operate on the mind by the force which remains."—There is a metaphysical, I had almost said, a magical *balance* and *arithmetic*, for the weighing and subtracting of evidence, to which he frequently recurs, and with which he seems to fancy he can perform wonders. I wish he had been a little more explicit in teaching us how these rare inventions must be used. When a writer of genius and elocution expresses himself in general terms, he will find it an easy matter to give a plausible appearance to things the most unintelligible in nature. Such sometimes is this author's way of writing. In the instance before us, he is particularly happy in his choice of metaphors. They are such as are naturally adapted to prepossess a reader in his favor. What candid person can think of suspecting the impartiality of an inquirer, who is for *weighing* in the *scales* of reason all the arguments on both sides? Who can suspect his exactness, who determines every thing by a *numerical computation?* Hence it is, that to a superficial view his reasoning appears scarcely inferior to demonstration; but, when narrowly canvassed, it is impracticable to find an application, of which, in a consistency with good sense, it is capable.

In confirmation of the remark just now made, let us try how his manner of arguing on this point can be applied to a particular instance. For this purpose I make the following supposition. I have lived for some years near a ferry. It consists with my knowledge, that the passage-boat has a thousand times crossed the river, and as many times returned safe. An unknown man, whom I have just now met, tells me, in a serious manner, that it is lost; and affirms, that he himself, standing on the bank, was a spectator of the scene; that he saw the passengers carried down the stream, and the boat overwhelmed. No person who is influenced in his judgment of things, not by philosophical subtilties, but by common sense, a much surer guide, will hesitate to declare, that in such a testimony I have probable evidence of the fact asserted. But if, leaving common sense, I shall recur to metaphysics, and submit to be tutored in my way of judging by the Essayist, he will remind me, "that there is here a contest of two opposite experiences, of which the one destroys the other, as far as its force goes, and the superior can only operate on the mind by the force which remains." I am warned, that "the very same principle of experience, which gives me a certain degree of assurance in the testimony of the witness, gives me also, in this case, another degree of assurance against the fact which he endeavors to establish; from which contradiction there arises a counterpoise, and mutual destruction of belief and authority." Well, I would know the truth, if possible; and that I may conclude fairly and philosophically, how must I balance these opposite experiences, as you are pleased to term them? Must I set the thousand, or rather the two thousand instances of the one side, against the single instance of the other? In that case, it is easy to see, I have nineteen hundred and ninety-nine degrees of evidence, that my information is false. Or is it necessary, in order to make it credible, that the single instance have two thousand times as much evidence as any of the opposite instances, supposing them equal among themselves; or supposing them unequal, as much as all the two thousand put together, that there may be at least an equilibrium? This is impossible: I had for some of those instances the evidence of sense, which hardly any testimony can equal, much less exceed. Once more, must the evidence I have of the veracity of the witness, be a full equivalent to the two thousand instances which oppose the fact attested? By the supposition, I have no positive evidence for or against his veracity, he being a person whom I never saw before. Yet if none of these be the balancing which the Essay writer means, I despair of being able to discover his meaning.

Is then so weak a proof from testimony incapable of being refuted? I am far from thinking so; though even so weak a proof could not be overturned by such a contrary experience. How then may it be overturned? *First*, By contradictory testimony. Going homewards I meet another person, whom I know as little as I did the former: finding that he comes from the ferry, I ask him concerning the truth of the report. He affirms, that the whole is a fiction; that he saw the boat, and all in it, come safe to land. This would do more to turn the scale, than fifty thousand such contrary instances as were supposed. Yet this would not remove suspicion. Indeed, if we were to consider the matter abstractly, one would think that all suspicion would be removed; that the two opposite testimonies would destroy each other, and leave the mind entirely under the influence of its former experience, in the same state as if neither testimony had been given. But this is by no means consonant to fact.

When once testimonies are introduced, former experience is generally of no account in the reckoning; it is but like the dust of the balance, which hath not any sensible effect upon the scales. The mind hangs in suspense between the two contrary declarations, and considers it as one to one, or equal in probability, that the report is true, or that it is false. Afterwards a third, and a fourth, and a fifth, confirm the declaration of the second. I am then quite at ease. Is this the only effectual way of confuting false testimony? No. I suppose *again*, that instead of meeting with any person who can inform me concerning the fact, I get from some, who are acquainted with the witness, information concerning his character. They tell me, he is notorious for lying; and that his lies are commonly forged, not with a view to interest, but merely to gratify a malicious pleasure which he takes in alarming strangers. This, though not so direct a refutation as the former, will be sufficient to discredit his report. In the former, where there is testimony contradicting testimony, the author's metaphor of a balance may be used with propriety. The things weighed are homogeneal: And when contradictory evidences are presented to the mind, tending to prove positions which cannot be both true, the mind must decide on the comparative strength of the opposite evidences, before it yield to either.

But is this the case in the supposition first made? By no means. The two thousand instances formerly known, and the single instance attested, as they relate to different facts, though of a contrary nature, are not contradictory. There is no inconsistency in believing both. There is no inconsistency in receiving the last on weaker evidence, (if it be sufficient evidence), not only than all the former together, but even than any of them singly. Will it be said, that though the former instances are not themselves contradictory to the fact recently attested, they lead to a conclusion that is contradictory? I answer, It is true, that the experienced frequency of the conjunction of any two events, leads the mind to infer a similar conjunction in time to come: But let it at the same time be remarked, that no man considers this inference, as having equal evidence with any one of those past events on which it is founded, and for the belief of which we have had sufficient testimony. Before, then, the method recommended by this author can turn to any account, it will be necessary for him to compute and determine, with precision, how many hundreds, how many thousands, I might say how many myriads of instances, will confer such evidence on the conclusion founded on them, as will prove an equipoise for the testimony of one ocular witness, a man of probity, in a case of which he is allowed to be a competent judge.

There is in *arithmetic* a rule called REDUCTION, by which numbers of different denominations are brought to the same denomination. If this ingenious author shall invent a rule in *logic* analogous to this, for reducing different classes of evidence to the same class, he will bless the world with a most important discovery. Then indeed he will have the honor to establish an everlasting peace in the republic of letters; then we shall have the happiness to see controversy of every kind, theological, historical, philosophical, receive its mortal wound: for though, in every question, we could not even then determine, with certainty, on which side the truth lay, we could always determine (and that is the utmost the nature of the thing admits) with as much accuracy as geometry and algebra can afford, on which side the probability lay, and in what degree. But till this metaphysical *reduction* be discovered, it will be impossible, where the evidences are of different orders, to ascertain by *subtraction* the superior evidence. We would not but esteem him a novice in arithmetic, who being asked, whether seven pounds or eleven pence make the greater sum, and what is the difference? Should, by attending solely to the numbers, and overlooking the value, conclude that eleven pence were the greater, and that it exceeded the other by four. Must we not be equal novices in reasoning, if we follow the same method? Must we not fall into as great blunders? Of as little significancy do we find the balance. Is the value of things heterogeneal to be determined merely by weight? Shall silver be weighed against lead, or copper against iron? If, in exchange for a piece of gold, I were offered some counters of baser metal, is it not obvious, that till I know the comparative value of the metals, in vain shall I attempt to find what is equivalent, by the assistance either of scales or of arithmetic?

It is an excellent observation, and much to the purpose, which the late learned and pious Bishop of Durham, in his admirable performance on the Analogy of Religion to the Course of Nature, hath made on this subject. "There is a very strong presumption," says he, "against the most ordinary facts, before the proof of them, which yet is overcome by almost any proof. There is a presumption of millions to one against the story of Caesar, or of any other man. For suppose a number of common facts, so and so circumstanced, of which one had no kind of proof, should happen to come into one's thoughts, every one would, without any possible doubt, conclude them to be false. The like may be said of a single common fact." What then, I may subjoin, shall be said of an uncommon fact? And that an uncommon fact may be proved by testimony, has not *yet* been made a question. But, in order to illustrate the observation above cited, suppose, first, one at random mentions, that at such an hour, of such a day, in such a part of the heavens, a comet *will* appear; the conclusion from experience would not be as millions, but as infinite to one, that the proposition is false. Instead of this, suppose you have the testimony of but one ocular witness, a man of integrity, and skilled in astronomy, that at such an hour, of such a day, in such a part of the heavens, a comet *did* appear; you will not hesitate one moment to give him credit. Yet all the presumption that was against the truth of the first supposition, though almost as strong evidence as experience can afford, was also against the truth of the second, before it was thus attested.

Is it necessary to urge further, in support of this doctrine, that as the water in the canal cannot be made to rise higher than the fountain whence it flows, so it is impossible that the evidence of testimony, if it proceeded from experience, should ever exceed that of experience, which is its source? Yet that it greatly exceeds this evidence, appears not only from what has been observed already, but still more from what I shall have occasion to observe in the sequel. One may safely affirm, that no conceivable conclusion from experience can possess stronger evidence, than that which ascertains us of the regular succession and duration of day and night. The reason is, the instances on which this experience is founded, are both without number and without exception. Yet even this conclusion, the author admits, as we shall see in the third section, may, in a particular instance, not only be surmounted, but even annihilated by testimony.

· · · · · · · · ·

FROM what has been said, the attentive reader will easily discover, that the author's argument against *miracles* has not the least affinity to the argument used by Dr. Tillotson against *transubstantiation*, with which Mr. Hume has introduced his subject. Let us hear the argument, as it is related in the Essay, from the writings of the Archbishop. "It is acknowledged on all hands," says that learned prelate, "that the authority either of the scripture or of tradition is founded merely on the testimony of the apostles, who were eye-witnesses to those miracles of our Savior by which he proved his divine mission. Our evidence then for the truth of the Christian religion is less than the evidence for the truth of our senses; because even in the first authors of our religion it was no greater; and it is evident, it must diminish in passing from them to their disciples; nor can any one be so certain of the truth of their testimony, as of the immediate objects of his senses. But a weaker evidence can never destroy a stronger; and therefore, were the doctrine of the real presence ever so clearly revealed in scripture, it were directly contrary to the rules of just reasoning to give our assent to it. It contradicts sense, though both the scripture and tradition, on which it is supposed to be built, carry not such evidence with them as sense, when they are considered merely as external evidences, and are not brought home to every one's breast by the immediate operation of the Holy Spirit." That the evidence of *testimony* is less than the evidence of *sense*, is undeniable.—*Sense* is the source of that evidence, which is first transferred to the *memory* of the individual, as to a general reservoir, and thence transmitted to others by the channel of *testimony*. That the original evidence can never gain any thing, but must lose, by the transmission, is beyond dispute. What has been rightly perceived, may be misremembered; what is rightly remembered, may, through incapacity, or through ill intention, be misreported; and what is rightly reported, may be misunderstood. In any of these four ways, therefore, either by defect of memory, of elocution, or of veracity in the relater, or by misapprehension in the hearer, there is a chance that the truth received by the information of the senses may be misrepresented or mistaken: now, every such chance occasions a real diminution of the evidence. That the sacramental elements are bread and wine, not flesh and blood, our sight and touch and taste and smell concur in testifying.

If these senses are not to be credited, the apostles themselves could not have evidence of the mission of their Master. For the greatest external evidence they had, or could have, of his mission, was that which their senses gave them of the reality of his miracles. But whatever strength there is in this argument, with regard to the apostles, the argument, with regard to us, who, for those miracles, have only the evidence, not of our own senses, but of their testimony, is incomparably stronger. In their case, it is sense contradicting sense; in ours, it is sense contradicting testimony. But what relation has this to the author's argument? None at all. Testimony, it is acknowledged, is a weaker evidence than sense. But it has been already evinced, that its evidence for particular facts is infinitely stronger than that which the general conclusions from experience can afford us. Testimony holds directly of memory and sense. Whatever is duly attested, must be remembered by the witness; whatever is duly remembered, must once have been perceived. But nothing similar takes place with regard to experience, nor can testimony, with any appearance of meaning, be said to hold of it.

.   .   .   .   .   .   .   .

## Section II. Mr. Hume charged with some fallacies in his way of managing the argument.

IN the Essay there is frequent mention of the word *experience*, and much use made of it. It is strange that the author has not favored us with the definition of a term of so much moment to his argument. This defect I shall endeavor to supply; and the rather, as the word appears to be equivocal, and to be used by the Essayist in two very different senses. The first and most proper signification of the word, which, for distinction's sake, I shall call *personal* experience, is that given in the preceding section. "It is," as was observed, "founded in *memory*, and consists solely of the general maxims or conclusions that each individual hath formed from the comparison of the particular facts remembered by him." In the other signification, in which the word is sometimes taken, and which I shall distinguish by the term *derived*, it may be thus defined:—"It is founded in *testimony*, and consists not only of all the experiences of others, which have, through that channel, been communicated to us, but of all the general maxims or conclusions we have formed, from the comparison of particular facts attested."

In proposing his argument, the author would surely be understood to mean only *personal* experience; otherwise, his making testimony derive its light from an experience which derives its light from testimony, would be introducing what logicians term a *circle in causes*. It would exhibit the same things alternately, as causes and effects of each other. Yet nothing can be more limited than the sense which is conveyed under the term *experience*, in the first acceptation. The merest clown or peasant derives incomparably more knowledge from testimony, and the communicated experience of others, than, in the longest life, he could have amassed out of the treasure of his own memory. Nay, to such a scanty portion the savage himself is not confined. If that therefore must be the rule, the only rule, by which every testimony is ultimately to be judged, our belief in matters of fact must have very narrow bounds. No testimony ought to have any weight with us, that does not relate an event, similar at least to some one observation which we ourselves have made. For example, that there are such people on the earth as negroes, could not, on that hypothesis, be rendered credible to one who had never seen a negro, not even by the most numerous and the most unexceptionable attestations. Against the admission of such testimony, however strong, the whole force of the author's argument evidently operates. But that innumerable absurdities would flow from this principle, I might easily evince, did I not think the task superfluous.

The author himself is aware of the consequences; and therefore, in whatever sense he uses the term *experience* in proposing his argument, in prosecuting it, he, with great dexterity, shifts the sense, and, ere the reader is apprised, insinuates another. "It is a miracle," says he, "that a dead man should come to life, because that has never been observed in any age or country. There must therefore be an uniform experience against every miraculous event, otherwise the event would not merit that appellation." Here the phrase, *an uniform experience against an event*, in the latter clause, is implicitly defined in the former, not what has never been observed BY US, but (mark his words) *what has never been observed* IN ANY AGE OR COUNTRY. Now, what has been observed, and what has not been observed, in all ages and countries, pray how can you, Sir, or I, or any man, come to the knowledge of? Only I suppose by testimony, oral or written. The personal experience of every individual is limited to but a part of one age, and commonly to a narrow spot of one country. If there be any other way of being made acquainted with facts, it is to me, I own, an impenetrable secret; I have no apprehension of it. If there be not any, what shall we make of that cardinal point, on which your argument turns? It is in plain language, "Testimony is not entitled to the least degree of faith, but as far as it is supported by such an extensive experience as, if we had not had a previous and independent faith in testimony, we could never have acquired."

How natural is the transition from one sophism to another! You will soon be convinced of this, if you attend but a little to the strain of the argument. "A miracle," says he, "is a violation of the laws of nature; and as a firm and unalterable experience hath established these laws, the proof against a miracle is as entire as any argument from experience can possibly be imagined." Again, "As an uniform experience amounts to a proof, there is here a direct and full proof, from the nature of the fact, against the existence of any miracle." I must once more ask the author, What is the precise meaning of the words *firm, unalterable, uniform?* An experience that admits no exception, is surely the only experience which can with propriety be termed *uniform, firm, unalterable*. Now since, as was remarked above, the far greater part of this experience, which comprises every age and every country, must be derived to us from testimony; that the experience may be *firm, uniform, unalterable*, there must be no contrary testimony whatever. Yet, by the author's own hypothesis, the miracles he would thus confute are supported by testimony. At the same time, to give strength to his argument, he is under a necessity of supposing, that there is no exception from the testimonies against them. Thus he falls into that paralogism, which is called *begging the question*. What he gives with one hand, he takes with the other. He admits, in opening his design, what in his argument he implicitly denies.

But that this, if possible, may be still more manifest, let us attend a little to some expressions, which one would imagine he had inadvertently dropt. "So long," says he, "as the world endures, I presume, will the accounts of miracles and prodigies be found in all profane history." Why does he presume so? A man so much attached to experience, can hardly be suspected to have any other reason than this—because such accounts have hitherto been found in all the histories, profane as well as sacred, of times past. But we need not recur to an inference to obtain this acknowledgment: it is often to be met with in the Essay. In one place we learn, that the witnesses for miracles are an infinite number; in another, that all religious records of whatever kind abound with them. I leave it therefore to the author to explain, with what consistency he can assert that the laws of nature are established by an uniform experience, (which experience is chiefly the result of testimony), and at the same time allow that almost all human histories are full of the relations of miracles and prodigies, which are violations of those laws. Here is, by his own confession, testimony against testimony, and very ample on both sides. How then can one side claim a firm, uniform, and unalterable support from testimony?

.   .   .   .   .   .   .   .

I shall remark one other fallacy in this author's reasoning, before I conclude this section. "The Indian prince," says he, "who refused to believe the first relations concerning the effects of frost, reasoned justly; and it naturally required very strong testimony to engage his assent to facts, which arose from a state of nature with which he was unacquainted, and bore so little analogy to those events of which he had had constant and uniform experience: Though they were not contrary to his experience, they were not conformable to it." Here a distinction is artfully suggested, between what is *contrary* to experience, and what is *not conformable* to it. The latter he allows may be proved by testimony, but not the former. A distinction, for which the author seems to have so great use, it will not be improper to examine.

If my reader happen to be but little acquainted with Mr. Hume's writings, or even with the piece here examined, I must entreat him, ere he proceed any farther, to give the Essay an attentive perusal; and to take notice particularly, whether, in one single passage, he can find any other sense given to the terms *contrary to experience*, but that which has *not* been *experienced*. Without this aid, I should not be surprised that I found it difficult to convince the judicious, that a man of so much acuteness, one so much a philosopher as this author, should, with such formality, make a distinction, which not only the Essay, but the whole tenor of his philosophical writings, shows evidently to have no meaning. Is that which is contrary to experience, a synonymous phrase for that which implies a contradiction? If this were the case, there would be no need to recur to experience for a refutation; it would refute itself. But it is equitable that the author himself be heard, who ought to be the best interpreter of his own words. "When the fact attested," says he, "is such a one as has seldom fallen under our observation, here is a contest of two opposite experiences." In this passage, not the being *never* experienced, but even the being *seldom* experienced, constitutes an *opposite* experience. I can conceive no way but one, that the author can evade the force of this quotation; and that is, by obtruding on us some new distinction between an *opposite* and a *contrary* experience. In order to preclude such an attempt, I shall once more recur to his own authority. "It is no miracle that a man in seeming good health should die of a sudden." Why? "Because such a kind of death, though more unusual than any other, hath yet been frequently observed to happen. But it is a miracle that a dead man should come to life." Why? Not because of any inconsistency in the thing. That a body should be this hour inanimate and the next animated, is no more inconsistent than the reverse, that it should be this hour animated and the next inanimate; though the one be common, and not the other. But the author himself answers the question: "Because that has never been observed in any age or country." All the contrariety then that there is in miracles to experience, does, by his own concession, consist solely in this, that they have never been observed; that is, they are not conformable to experience. To his experience, personal or derived, he must certainly mean; to what he has learned of different ages and countries. To speak beyond the knowledge he has attained, would be ridiculous. It would be first supposing a miracle, and then inferring a contrary experience, instead of concluding, from experience, that the fact is miraculous.

Now I insist, that, as far as regards the author's argument, a fact perfectly unusual, or not conformable to our experience, such a fact as, for aught we know, was never observed in any age or country, is as incapable of proof from testimony as miracles are; that, if this writer would argue consistently, he could never, on his own principles, reject one, and admit the other. Both ought to be rejected, or neither. I would not by this be thought to signify, that there is no difference between a miracle and an extraordinary event. I know that the former implies the interposal of an invisible agent, which is not implied in the latter. All that I intend to assert is, that the author's argument equally affects them both. Why does such interposal appear to him incredible? Not from any incongruity he discerns in the thing itself: he does not pretend it: but it is not conformable to his experience. "A miracle," says he, "is a transgression of a law of nature." But how are the laws of nature known to us? By experience. What is the criterion whereby we must judge whether the laws of nature are transgressed? Solely the conformity or disconformity of events to our experience. This writer surely will not pretend, that we can have any knowledge *a priori*, either of the law or of the violation.

Let us then examine, by his own principles, whether the King of Siam, of whom the story he alludes to is related by Locke, could have sufficient evidence, from testimony, of a fact so contrary to his experience as the freezing of water. He could just say as much of this event, as the author can say of a dead man's being restored to life: "Such a thing was never observed, as far as I could learn, in any age or country." If the things themselves too be impartially considered, and independently of the notions acquired by us in these northern climates, we should account the first at least as extraordinary as the second.—That so pliant a body as water should become hard like pavement, so as to bear up an elephant on its surface, is as unlikely, in itself, as that a body inanimate today should be animated tomorrow. Nay, to the Indian monarch, I must think, that the first would appear more a miracle, more contrary to experience, than the second. If he had been acquainted with *ice* or frozen water, and afterwards seen it become fluid, but had never seen nor learned, that after it was melted it became hard again, the relation must have appeared marvelous, as the process from fluidity to hardness never had been experienced, though the reverse often had. But I believe nobody will question, that on this supposition it would not have appeared quite so strange as it did. Yet this supposition makes the instance more parallel to the restoring of the dead to life. The process from animate to inanimate we are all acquainted with; and what is such a restoration, but the reversing of this process? So little reason had the author to insinuate, that the one was only *not conformable*, the other *contrary* to experience. If there be a difference in this respect, the first, to one alike unacquainted with both, must appear the more contrary of the two.

Does it alter the matter, that he calls the former "a fact which arose from a state of nature with which the Indian was unacquainted?" Was not such a state quite unconformable, or (which in the author's language I have shown to be the same) contrary to his experience? Is then a state of nature, which is contrary to experience, more credible than a single fact contrary to experience? I want the solution of one difficulty: the author, in order to satisfy me, presents me with a thousand others. Is this suitable to the method he proposes in another place, of admitting always the less miracle, and rejecting the greater? Is it not, on the contrary, admitting without any difficulty the greater miracle, and thereby removing the difficulty which he otherwise would have had in admitting the less? Does he forget, that to exhibit a state of nature entirely different from what we experience at present, is one of those enormous prodigies, which, in his account, render the Pentateuch unworthy of credit? "No Indian," says he in the note, "it is evident, could have experience that water did not freeze in cold climates. This is placing nature in a situation quite unknown to him; and it is impossible for him to tell, *a priori*, what will result from it." This is precisely as if, in reply to the author's objection from experience against the raising of a dead man (suppose Lazarus) to life, I should retort: "Neither you, Sir, nor any who live in this century, can have experience, that a dead man could not be restored to life at the command of one divinely commissioned to give a revelation to men. This is placing nature in a situation quite unknown to you ; and it is impossible for you to tell, *a priori*, what will result from it. This therefore is not contrary to the course of nature, in cases where all the circumstances are the same. As you never saw one vested with such a commission, you are as unexperienced, as ignorant of this point, as the inhabitants of Sumatra are of the frosts in Muscovy; you cannot therefore reasonably, any more than they, be positive as to the consequences." Should he rejoin, as doubtless he would, "This is not taking away the difficulty; but, like the elephant and the tortoise, in the account given by some barbarians of the manner in which the earth is supported, it only shifts the difficulty a step further back: My objection still recurs—That any man should be endowed with such power is contrary to experience, (or, as I have shewn to be the same in this author's language, is not conformable to my experience), and therefore incredible:"—Should he, I say, rejoin in this manner, I could only add, "Pray, Sir, revise your own words lately quoted, and consider impartially, whether they be not as glaringly exposed to the like reply." For my part, I can only perceive one difference that is material between the two cases. You frankly confess, that with regard to the freezing of water, beside the absolute want of experience, there would be from analogy a presumption against it, which ought to weigh with a rational Indian. I think, on the contrary, in the case supposed by me, of one commissioned by Heaven, there is at least no presumption against the exertion of such a miraculous power; there is rather a presumption in its favor.

Does the author then say, that no testimony could give the King of Siam sufficient evidence of the effects of cold on water? No. By implication he says the contrary: "It required very strong testimony." Will he say, that those most astonishing effects of electricity lately discovered, so entirely unanalogous to every thing before experienced—will he say, that such facts no reasonable man could have sufficient evidence from testimony to believe? No. We may presume he will not, from his decision in the former case; and if he should, the common sense of mankind would reclaim against such extravagance. Yet it is obvious to every considerate reader, that this argument concludes equally against those truly marvelous, as against miraculous events; both being alike unconformable, or alike contrary, to former experience.

Thus I think I have shown, that the author is chargeable with some fallacies in his way of managing the argument;—that he all along avails himself of an ambiguity in the word *experience*;—that his reasoning includes a *petitio principii* in the bosom of it;—and that, in supporting his argument, he must have recourse to distinctions, where, even himself being judge, there is no difference.

## Section III. Mr. Hume himself gives up his favourite argument.

"Mr. Hume himself," methinks I hear my reader repeating with astonishment, "gives up his favourite argument!" To prove this point is indeed a very bold attempt: Yet that this attempt is not altogether so arduous as, at first hearing, he will possibly imagine, I hope, if favored a while with his attention, fully to convince him. If to acknowledge, after all, that there may be miracles which admit of proof from human testimony; if to acknowledge, that such miracles ought to be received, not as probable only, but as absolutely certain; or, in other words, that the proof from human testimony may be such, as that all the contrary uniform experience should not only be overbalanced, but, to use the author's expression, should be annihilated: if such acknowledgments as these are subversive of his own principles; if, by making them, he abandons his darling argument; this strange part the Essayist evidently acts.

"I own," these are his words, "there may possibly be miracles, or violations of the usual course of nature, of such a kind as to admit a proof from human testimony, though perhaps" (in this he is modest enough, he avers nothing; *perhaps*) "it will be impossible to find any such in all the records of history." To this declaration he subjoins the following supposition:—"Suppose all authors, in all languages, agree, that from the 1st of January 1600 there was a total darkness over the whole earth for eight days; suppose that the tradition of this extraordinary event is still strong and lively among the people; that all travellers, who return from foreign countries, bring us accounts of the same tradition, without the least variation or contradiction—it is evident that our present philosophers, instead of doubting of that fact, ought to receive it for certain, and ought to search for the causes whence it might be derived."

Could one imagine that the person who had made the above acknowledgment, a person too who is justly allowed, by all who are acquainted with his writings, to possess uncommon penetration and philosophical abilities, that this were the same individual who had so short while before affirmed, that a "miracle," or a violation of the usual course of nature, "supported by any human testimony, is more properly a subject of derision than of argument;" who had insisted, that "it is not requisite, in order to reject the fact, to be able accurately to disprove the testimony, and to trace its falsehood; that such an evidence carries falsehood on the very face of it;" that "we need but oppose, even to a cloud of witnesses, the absolute impossibility, or," which is all one, "miraculous nature of the events which they relate; that this, in the eyes of all reasonable people will alone be regarded as a sufficient refutation;" and who, finally, to put an end to all altercation on the subject, had pronounced this *oracle*, "NO

TESTIMONY FOR ANY KIND OF MIRACLE CAN EVER POSSIBLY AMOUNT TO A PROBABILITY, MUCH LESS TO A PROOF." Was there ever a more glaring contradiction?

Yet for the event supposed by the Essayist, the testimony, in his judgment, would amount to a *probability*; nay, to more than a probability, to a *proof*: let not the reader be astonished, or, if he cannot fail to be astonished, let him not be incredulous, when I add, to *more than a proof*, more than a full, entire, and direct proof—for even this I hope to make evident from the author's principles and reasoning. "And even supposing," says he, that is, granting for argument's sake, "that the testimony for a miracle amounted to a proof, it would be opposed by another proof, derived from the very nature of the fact which it would endeavor to establish." Here is then, by his own reasoning, proof against proof, from which there could result no belief or opinion, unless the one is conceived to be in some degree superior to the other. "Of which proofs," says he, "the strongest must prevail, but still with a diminution of its force, in proportion to that of its antagonist." Before the author could believe such a miracle as he supposes, he must at least be satisfied that the proof of it from testimony is stronger than the proof against it from experience. That we may form an accurate judgment of the strength he here ascribes to testimony, let us consider what, by his own account, is the strength of the opposite proof from experience. "A miracle is a violation of the laws of nature; and as a firm and unalterable experience has established these laws, the proof against a miracle, from the very nature of the fact, is as *entire* as any argument from experience can possibly be imagined." Again, "As an uniform experience amounts to a proof, there is here a *direct* and *full* proof, from the nature of the fact, against the existence of any miracle." The proof then which the Essayist admits from testimony, is, by his own estimate, not only superior to a *direct* and *full* proof, but even superior to as *entire* a proof as any argument from experience can possibly be imagined. Whence, I pray, doth testimony acquire such amazing evidence? "Testimony," says the author, "hath no evidence, but what it derives from experience. These differ from each other only as the species from the genus." Put then for *testimony* the word *experience*, which in this case is equivalent, and the conclusion will run thus: *Here is a proof from experience, which is superior to as entire a proof from experience as can possibly be imagined*. This deduction from the author's words, the reader will perceive, is strictly logical. What the meaning of it is, I leave to Mr. Hume to explain.

What has been above deduced, how much soever it be accounted, is not all that is implied in the concession made by the author. He further says, that the miraculous fact, so attested, ought not only to be received, but to be received *for certain*. Is it not enough, Sir, that you have shown that your most full, most direct, most perfect argument may be overcome? Will nothing satisfy you now but its destruction? One would imagine, that you had conjured up this demon, by whose irresistible arm you proposed to give a mortal blow to religion, and render skepticism triumphant, (that you had conjured him up, I say), for no other purpose, but to show with what facility you could lay him. To be serious, does not this author remember, that he had oftener than once laid it down as a maxim, That when there is proof against proof, we must incline to the superior, still with a diminution of assurance, in proportion to the force of its antagonist? But when a fact is received *for certain*, there can be no sensible diminution of assurance, such diminution always implying some doubt and *uncertainty*. Consequently the general proof from experience, though as entire as any argument from experience can possibly be imagined, is not only surmounted, but is really in comparison as nothing, or, in Mr. Hume's phrase, undergoes annihilation, when balanced with the particular proof from testimony. Great indeed, it must be acknowledged, is the force of truth. This conclusion, on the principles I have been endeavoring to establish, has nothing in it but what is conceivable and just; but, on the principles of the Essay, which deduce all the force of testimony from experience, serves only to confound the understanding, and to involve the subject in midnight darkness.

It is therefore manifest, that either this author's principles condemn his own method of judging with regard to miraculous facts; or that his method of judging subverts his principles, and is a tacit desertion of them. Thus that impregnable fortress, the asylum of infidelity, which he so lately gloried in having erected, is in a moment abandoned by him as a place untenable.

.    .    .    .    .    .    .    .    .

## Section VI. Inquiry into the meaning and propriety of one of Mr. Hume's favourite maxims.

THERE is a method truly curious, suggested by the author, for extricating the mind, should the evidence from testimony be so great, that its falsehood might, as he terms it, be accounted miraculous. In this puzzling case, when a man is so beset with miracles that he is under the necessity of admitting one, he must always take care it be the smallest; for it is an *axiom* in this writer's DIALECTIC, That *the probability of the fact is in the inverse ratio of the quantity of miracle there is in it*. "I weigh," says he, "the one miracle against the other, and according to the superiority which I discover, I pronounce my decision, and always reject the greater miracle."

.    .    .    .    .    .    .    .    .

But though the maxim laid down by the author were just, I cannot discover in what instance, or by what application, it can be rendered of any utility. Why? Because we have no rule whereby we can judge of the greatness of miracles. I allow that, in such a singular instance as that above quoted from the Essay, we may judge safely enough. But that can be of no practical use. In almost every case that will occur, I may warrantably aver, that it will be impossible for the acutest intellect to decide which of the two is the greatest miracle. As to the author, I cannot find that he has favored us with any light in so important and so critical a question. Have we not then some reason to dread, that the task will not be less difficult to furnish us with a *measure* by which we can determine the magnitude of miracles, than to provide us with a *balance* by which we can ascertain the comparative weight of testimonies and experiences?

If, leaving the speculations of the Essayist, we shall, in order to be assisted on this subject, recur to his example and decisions; let us consider the miracle which was recited in the third section, and which, he declares, would, on the evidence of such testimony as he supposes, not only be probable but certain. For my part, it is not in my power to conceive a greater miracle than that is. The whole universe is affected by it; the earth, the sun, the moon, the stars. The most invariable laws of nature with which we are acquainted, even those which regulate the motions of the heavenly bodies, and dispense darkness and light to worlds, are violated. I appeal to the author himself, whether it could be called a greater, or even so great a miracle, that all the writers at that time, or even all mankind, had been seized with a new species of epidemical delirium, which had given rise to this strange illusion. But in this the author is remarkably unfortunate, that the principles by which he in fact regulates his judgment and belief, are often the reverse of those which he endeavors to establish in his theory.

Shall I hazard a conjecture? It is, that the word *miracle*, as thus used by the author, is used in a vague and improper sense, as a synonymous term for *improbable*; and that believing the *less*, and rejecting the *greater miracle*, denote simply believing what is *least*, and rejecting what is *most improbable*; or still more explicitly, believing what we think *most worthy of belief*, and rejecting what we think *least worthy*. I am aware, on a second perusal of the author's words, that my talent in guessing may be justly questioned. He has in effect told us himself what he means. "When any one," says he, "tells me that he saw a dead man restored to life, I immediately consider with myself, whether it be more *probable* that this person should either deceive or be deceived, or that the fact he relates should really have happened. I weigh the one *miracle* against the other; and, according to the superiority which I discover, I pronounce my decision, and always reject the greater miracle. If the falsehood of his testimony would be more miraculous than the event which he relates; then, and not till then, can he pretend to command my belief or opinion." At first, indeed, one is ready to exclaim, What a strange *revolution* is here! The belief of miracles then, even by Mr. Hume's account, is absolutely inevitable. Miracles themselves too, so far from being impossible, or even extraordinary, are the commonest things in nature; so common, that when any miraculous fact is attested to us, we are equally under a necessity of believing a miracle, whether we believe the fact or deny it. The whole difference between the Essayist and us is at length reduced to this single point, Whether greater or smaller miracles are entitled to the preference? This mystery however vanishes on a nearer inspection. The style, we find, is figurative, and the author is all the while amusing both his readers and himself with an unusual application of a familiar term. What is called the weighing of *probabilities* in one sentence, is the weighing of *miracles* in the next. If it were asked, For what reason did not Mr. Hume express his sentiment in ordinary and proper words? I could only answer, I know no reason but one, and that is, To give the appearance of novelty and depth to one of those very harmless propositions which by philosophers are called *identical*; and which, to say the truth, need some disguise to make them pass upon the world with tolerable decency.

What then shall be said of the conclusion which he gives as the sum and quintessence of the first part of the Essay? The best thing, for aught I know, that can be said is, that it contains a most certain truth, though at the same time the least significant, that ever perhaps was ushered into the world with so much solemnity. In order therefore to make *plainer English* of his *plain consequence*, let us only change the word *miraculous*, as applied to the falsehood of human testimony, into *improbable*, which in this passage is entirely equivalent, and observe the effect produced by this elucidation. "The plain consequence is, and it is a GENERAL MAXIM, *worthy of our attention*, That NO TESTIMONY IS SUFFICIENT TO ESTABLISH A MIRACLE; UNLESS THE TESTIMONY BE OF SUCH A KIND, THAT ITS FALSE-HOOD WOULD BE MORE IMPROBABLE THAN THE FACT WHICH IT ENDEAVORS TO ESTABLISH." If the reader think himself instructed by this discovery, I should be loth to envy him the pleasure he may derive from it.


## Anonymous (George Hooper?), "A Calculation of the Credibility of Human Testimony" (1699)

*Moral Certitude Absolute*, is that in which the Mind of Man entirely acquiesces, requiring no further Assurance: As if one in whom I absolutely confide, shall bring me word of 1200 £ accruing to me by Gift, or a Ships Arrival; and for which therefore I would not give the least valuable Consideration to be Ensur'd.

*Moral Certitude Incompleat*, has its several Degrees to be estimated by the Proportion it bears to the *Absolute*, As if one in whom I have that degree of Confidence, as that I would not give above One in Six to be ensur'd of the Truth of what he says, shall inform me, as above, concerning 1200 £: I may then reckon that I have as good as the Absolute Certainty of a 1000 £, or five sixths of Absolute Certainty for the whole Summ.

The *Credibility* of any *Reporter* is to be rated (1) by his *Integrity*, or Fidelity; and (2) by his *Ability*: and a double *Ability* is to be considered; both that of *Apprehending*, what is deliver'd; and also of *Retaining* it afterwards, till it be transmitted.

## Propos. II: *Concerning* Concurrent *Testifications*

IF Two Concurrent Reporters have, each of them, as (1/6)ths of Certainty; they will both give me an Assurance of (35/36)ths, or of 35 to one: If Three; an Assurance of (215/216)ths, or of 215 to one.

For if one of them gives a Certainty for 1200 £, as of (5/6)ths there remains but an Assurance of (1/6)th, or of 200 £ wanting to me, for the whole. And towards that the Second Attester contributes, according to his Proportion of Credibility: That is to 'ths of Certainty before had, he adds (5/6)ths of the (1/6)th which was wanting: So that there is now wanting but (1/6)th of (1/6)th that is (1/36)th; and consequently I have, from them both, (35/36)ths of Certainty. So from Three, 215/216, etc.

That is, if the First Witness gives me a/(a+c) of Certainty and there is wanting of it c/(a+c); the Second Attester will add a/(a+c); of that, c/(a+c); and consequently leave nothing wanting but c/(a+c) of that a/(a+c) = $c^2/(a+c)^2$. And in like manner the third Attester adds his a/(a+c) of that $c^2/(a+c)^2$, and leaves wanting only $c^3/(a+c)^3$. Etc.

Corollary: Hence it follows, that if a single Witness should be only so far Credible, as to give me the Half of a full Certainty; a Second of the fame Credibility, would (joined with the first) give me (3/4)ths; a Third, (7/8)ths; etc: So that the Coattestation of a Tenth would give me (1023/1024)ths of Certainty; and the Coattestation of a Twentieth, (1096999/1097000)ths or above Two Millions to one. etc.

## *Pierre Simon Laplace,* A Philosophical Essay on Probability *(1814), Chapter II* "*Concerning the Probabilities of Testimonies*"

The majority of our opinions being founded on the probability of proofs it is indeed important to submit it to calculus. Things it is true often become impossible by the difficulty of appreciating the veracity of witnesses and by the great number of circumstances which accompany the deeds they attest; but one is able in several cases to resolve the problems which have much analogy with the questions which are proposed and whose solutions may be regarded as suitable approximations to guide and to defend us against the errors and the dangers of false reasoning to which we are exposed. An approximation of this kind, when it is well made, is always preferable to the most specious reasonings. Let us try then to give some general rules for obtaining it.

A single number has been drawn from an urn which contains a thousand of them. A witness to this drawing announces that number 79 is drawn; one asks the probability of drawing this number. Let us suppose that experience has made known that this witness deceives one time in ten, so that the probability of his testimony is $1/10$. Here the event observed is the witness attesting that number 79 is drawn. This event may result from the two following hypotheses, namely: that the witness utters the truth or that he deceives. Following the principle that has been expounded on the probability of causes drawn from events observed it is necessary first to determine *à priori* the probability of the event in each hypothesis. In the first, the probability that the witness will announce number 79 is the probability itself of the drawing of this number, that is to say, $1/1000$. It is necessary to multiply it by the probability $9/10$ of the veracity of the witness; one will have then $9/10000$ for the probability of the event observed in this hypothesis. If the witness deceives, number 79 is not drawn, and the probability of this case is $999/1000$. But to announce the drawing of this number the witness has to choose it among the 999 numbers not drawn; and as he is supposed to have no motive of preference for the ones rather than the others, the probability that he will choose number 79 is $1/999$; multiplying, then, this probability by the preceding one, we shall have $1/1000$ for the probability that the witness will announce number 79 in the second hypothesis. It is necessary again to multiply this probability by $1/10$ of the hypothesis itself, which gives $1/10000$ for the probability of the event relative to this hypothesis. Now if we form a fraction whose numerator is the probability relative to the first hypothesis, and whose denominator is the sum of the probabilities relative to the two hypotheses, we shall have, by the sixth principle, the probability of the first hypothesis, and this probability will be $9/10$; that is to say, the veracity itself of the witness. This is likewise the probability of the drawing of number 79. The probability of the falsehood of the witness and of the failure of drawing this number is $1/10$.

If the witness, wishing to deceive, has some interest in choosing number 79 among the numbers not drawn,—if he judges, for example, that having placed upon this number a considerable stake, the announcement of its drawing will increase his credit, the probability that he will choose this number will no longer be as at first, $1/999$, it will then be $1/2$, $1/3$, etc., according to the interest that he will have in announcing its drawing. Supposing it to be $1/9$, it will be necessary to multiply by this fraction the probability $999/1000$ in order to get in the hypothesis of the falsehood the probability of the event observed, which it is necessary still to multiply by $1/10$, which gives $111/10000$ for the probability of the event in the second hypothesis. Then the probability of the first hypothesis, or of the drawing of number 79, is reduced by the preceding rule to $9/120$. It is then very much decreased by the consideration of the interest which the witness may have in announcing the drawing of number 79. In truth this same interest increases the probability $9/10$ that the witness will speak the truth if number 79 is drawn. But this probability cannot exceed unity or $10/10$; thus the probability of the drawing of number 79 will not surpass $10/121$. Common sense tells us that this interest ought to inspire distrust, but calculus appreciates the influence of it.

The probability *à priori* of the number announced by the witness is unity divided by the number of the numbers in the urn; it is changed by virtue of the proof into the veracity itself of the witness; it may then be decreased by the proof. If, for example, the urn contains only two numbers, which gives 1/2 for the probability *à priori* of the drawing of number 1, and if the veracity of a witness who announces it is 4/10, this drawing becomes less probable. Indeed it is apparent, since the witness has then more inclination towards a falsehood than towards the truth, that this testimony ought to decrease the probability of the fact attested every time that this probability equals or surpasses 1/2. But if there are three numbers in the urn the probability *à priori* of the drawing of number 1 is increased by the affirmation of a witness whose veracity surpasses 1/3.

Suppose now that the urn contains 999 black balls and one white ball, and that one ball having been drawn a witness of the drawing announces that this ball is white. The probability of the event observed, determined *à priori* in the first hypothesis, will be here, as in the preceding question, equal to 9/10000. But in the hypothesis where the witness deceives, the white ball is not drawn and the probability of this case is 999/1000. It is necessary to multiply it by the probability 1/10 of the falsehood, which gives 999/10000 for the probability of the event observed relative to the second hypothesis. This probability was only 1/10000 in the preceding question; this great difference results from this—that a black ball having been drawn the witness who wishes to deceive has no choice at all to make among the 999 balls not drawn in order to announce the drawing of a white ball. Now if one forms two fractions whose numerators are the probabilities relative to each hypothesis, and whose common denominator is the sum of these probabilities, one will have 9/1008 for the probability of the first hypothesis and of the drawing of a white ball, and 999/1008 for the probability of the second hypothesis and of the drawing of a black ball. This last probability strongly approaches certainty; it would approach it much nearer and would become 999999/1000008 if the urn contained a million balls of which one was white, the drawing of a white ball becoming then much more extraordinary. We see thus how the probability of the falsehood increases in the measure that the deed becomes more extraordinary.

We have supposed up to this time that the witness was not mistaken at all; but if one admits, however, the chance of his error the extraordinary incident becomes more improbable. Then in place of the two hypotheses one will have the four following ones, namely: that of the witness not deceiving and not being mistaken at all; that of the witness not deceiving at all and being mistaken; the hypothesis of the witness deceiving and not being mistaken at all; finally, that of the witness deceiving and being mistaken. Determining *à priori* in each of these hypotheses the probability of the event observed, we find by the sixth principle the probability that the fact attested is false equal to a fraction whose numerator is the number of black balls in the urn multiplied by the sum of the probabilities that the witness does not deceive at all and is mistaken, or that he deceives and is not mistaken, and whose denominator is this numerator augmented by the sum of the probabilities that the witness does not deceive at all and is not mistaken at all, or that he deceives and is mistaken at the same time. We see by this that if the number of black balls in the urn is very great, which renders the drawing of the white ball extraordinary, the probability that the fact attested is not true approaches most nearly to certainty.

Applying this conclusion to all extraordinary deeds it results from it that the probability of the error or of the falsehood of the witness becomes as much greater as the fact attested is more extraordinary. Some authors have advanced the contrary on this basis that the view of an extraordinary fact being perfectly similar to that of an ordinary fact the same motives ought to lead us to give the witness the same credence when he affirms the one or the other of these facts. Simple common sense rejects such a strange assertion; but the calculus of probabilities, while confirming the findings of common sense, appreciates the greatest improbability of testimonies in regard to extraordinary facts.

These authors insist and suppose two witnesses equally worthy of belief, of whom the first attests that he saw an individual dead fifteen days ago whom the second witness affirms to have seen yesterday full of life. The one or the other of these facts offers no improbability. The reservation of the individual is a result of their combination; but the testimonies do not bring us at all directly to this result, although the credence which is due these testimonies ought not to be decreased by the fact that the result of their combination is extraordinary.

But if the conclusion which results from the combination of the testimonies was impossible one of them would be necessarily false; but an impossible conclusion is the limit of extraordinary conclusions, as error is the limit of improbable conclusions; the value of the testimonies which becomes zero in the case of an impossible conclusion ought then to be very much decreased in that of an extraordinary conclusion. This is indeed confirmed by the calculus of probabilities.

In order to make it plain let us consider two urns, A and B, of which the first contains a million white balls and the second a million black balls. One draws from one of these urns a ball, which he puts back into the other urn, from which one then draws a ball. Two witnesses, the one of the first drawing, the other of the second, attest that the ball which they have seen drawn is white without indicating the urn from which it has been drawn. Each testimony taken alone is not improbable; and it is easy to see that the probability of the fact attested is the veracity itself of the witness. But it follows from the combination of the testimonies that a white ball has been extracted from the urn A at the first draw, and that then placed in the urn B it has reappeared at the second draw, which is very extraordinary; for this second urn, containing then one white ball among a million black balls, the probability of drawing the white ball is 1/1000001. In order to determine the diminution which results in the probability of the thing announced by the two witnesses we shall notice that the event observed is here the affirmation by each of them that the ball which he has seen extracted is white. Let us represent by 9/10 the probability that he announces the truth, which can occur in the present case when the witness does not deceive and is not mistaken at all, and when he deceives and is mistaken at the same time. One may form the four following hypotheses:

1st. The first and second witness speak the truth. Then a white ball has at first been drawn from the urn A, and the probability of this event is 1/2, since the ball drawn at the first draw may have been drawn either from the one or the other urn. Consequently the ball drawn, placed in the urn B, has reappeared at the second draw; the probability of this event is 1/1000001 the probability of the fact announced is then 1/2000002. Multiplying it by the product of the probabilities 9/10 and 9/10 that the witnesses speak the truth one will have 81/200000200 for the probability of the event observed in this first hypothesis.

2nd. The first witness speaks the truth and the second does not, whether he deceives and is not mistaken or he does not deceive and is mistaken. Then a white ball has been drawn from the urn A at the first draw, and the probability of this event is 1/2. Then this ball having been placed in the urn B a black ball has been drawn from it: the probability of such drawing is 1000000/1000001; one has then 1000000/2000002 for the probability of the compound event. Multiplying it by the product of the two probabilities 9/10 and 1/10 that the first witness speaks the truth and that the second does not, one will have 9000000/200000200 for the probability for the event observed in the second hypothesis.

3rd. The first witness does not speak the truth and the second announces it. Then a black ball has been drawn from the urn B at the first drawing, and after having been placed in the urn A a white ball has been drawn from this urn. The probability of the first of these events is 1/2 and that of the second is 1000000/1000001; the probability of the compound event is then 10000/2000002. Multiplying it by the product of the probabilities 1/10 and 9/10 that the first witness does not speak the truth and that the second announces it, one will have 9000000/200000200 for the probability of the event observed relative to this hypothesis.

4th. Finally, neither of the witnesses speaks the truth. Then a black ball has been drawn from the urn B at the first draw; then having been placed in the urn A it has reappeared at the second drawing: the probability of this compound event is 1/2000002. Multiplying it by the product of the probabilities 1/10 and 1/10 that each witness does not speak the truth one will have 1/200000200 for the probability of the event observed in this hypothesis.

Now in order to obtain the probability of the thing announced by the two witnesses, namely, that a white ball has been drawn at each draw, it is necessary to divide the probability corresponding to the first hypothesis by the sum of the probabilities relative to the four hypotheses; and then one has for this probability 81/18000082, an extremely small fraction.

If the two witnesses affirm the first, that a white ball has been drawn from one of the two urns A and B; the second that a white ball has been likewise drawn from one of the two urns A' and B', quite similar to the first ones, the probability of the thing announced by the two witnesses will be the product of the probabilities of their testimonies, or 81/100; it will then be at least a hundred and eighty thousand times greater than the preceding one. One sees by this how much, in the first case, the reappearance at the second draw of the white ball drawn at the first draw, the extraordinary conclusion of the two testimonies decreases the value of it.

We would give no credence to the testimony of a man who should attest to us that in throwing a hundred dice into the air they had all fallen on the same face. If we had ourselves been spectators of this event we should believe our own eyes only after having carefully examined all the circumstances, and after having brought in the testimonies of other eyes in order to be quite sure that there had been neither hallucination nor deception. But after this examination we should not hesitate to admit it in spite of its extreme improbability; and no one would be tempted, in order to explain it, to recur to a denial of the laws of vision. We ought to conclude from it that the probability of the constancy of the laws of nature is for us greater than this, that the event in question has not taken place at all—a probability greater than that of the majority of historical facts which we regard as incontestable. One may judge by this the immense weight of testimonies necessary to admit a suspension of natural laws, and how improper it would be to apply to this case the ordinary rules of criticism. All those who without offering this immensity of testimonies support this when making recitals of events contrary to those laws, decrease rather than augment the belief which they wish to inspire; for then those recitals render very probable the error or the falsehood of their authors. But that which diminishes the belief of educated men increases often that of the uneducated, always greedy for the wonderful.

There are things so extraordinary that nothing can balance their improbability. But this, by the effect of a dominant opinion, can be weakened to the point of appearing inferior to the probability of the testimonies; and when this opinion changes an absurd statement admitted unanimously in the century which has given it birth offers to the following centuries only a new proof of the extreme influence of the general opinion upon the more enlightened minds. Two great men of the century of Louis XIV—Racine and Pascal—are striking examples of this. It is painful to see with what complaisance Racine, this admirable painter of the human heart and the most perfect poet that has ever lived, reports as miraculous the recovery of Mlle. Perrier, a niece of Pascal and a day pupil at the monastery of Port-Royal; it is painful to read the reasons by which

Pascal seeks to prove that this miracle should be necessary to religion in order to justify the doctrine of the monks of this abbey, at that time persecuted by the Jesuits. The young Perrier had been afflicted for three years and a half by a lachrymal fistula; she touched her afflicted eye with a relic which was pretended to be one of the thorns of the crown of the Saviour and she had faith in instant recovery. Some days afterward the physicians and the surgeons attest the recovery, and they declare that nature and the remedies have had no part in it. This event, which took place in 1656, made a great sensation, and "all Paris rushed," says Racine, "to Port-Royal. The crowd increased from day to day, and God himself seemed to take pleasure in authorizing the devotion of the people by the number of miracles which were performed in this church." At this time miracles and sorcery did not yet appear improbable, and one did not hesitate at all to attribute to them the singularities of nature which could not be explained otherwise.

This manner of viewing extraordinary results is found in the most remarkable works of the century of Louis XIV.; even in the Essay on the Human Understanding by the philosopher Locke, who says, in speaking of the degree of assent: "Though the common experience and the ordinary course of things have justly a mighty influence on the minds of men, to make them give or refuse credit to anything proposed to their belief; yet there is one case, wherein the strangeness of the fact lessens not the assent to a fair testimony of it. For where such supernatural events are suitable to ends aimed at by him who has the power to change the course of nature, there, under such circumstances, they may be the fitter to procure belief, by how much the more they are beyond or contrary to ordinary observation." The true principles of the probability of testimonies having been thus misunderstood by philosophers to whom reason is principally indebted for its progress, I have thought it necessary to present at length the results of calculus upon this important subject.

There comes up naturally at this point the discussion of a famous argument of Pascal, that Craig, an English mathematician, has produced under a geometric form. Witnesses declare that they have it from Divinity that in conforming to a certain thing one will enjoy not one or two but an infinity of happy lives. However feeble the probability of the proofs may be, provided that it be not infinitely small, it is clear that the advantage of those who conform to the prescribed thing is infinite since it is the product of this probability and an infinite good; one ought not to hesitate then to procure for oneself this advantage.

This argument is based upon the infinite number of happy lives promised in the name of the Divinity by the witnesses; it is necessary then to prescribe them, precisely because they exaggerate their promises beyond all limits, a consequence which is repugnant to good sense. Also calculus teaches us that this exaggeration itself enfeebles the probability of their testimony to the point of rendering it infinitely small or zero. Indeed this case is similar to that of a witness who should announce the drawing of the highest number from an urn filled with a great number of numbers, one of which has been drawn and who would have a great interest in announcing the drawing of this number. One has already seen how much this interest enfeebles his testimony. In evaluating only at 1/2 he probability that if the witness deceives he will choose the largest number, calculus gives the probability of his announcement as smaller than a fraction whose numerator is unity and whose denominator is unity plus the half of the product of the number of the numbers by the probability of falsehood considered *à priori* or independently of the announcement. In order to compare this case to that of the argument of Pascal it is sufficient to represent by the numbers in the urn all the possible numbers of happy lives which the number of these numbers renders infinite; and to observe that if the witnesses deceive they have the greatest interest, in order to accredit their falsehood, in promising an eternity of happiness. The expression of the probability of their testimony becomes then infinitely small. Multiplying it by the infinite number of happy lives promised, infinity would disappear from the product which expresses the advantage resultant from this promise which destroys the argument of Pascal.

Let us consider now the probability of the totality of several testimonies upon an established fact. In order to fix our ideas let us suppose that the fact be the drawing of a number from an urn which contains a hundred of them, and of which one single number has been drawn. Two witnesses of this drawing announce that number 2 has been drawn, and one asks for the resultant probability of the totality of these testimonies. One may form these two hypotheses: the witnesses speak the truth; the witnesses deceive. In the first hypothesis the number 2 is drawn and the probability of this event is 1/100. It is necessary to multiply it by the product of the veracities of the witnesses, veracities which we will suppose to be 9/10 and 7/10: one will have then 63/10000 for the probability of the event observed in this hypothesis. In the second, the number 2 is not drawn and the probability of this event is 99/100. But the agreement of the witnesses requires then that in seeking to deceive they both choose the number 2 from the 99 numbers not drawn: the probability of this choice if the witnesses do not have a secret agreement is the product of the fraction 1/99 by itself; it becomes necessary then to multiply these two probabilities together, and by the product of the probabilities 1/10 and 3/10 that the witnesses deceive; one will have thus 1/330000 for the probability of the event observed in the second hypothesis. Now one will have the probability of the fact attested or of the drawing of number 2 in dividing the probability relative to the first hypothesis by the sum of the probabilities relative to the two hypotheses; this probability will be then 2079/2080, and the probability of the failure to draw this number and of the falsehood of the witnesses will be 1/2080.

If the urn should contain only the numbers 1 and 2 one would find in the same manner 21/22 for the probability of the drawing of number 2, and consequently 1/22 for the probability of the falsehood of the witnesses, a probability at least ninety-four times larger than the preceding one. One sees by this how much the probability of the falsehood of the witnesses diminishes when the fact which they attest is less probable in itself. Indeed one conceives that then the accord of the witnesses, when they deceive, becomes more difficult, at least when they do not have a secret agreement, which we do not suppose here at all.

In the preceding case where the urn contained only two numbers the *à priori* probability of the fact attested is 1/2, the resultant probability of the testimonies is the product of the veracities of the witnesses divided by this product added to that of the respective probabilities of their falsehood.

It now remains for us to consider the influence of time upon the probability of facts transmitted by a traditional chain of witnesses. It is clear that this probability ought to diminish in proportion as the chain is prolonged. If the fact has no probability itself, such as the drawing of a number from an urn which contains an infinity of them, that which it acquires by the testimonies decreases according to the continued product of the veracity of the witnesses. If the fact has a probability in itself; if, for example, this fact is the drawing of the number 2 from an urn which contains an infinity of them, and of which it is certain that one has drawn a single number; that which the traditional chain adds to this probability decreases, following a continued product of which the first factor is the ratio of the number of numbers in the urn less one to the same number, and of which each other factor is the veracity of each witness diminished by the ratio of the probability of his falsehood to the number of the numbers in the urn less one; so that the limit of the probability of the fact is that of this fact considered *à priori*, or independently of the testimonies, a probability equal to unity divided by the number of the numbers in the urn.

The action of time enfeebles then, without ceasing, the probability of historical facts just as it changes the most durable monuments. One can indeed diminish it by multiplying and conserving the testimonies and the monuments which support them. Printing offers for this purpose a great means, unfortunately unknown to the ancients. In spite of the infinite advantages which it procures the physical and moral revolutions by which the surface of this globe will always be agitated will end, in conjunction with the inevitable effect of time, by rendering doubtful after thousands of years the historical facts regarded to-day as the most certain.

Craig has tried to submit to calculus the gradual enfeebling of the proofs of the Christian religion; supposing that the world ought to end at the epoch when it will cease to be probable, he finds that this ought to take place 1454 years after the time when he writes. But his analysis is as faulty as his hypothesis upon the duration of the moon is bizarre.

## Charles Babbage, Ninth Bridgewater Treatise *(2d ed. 1838), Chapter 10, "On Hume's Argument against Miracles"*

Few arguments have excited greater attention, and produced more attempts at refutation, than the celebrated one of David Hume, respecting miracles; and it might be added, that more sophistry has been advanced against it, than its author employed in the whole of his writings.

It must be admitted that in the argument, as originally developed by its author, there exists some confusion between personal experience and that which is derived from testimony; and that there are several other points open to criticism and objection; but the main argument, divested of its less important adjuncts, never has, and never will be refuted. Dr. Johnson seems to have been of this opinion, as the following extract from his life by Boswell proves:—

"Talking of Dr. Johnson's unwillingness to believe extraordinary things, I ventured to say—

" 'Sir, you come near to Hume's argument against miracles—That it is more probable witnesses should lie, or be mistaken, than that they should happen.'

"Johnson.—'Why, Sir, Hume, taking the proposition simply, is right. But the Christian revelation is not proved by miracles alone, but as connected with prophecies, and with the doctrines in confirmation of which miracles were wrought.' " [1]

Hume contends that a miracle is a violation of the laws of nature; and as a firm and unalterable experience has established these laws, the proof against a miracle from the very nature of the fact, is as entire as any argument from experience can possibly be imagined.

> The plain consequences is (and it is a general maxim worthy of our attention), that no testimony is sufficient to establish a miracle, unless the testimony be of such a kind, that its falsehood would be more miraculous than the fact which it endeavors to establish: and even in that case there is a mutual destruction of arguments, and the superior only gives us an assurance suitable to that degree of force which remains after deducting the inferior. [2]

The word *miraculous* employed in this passage is evidently equivalent to *improbable*, although the improbability is of a very high degree.

The condition, therefore, which, it is asserted by the argument of Hume, must be fulfilled with regard to the testimony, is that the *improbability* of its falsehood must be GREATER than the *improbability* of the occurrence of the fact.

This is a condition which, when the terms in which it is expressed are understood, immediately commands our assent. It is in the subsequent stage of the reasoning that the fallacy is introduced. Hume asserts, that this condition cannot be fulfilled by the evidence of *any number* of witnesses, because our experience of the truth of human testimony is not uniform and without any exceptions; whereas, our experience of the course of nature, or our experience against miracles, is uniform and uninterrupted.

The only sound way of trying the validity of this assertion is to *measure* the numerical value of the two improbabilities, one of which it is admitted must be greater than the other; and to ascertain whether, by making any hypothesis respecting the veracity of each witness, it is possible to fulfil that condition by any finite number of such witnesses.

Hume appears to have been but very slightly acquainted with the doctrine of probabilities, and, indeed, at the period when he wrote, the details by which the conclusion he had arrived at could be proved or refuted were yet to be examined and arranged. It is, however, remarkable that the opinion he maintained respecting our knowledge of causation is one which eminently brings the whole question within the province of the calculus of probabilities. In fact, its solution can only be *completely* understood by those who are acquainted with that most difficult branch of science. By those who are not so prepared, certain calculations, which will be found more fully developed in the Note (E), must be taken for granted; and all that can be attempted will be, to convey to them a general outline of the nature of the principles on which these enquiries depend.

A miracle is, according to Hume, an event which has never happened within the experience of the whole human race. Now, the improbability of the future happening of such an occurrence may be calculated according to two different views.

We may conceive an urn, containing *only* black and white balls, from which *m* black balls have been successively drawn and replaced, one by one; and we may calculate the probability of appearance of a white ball at the next drawing. This would be analogous to the case of one human being raised from the dead after *m* instances to the contrary.

Looking, in another point of view, at a miracle, we may imagine an urn to contain a very large number of tickets, on each of which is written one of the series of natural numbers. These being thoroughly mixed together, a single ticket is drawn: the prediction of the particular number inscribed on the ticket about to be drawn may be assimilated to the occurrence of a miracle.

According to either of these views, the probability of the occurrence of such an event by mere accident may be calculated. Now, the reply to Hume's argument is this: Admitting at once the essential point, viz. that the improbability of the concurrence of the witnesses in falsehood must be *greater* than the improbability of the miracle, it may be denied that this does not take place. Hume has asserted that, in order to prove a miracle, a certain improbability must be *greater* than another; and he has also asserted that this *never* can take place.

Now, as each improbability can be truly measured by number, the *only* way to refute Hume's argument is by examining the *magnitude* of these numbers. This examination depends on known and admitted principles, for which the reader, who is prepared by previous study, may refer to the work of Laplace, *Théorie Analytique des Probabilités;* Poisson, *Recherches sur la Probabilité des Jugements,* 1837; or he may consult the article *Probabilities,* by Mr. De Morgan, in the Encyclopaedia Metropolitana, in which he will find this subject examined.

One of the most important principles on which the question rests, is the concurrence of the testimony of independent witnesses. This principle has been stated by Campbell, and has been employed by the Archbishop of Dublin,[3] and also by Dr. Chalmers.[4] It requires however to be combined with another principle, in order to obtain the numerical values of the quantities spoken of in the argument. The following example may be sufficient for a popular illustration.

Let us suppose that there are witnesses who will speak the truth, and who are not themselves deceived in ninety-nine cases out of a hundred. Now, let us examine what is the probability of the falsehood of a statement about to be made by two such persons absolutely unknown to and unconnected with each other.

Since the order in which independent witnesses give their testimony does not affect their credit, we may suppose that, in a given number of statements, both witnesses tell the truth in the ninety-nine first cases, and the falsehood in the hundredth.

Then the first time the second witness B testifies, he will agree with the testimony of the first witness A, in the ninety-nine first cases, and differ from him in the hundredth. Similarly, in the second testimony of B, he will again agree with A in ninety-nine cases, and differ in the hundredth, and so on for ninety-nine times; so that, after A has testified a hundred, and B ninety-nine times, we shall have 99 × 99 cases in which both agree, 99 cases in which they differ, A being wrong. Now, in the hundredth case in which B testifies, he is wrong; and, if we combine this with the testimony of A, we have ninety-nine cases in which A will be right and B wrong; and one case only in which both A and B will agree in error. The whole number of cases, which amounts to ten thousand, may be thus divided:—

99 × 99 = 9801 cases in which A and B agree in truth,
　1 × 99 = 99 cases in which B is true and A false,
99 × 1 = 99 cases in which A is true and B false,
　　1 × 1 = 1 case in which both A and B agree in falsehood.

———————————
　　　10,000 cases.

As there is only one case in ten thousand in which two such independent witnesses can agree in error, the probability of their future testimony being false is $1/10,000$ or $1/(100)^2$.

The reader will already perceive how great a reliance is due to the *future* concurring testimony of two independent witnesses of tolerably good character and understanding. It appears that, previously to the testimony, the chance of one such witness being in error is $1/100$; that of two concurring in the same error is $1/(100)^2$; and if the same reasoning be applied to three independent witnesses, it will be found that the probability of their agreeing in error is $1/(100)^3$; or that the odds are 999,999 to 1 against the agreement.

Pursuing the same reasoning, the probability of the falsehood of a fact which six such independent witnesses attest is, previously to the testimony, $1/(100)^6$ or it is, in round numbers, 1,000,000,000,000 to 1 against the falsehood of their testimony.

The improbability of the miracle of a dead man being restored, is, on the principles stated by Hume, $1/20(100)^5$; or it is—200,000,000,000 to 1 against its occurrence.

It follows, then, that the chances of accidental or other independent concurrence of only *six* such independent witnesses, is already *five times* as great as the improbability against the miracle of a dead man's being restored to life, deduced from Hume's method of estimating its probability solely from experience.

This illustration shows the great accumulation of probability arising from the concurrence of independent witnesses: we must however combine this principle with another, before we can arrive at the real numerical value of the improbabilities referred to in the argument.

The calculation of the numerical values of these improbabilities I have given in Note (E.)

From this it results that, provided we assume that independent witnesses can be found of whose testimony it can be stated that it is more probable that it is true than that it is false, *we can always assign a number of witnesses which will, according to Hume's argument, prove the truth of a miracle.*


## Note E

The reader will observe, that throughout the chapter to which this note refers, as well as in the note itself, the argument of Hume is taken strictly according to his own interpretation of the terms he uses, and the calculations are founded on them; so that it is from the very argument itself, when fairly pursued to its full extent, that the refutation results.

Both our belief in the truth of human testimony, and our belief in the permanence of the laws of nature, are, according to Hume, founded on experience; we may, therefore, in the complete ignorance in which he assumes we are, with respect to the causes of either, treat the question as one of the probability of an event deduced solely from observations of the past. The argument of Hume asserts, that one improbability, namely, that of the falsehood of the testimony in favour of a miracle, must always be *greater* than another improbability, namely, that of the occurrence of the miracle itself; and also, that, from the very nature of human experience, this preponderance can *never* take place.

Now the ONLY POSSIBLE mode of disproving the assertion, that one thing cannot, under any circumstances, be greater than another, is to measure, under all circumstances, the numerical value of the two things so compared, and the truth or falsehood of the assertion will then appear. The doctrine of chances, which has been much improved since the time of Hume, now enables us to apply precise measures to this argument; and it is the object of this Note to state the outlines of the calculation, and the results to which it leads. Previously to this, however, it may not be amiss to offer a few remarks on the Principles about to be employed.

In the great work of Laplace, "Theorie Analytique des Probabilités," those principles are established, and they are not merely undisputed, but are admitted by other writers of the highest authority on this subject. They form a part of the received knowledge of the present day, and, as such, they are employed in the present work, in which I propose to use, not to discuss them. I state this, because it has occasionally been asserted by persons unacquainted with the doctrine of chances, that the argument respecting the probability or improbability of miracles does not admit of the application of numbers. The received foundations of science are not to be put aside by such opinions, however highly skilled their authors may be in other branches of knowledge, and however powerful the intellect by which they may have attained those acquirements. The conclusions arrived at by the application of pure analysis must ever rest on the truth of the principles assumed at the commencement of the inquiry; and although a knowledge of mathematics may not appear necessary for forming a right judgment of the accuracy of those principles, yet it is observed, that a clear apprehension of them is not often found in the minds of those who are unacquainted with that science. When, however, the grounds on which the principles employed in the doctrine of chances are called in question by competent authority, it will be time enough to examine the question; and none will more eagerly enter upon that examination than those best versed in it, for none are so well aware of the extreme difficulty and delicacy of the subject.

As confusion sometimes arises from the difference in the meaning of the words *probable* and *improbable* in popular language and in mathematical inquiries, it may be convenient to point it out; and to state, that in this Note it is used in the mathematical sense, unless the reader's attention is directly called to a question relating to its popular sense.

In common language, an event is said to be *probable* when it is more likely to happen than to fail: it is said to be *improbable* when it is more likely to fail than to happen.

Now, an event whose probability is, in mathematical language $1/p$, will be called probable or improbable, in ordinary language, according as $p$ is less or greater than 2.

If, in mathematical language, $1/p$ expresses the *probability* of an event happening, $1 - 1/p$ expresses the probability of its failing, or the *improbability* of its happening.

It has been stated in the text, that two views may be taken of those extraordinary deviations from the usual course of nature, called miracles. According to the first of these, we have to calculate the probability that a *white* ball has been drawn from an urn (containing only white and black balls, out of which $m$ balls have been drawn all black), as deduced from the testimony of witnesses whose probability of speaking truth is known:—or, of the analogous case; it having been observed that $m$ persons have died without any restoration to life, what is the probability that such a resurrection has happened, it having been asserted by $n$ independent witnesses, the probability of each of whose speaking false is $1/p$?

The probability of the death without resurrection of the $(m+1)$th is $(m+1)/(m+2)$, and the improbability of such an occurrence, independently of testimony, is $1/(m+2)$; which is therefore the probability of a contrary occurrence, or that of a person being raised from the dead.

Now only two hypotheses can be formed, collusion being, by hypothesis, out of the question: either the event did happen, and the witnesses agree in speaking the truth, the probability of their concurrence being $(1—1/p)^n$, and of that of the hypothesis being $1/(m+2)$; or the event did not happen, and the witnesses agree in a falsehood, the probability of their concurrence being $(1/p)^n$, and that of the hypothesis $(m+1)/(m+2)$.

The probability of the witnesses speaking truth, and the event occurring, is therefore,

$$\frac{(1 - 1/p)^n(1/(m+2))}{(1 - 1/p)^n(1/(m+2)) + (1/p)^n((m+1)/(m+2))} \qquad (A.)$$
$$= \frac{(p - 1)^n}{(p - 1)^n + m + 1};$$

and the probability of their falsehood is,

$$\frac{(1/p)^n((m + 1)/(m + 2))}{(1 - 1/p)^n(1/(m + 2)) + (1/p)^n((m + 1)/(m + 2))} \qquad (B.)$$
$$= \frac{m + 1}{(p - 1)^n + m + 1}.$$

If we interpret Hume's assertion, "that the falsehood of the witnesses must be more improbable than the occurrence of the miracle," according to the mathematical meaning of the word improbable, then we must have,

$$\frac{m + 1}{(p - 1)^n + m + 1} < \frac{1}{m + 2};$$

or,

$$(m + 1)(m + 2) < (p - 1)^n + m + 1;$$

hence,

$$(p - 1)^n > (m + 1)(m + 2) - (m + 1) > (m + 1)^2,$$

from which we find,

$$n > \frac{2\log(m + 1)}{\log(p - 1)}.$$

If $p$ is any number greater than two, this equation can always be satisfied.

It follows, therefore, that however large $m$ may be, or however great the quantity of experience against the occurrence of a miracle, (provided only that there are persons whose statements are more frequently correct than incorrect, and who give their testimony in favour of it without collusion,) a certain number $n$ can ALWAYS be found; so that *it shall be a greater improbability that their unanimous statement shall be a falsehood, than that the miracle shall have occurred.*

Let us now suppose each witness to state one falsehood for every ten truths, or $p = 11$, and $m = 1000,000,000,000$; then

$$n > \frac{2\log(10^{12} + 1)}{\log(10)} > 24.$$

or twenty-five such witnesses are sufficient.

If the witnesses only state one falsehood for every hundred truths, then thirteen such witnesses are sufficient.

Another view of the question might be taken; and it might be asserted that, in order to believe in the miracle, the probability of its truth must be greater than the probability of its falsehood; in this case the expression $(A)$ must be greater than $(B)$; or,

$$\frac{(p - 1)^n}{(p - 1)^n + m + 1} > \frac{m + 1}{(p - 1)^n + m + 1};$$

hence,

$$(p - 1)^n > m + 1,$$

and

$$n > \frac{\log(m + 1)}{\log(p - 1)}.$$

In this case also, under the same circumstances, the condition can always be fulfilled of finding a sufficient number of witnesses to render the miracle probable, or even to give to it any required degree of probability.

If $p = 11$, and $m = 1000,000,000,000$, as before, then

$$n > \frac{\log(10^{12} + 1)}{\log(10)} > 12.$$

According to the second view stated in the text, a miracle may be assimilated to the drawing of a given number $i$ out of an urn, containing all numbers from one to $m$.

In this case the probability of the occurrence of the event is $1/m$, and the probability of the concurrence of $n$ witnesses in falsehood is $(1/p)^n$.

Hence the probability that the particular number $i$ was drawn, as deduced from the testimony of $n$ witnesses, each of whose probability of falsehood is $1/p$, is expressed by,

$$\frac{(1 - 1/p)^n(1/m)}{(1 - 1/p)^n(1/m) + (1/p)^n(1 - 1/m)[1/(m - 1)]^n}$$
$$= \frac{(p - 1)^n}{(p - 1)^n + (m - 1)[1/(m - 1)]^n} \qquad (C.)$$
$$= \frac{1}{1 + (m - 1)[1/((m - 1)(p - 1))]^n}$$

and the probability of the number $i$ not having been drawn, or of their falsehood, is

$$\frac{(1/p)^n(1 - 1/m)[1/(m - 1)]^n}{(1 - 1/p)^n(1/m) + (1/p)^n(1 - 1/m)[1/(m - 1)]^n}$$
$$= \frac{(m - 1)[1/(m - 1)]^n}{(p - 1)^n + (m - 1)[1/(m - 1)]^n} \qquad (D.)$$
$$= \frac{m - 1}{[(p - 1)(m - 1)]^n + (m - 1)}$$

Hence the improbability of the testimony must, according to Hume, be greater than that of the occurrence of the event; or;

$$\frac{m - 1}{[(p - 1)(m - 1)]^n + m - 1} < \frac{1}{m}.$$

Hence,

$$m(m - 1) < [(p - 1)(m - 1)]^n + m - 1,$$

and

$$[(p - 1)(m - 1)]^n > m(m - 1) - m - 1 > (m - 1)^2,$$

or

$$n > \frac{2\log(m - 1)}{\log(p - 1) + \log(m - 1)}.$$

If $p = 11$ and $m = 1000,000,000,000$, as above,

$$n > \frac{2 \times 12}{1 + 12} > \frac{24}{13} > 2.$$

If it is only required that the probability of the occurrence of the miracle shall be greater than its improbability, then we must make (C) greater than (D); or,

$$\frac{1}{1 + (m - 1)[1/((m - 1)(p - 1))]^n} > \frac{m - 1}{[(p - 1)(m - 1)]^n + m - 1};$$

from which,

$$\frac{[(m - 1)(p - 1)]^n}{[(m - 1)(p - 1)]^n + m - 1} > \frac{m - 1}{[(p - 1)(m - 1)]^n + m - 1},$$

or

$$[(m - 1)(p - 1)]^n > m - 1.$$

Hence,

$$n > \frac{\log(m - 1)}{\log(m - 1) + \log(p - 1)}.$$

If $p = 11$, and $m = 1000,000,000,000$, $n > \dfrac{12}{12 + 1} > \dfrac{12}{13}$.

Hence in this view, also, a sufficient number of witnesses of given veracity may *always* be found to render the improbability of their concurrent independent testimony being false, greater than the improbability of the occurrence of the miracle.

There is, however, one other view, which it seems probable would have been that taken by Hume himself, had he applied numbers to his own argument. Considering the probability of the coincidence in falsehood of $n$ persons each having the probability $(p - 1)/p$ in favour of his truth, which is $1/p^n$ that probability ought to be less than that of the occurrence of the miracle; or,

$$\frac{1}{p^n} < \frac{1}{m + 2};$$

hence,

$$p^n > m + 2,$$

or,

$$n > \frac{\log(m + 2)}{\log(p)}.$$

According to this view also, if $m = 1000,000,000,000$, and $p = 11$, $n > \dfrac{12}{1.04} > 12.$[5]

This view of the question refers to the probability of the concurrence of the witnesses before they have given their testimony. The other four cases relate to the probability of the miracle having happened, as deduced from the fact of the testimony having been given. The last seems to have been that which Hume would have himself arrived at; the others represent the true methods of estimating the probabilities of the various cases: and the important conclusion follows, that, whichever be the interpretation given to the argument of Hume, if independent witnesses can be found, who speak truth more frequently than falsehood, it is ALWAYS *possible to assign a number of independent witnesses, the improbability of the falsehood of whose concurring testimony shall be greater than that of the improbability of the miracle itself.*

It is to be observed, the whole of this argument applies to *independent* witnesses. The possibility of the collusion, and the degree of credit to be assigned to witnesses under any given circumstances, depend on facts which have not yet been sufficiently collected to become the subject of mathematical inquiry. Some of those considerations which bear on this part of the subject, the reader will find treated in the work of Dr. Conyers Middelton, entitled "A Free Inquiry into the Miraculous Powers which are supposed to have subsisted in the Christian Church, from the time of the earliest Ages through several successive centuries." London, 1749.

*Notes*

1. Boswell's Life of Johnson. Oxford, 1826. vol. iii. p. 169.
2. Hume's Essays, Edinburgh, 1817, vol. ii. p. 117.
3. Elements of Rhetoric, by R. Whately, D. D. p. 57, 1832.
4. Evidence of Christia Revelation, vol. I. p. 129.
5. [Presumably this is a misprint for < 12.]

# Index

agnosticism, 72–73
American Revolution, 24
ampliative reasoning, 29, 73
*Analyst* (Berkeley), 25
Anglican Church, 10, 63
Annet, Peter, 7, 18, 19–20, 45, 42,
    62, 68, 80n.30, 83n.59, 85n.81
  text of *The Resurrection of Jesus*
    *Considered*, 132–40
anti-inductivism, 28–29
asymptotic certainty, of miracle
    occurrence, 57, 58–59
atheism, 9, 72–73

Babbage, Charles, 54–55, 56
  text from *Ninth Bridgewater Treatise*,
    203–12
Bayes, Thomas, 25–31, 82nn.42, 44
Bayesianism, 26–29, 48, 49, 54, 70,
    72–73
  belief and, 26–27, 30–31, 85n.78
  contrary miracles argument and,
    67–68
  religious doctrine probabilifying, 66,
    85n.79
Bayes-Laplace rule. *See* Laplace's rule
  of succession
Bayes' theorem, 27, 29, 43, 47, 69,
    82n.44
  diminution principle and, 49, 50,
    51, 84n.70
  multiple witnessing and, 54, 55, 60
  prior probability, 49, 82nn.50, 52
Berkeley, Bishop, 25
Berlitz, Charles, 3
*Bermuda Triangle, The* (Berlitz), 3
Blair, Hugh, 23, 32, 46, 59, 84n.68,
    85n.75

Boyle, Robert, 10
Boyl, John, 82n.43
Broad, C. D., 21–22, 79–80n.24, 82–
    83nn.54, 55
Burns, R. M., 63, 80–81nn.29, 32, 35
Butler, J., 83n.59

"Calculation of the Credibility of
    Human Testimony, A"
    (Anonymous), 53
  text from, 193–94
Campbell, George, 34, 6, 13, 59, 41–
    42, 43, 83nn.57, 61
  text from *A Dissertation on Miracles*,
    176–93
Carnap, R., 30, 31
causation
  Mill on law of, 37
  supernatural, 8, 13, 14, 22, 62–63
certainty
  asymptotic, 57, 58–59
  moral, 63, 67
Chandler, S., 18, 45
Chubb, Thomas, 67, 68
Clarke, Samuel, 10, 64
  text of "A Discourse Concerning the
    Unalterable Obligations of
    Natural Religion . . . ," 120–25
coincidence, miracles and, 10, 79n.17
conditionalization, rule of, 26–27, 30–
    31, 32, 48, 82nn.48, 49
  Hume's Maxim and, 39, 83–84n.66
confirmation, 27, 66–67, 68–69, 70,
    72
Confucianism, 85n.81
contrary miracles argument, 19, 43,
    67–70, 85–86nn.80, 81, 82
Craig, John, 53, 85n.72

credibility, 4, 13
  Locke on sources of, 15, 17
  of miracles, 5, 11, 18, 21–22, 32,
    38, 40–42, 44–48, 53, 61, 64
  of religious doctrines, 67
  of testimony, 8, 17–18, 25, 38, 69–
    70
Curd, Martin, 14

Dale, A. I., 85n.73
deception, 71
  diminution principle and, 49, 51–52
  miracle credibility and, 44, 47–48
  multiple witnesses and, 54
demarcation criterion, 3
determinism, 9
Dialogue Concerning Heresies (More), 33
Dialogues Concerning Natural Religion
    (Hume), 4–5, 77nn.7, 8
diminution principle, 49–53, 84n.70
"Discourse Concerning the
    Unalterable Obligations of
    Natural Religion, and the Truth
    and Certainty of the Christian
    Revelations, A" (Clarke), text of,
    120–25
"Discourse of Miracles, A" (Locke), 10
  text of, 114–20
Dissertation on Miracles, A (Campbell),
    6, 13, 59
  text from, 176–93
doctrinal credibility, 67
Donegan, Alan, 78–79n.15
Dutch book argument, 26, 82nn.47,
    48

Elisha, 78n.15
Elizabeth I, queen of England, 31, 47,
    56, 61
Elliot, Gilbert, 77n.7
empiricism
  constructive, 73
  logical, 71
Enquiry Concerning Human
    Understanding (Hume), 3, 4, 6–8,
    13, 22, 23, 34, 45, 49, 77n.1,
    84n.68, 86n.84, 140–57
  See also "Of Miracles"
Essay Concerning Human
    Understanding, An (Locke), 15, 17
  text from, 97–107

"Essay towards Solving a Problem in
    the Doctrine of Chances, A"
    (Bayes), 25
expectancy of evidence, 27
eyewitness testimony, 4, 33
  to miracles, 5, 8, 18–22, 35, 41, 44–
    45, 61, 62, 71
  by multiple witnesses, 25, 53–59,
    60
  Spinoza's views on scripture and,
    78–79n.15
  unreliability of, 49, 55

Four Dissertations (Price), 24, 25, 29,
    39–40, 45, 49
  text from, 157–76
Franklin, Alan, 72
Free Enquirer (Annet), 18
Free Inquiry (Middleton), 71

Gale, Richard, 85n.77
Gasking, J. C. A., 16, 80n.27
George III, king of Great Britain, 24
Gibson, Bishop, 16
Gillies, D., 40
God
  miracles and, 9, 10, 62–63, 67
  supports for existence of, 5, 72,
    85n.80
  See also theism
Gower, B., 82n.45
Grieg, J. Y. T., 85n.75

Hambourger, R., 84n.67
Hamilton, William, 6, 78n.11
Herodotus, 18
"Historical Doubts Relative to
    Napoleon Bonaparte" (Whately),
    33
History of England (Hume), 13, 33
Hobbes, Thomas, 5
Holder, Rodney, 86n.83
Home, Henry, 6–7, 16
Hooper, George, 85n.73, 193–94
Howson, Colin, 83nn.63, 64
Huber, Peter, 84n.70
Hume, David, 3, 4–5, 8–9, 11–14, 22–
    25, 28–32, 35–38, 44–45, 47–48,
    62, 71, 81–82nn.37, 38, 39, 41,
    44, 45
  text of "Of Miracles," 140–57

independence of witnesses, 54–55, 57–58, 60–61
independent and identically distributed (IID) trials, 27, 28
Indian prince (Hume example), 14–15, 32–38
induction, 20
    Bayesian perspective, 27, 28–29, 30
    Hume's account of, 3, 4, 5, 13, 22–24, 28–32, 35–37, 81–82nn.37–39
    straight rule of, 22–23, 29–32, 35–37, 81n.36

Jackson, J., 18, 45
Jansenist miracle stories, 31, 32
Jesus
    critiques of resurrection of, 7, 15–20, 45–46, 61, 62, 78–79n.15, 132–40
    dating of Second Coming of, 53
    miracles performed by, 5
Joshua, 78n.15

king of Siam (Locke character), 14, 17, 19, 33, 34
Kusche, Larry, 3

Laplace, Pierre Simon, 50, 51, 56, 85n.72
    text from A Philosophical Essay on Probability, 194–202
laws of nature, 17–18, 82–83nn.54–56
    miracles and, 8–14, 19–20, 22, 78n.14
law statements, 12, 13, 32, 36, 79nn.20, 21, 22, 23
    presumptive, 12, 13, 23–24, 38, 83n.56
    strongly presumptive, 35
Leibniz, G. W., 25, 62
Leviathan (Hobbes), 5
Lewis, David, 79n.21
likelihood of hypothesis, 27
Locke, John, 8, 10, 11, 14–15, 17, 19, 25, 33, 34, 35, 63, 64, 68, 79n.17, 80n.26, 84–86nn.71, 82
    text from Essay Concerning Human Understanding, 97–107

text of "Discourse of Miracles," 114–20
logical positivism, 3, 71
Looking for a Miracle (Nickell), 4

marvels, miracles vs., 11, 13, 21, 32, 33, 37, 49, 84n.68
Methods of Agreement, Difference, Residues and Concomitant Variation (Mill), 37
Meyers, Robert, 78n.10
Middleton, Conyers, 71, 86n.84
Mill, John Stuart, 37, 63
miracles, 4
    coincidence and, 10, 79n.17
    contrary argument, 19, 43, 67–70, 85–86nn.80, 81, 82
    credibility of, 5, 11, 13, 18, 21–22, 32, 38, 40–42, 44–48, 53, 61, 64
    eighteenth-century debate on, 14–20, 63
    evidence for, 19, 20, 41, 42
    eyewitness testimony to, 5, 8, 18–22, 35, 41, 44–45, 49, 61, 62, 71
    hard miracles, 38
    hard vs. soft, 38
    Hume's conception of, 8–9, 11–14, 45, 62. See also "Of Miracles"
    Hume's Maxim on, 22, 38–43, 54, 80n.32, 83–84n.66
    Hume's proof against, 6, 8, 11, 22–24, 32, 43
    Locke's conception of, 8, 10, 11, 14–15, 35, 63, 79n.17
    marvels vs., 11, 13, 21, 32, 33, 37, 49, 84n.68
    multiple witnesses to, 57, 58–59
    Price on historical evidence and, 157–76
    religious, 5, 38, 43–48, 52, 53, 61–62
    religious doctrine probabilifying and, 65–67
    soft miracles, 38
    Spinoza's conception of, 9–10, 11
    subjectivist conceptions of, 8, 11, 35
    supernatural causation of, 8, 13, 14, 22, 62–63
    varying conceptions of, 9–11
miracle statements, 12, 40, 41, 79n.22

moral certainty, 63, 67
More, Thomas, St., 33
multiple witnesses, 25, 53–59, 60, 71
*Mystery of the Bermuda Triangle-Solved, The* (Kusche), 3

negation principle, 41, 54, 66
Newton, Isaac, 10
Nickell, Joe, 4
*Ninth Bridgewater Treatise* (Babbage), 54
  text from, 203–12

*Observations on Reversionary Payments* (Price), 24
*Observations on the Nature of Civil Liberty* (Price), 24
"Of Miracles" (Hume), 3, 4, 6–8, 14–15, 18, 19, 20–23, 25, 29–32, 35–53, 54, 56, 59–64, 67–71, 73, 80n.32, 83–34n.66, 85–86nn.80, 81, 82
  text of, 140–57
"Of Probabilities" (Hume), 23
*Of the Principles and Duties of Natural Religion* (Wilkins), 63
"On the Importance of Christianity and the Nature of Historical Evidence, and Miracles" (Price), text from, 157–76
*Ophiomaches* (Skelton), 34
Oswald, James, 7
Owen, D., 80n.26

Pearce, Z., 45
Pearson, Karl, 54, 82n.42
personal experience, 35, 36, 64
*Philosophical Essay on Probability, A* (Laplace), 50
  text from, 194–202
posterior probability, 27, 41, 43, 47
  diminution principle and, 49–52
  multiple witnessing and, 54, 55–56, 60
presumptive hard laws, 38
presumptive law statements, 12, 13, 23–24, 38, 83n.56
Price, Richard, 21–22, 24–25, 28, 29–30, 33, 39–40, 41, 42, 45, 49–51, 82nn.41, 43
  text from *Four Dissertations*, 157–76

prior improbability, 33, 41, 42, 49
prior likelihood, 27
prior probability, 27–31, 33, 72
  Bayes' theorem, 49, 82nn.50, 52
  diminution principle and, 49–52
  Hume's Maxim and, 41
  multiple witnessing and, 60
  theism and, 66
probability calculus, 15, 25, 32, 44, 75–76
  Bayesianism and, 26–29, 30
prophecy, 10, 67
pseudo-science, 3, 77n.3

Raynor, D., 82n.44
Reichenbach, Hans, 22–23, 29, 71–72, 79n.21, 81n.36
relative likelihood, principle of, 84n.67
reliability of witnesses, 49, 55–56, 58, 61
resurrection, 38
  of Jesus, 7, 15–20, 45–46, 61, 62, 78–79n.15, 132–40
  as miracle, 12, 14, 33–34, 35, 64, 79–80n.19, 24
  of Queen Elizabeth (hypothetical), 31, 47, 56, 61
  Spinoza's views on, 78–79n.15
*Resurrection of Jesus Considered, The: In Answer to the Tryal of the Witnesses, The* (Annet), 18, 19
  text of, 132–40
Retz, Cardinal de, 31
*Review of the Principal Questions and Difficulties in Morals* (Price), 24
Royal Society, 10, 35, 63
rule of succession, 28, 29, 30

self-deception, 44, 47–48, 71
Sherlock, Thomas, 16–18, 45, 46, 83n.59
  text of *The Tryal of the Witnesses of the Resurrection of Jesus*, 125–32
*Six Discourses on the Miracles of Our Savior* (Woolston), 15–16, 80n.28
Skelton, P., 34
skepticism, 25–26, 29, 78n.15
Smith, Norman Kemp, 7
Sobel, J. H., 40, 41, 83–84n.66

Spinoza, Benedict de, 9–10, 11, 67, 78–
79nn.14, 15
text from *A Theologico-Political
Treatise*, 107–14
Stephen, Leslie, 16, 80nn.28, 30
straight rule of induction, 22–23, 29–
32, 35–37, 81n.36
strongly presumptive law statements,
35
succession, rule of, 28, 29, 30
supernatural causation, 8, 13, 14, 22,
62–63
Swinburne, Richard, 72, 79n.22
*System of Logic* (Mill), 37, 63

testimony, 34
chains of witnesses and, 53, 84–
85n.71
credibility of, 8, 13, 17–18, 25, 38,
69–70
diminution principle and, 49–53
on hard vs. soft miracles, 38
Hume's Maxim and, 22, 38–43, 54,
80n.32
miracle credibility and, 22, 32, 38,
44–47, 53, 61, 64
of multiple witnesses, 25, 53–59
and prior improbabilities, 33
religious doctrine probabilifying, 65–
67
Spinoza's view of, 78–79n.15
weakened elements of, 15, 71
*See also* eyewitness testimony
theism, 9, 14, 67
arguments based on probability, 26,
66
of Hume, 4–5
*Theologico-Political Treatise, A*
(Spinoza), 9
text from, 107–14

*Théorie Analytique des Probabilités*
(Laplace), 56
Thomas Aquinas, St., 9
Tillotson, J., 4, 20, 64, 77n.5, 80–
81n.33, 84–85n.71
total probability principle, 27, 47, 50,
51, 65, 66
transubstantiation, 4, 20, 80–81n.33,
84–85n.71
*Treatise of Human Nature* (Hume),
6–7, 13, 15, 16, 25, 53, 78nn.10,
12
*Tryal of the Witnesses of the
Resurrection of Jesus* (Sherlock),
16–18
text of, 125–32

uniform experience, 12, 13, 18, 21, 37
Hume's view of, 20, 23, 32, 34–35,
36, 47

Van der Loos, H., 63

Warburton, Bishop, 24
West, G., 18, 45
Whately, Richard, 33
Whiston, William, 10
Wilkins, John, 10, 63–64
witnesses
chains of testifiers, 53, 84–85n.71
independence of, 54–55, 57–58, 60–
61
multiple, 25, 53–59, 60, 71
reliability of, 49, 55–56, 58, 61
*See also* eyewitness testimony
Wollaston, W., 18
Woolston, Thomas, 7, 15–16, 18, 45,
62, 80nn.28, 29
Wootton, D., 19, 25–26, 80n.32